THE MAP
of
THE
TAROT

THE MAGICAL WORLD
of
THE
TAROT

FOURFOLD MIRROR
OF THE UNIVERSE

GARETH KNIGHT

SAMUEL WEISER, INC.
York Beach, Maine

First published in 1996 by
Samuel Weiser, Inc.
P.O. Box 612
York Beach, ME 03910-0612

Library of Congress Cataloging-in-Publication Data

Knight, Gareth.
    The magical world of the tarot : fourfold mirror of the
universe / Gareth Knight.
        p.   cm.
    Previously published: London : Aquarian Press, 1991.
    Includes index.
    ISBN 0-87728-873-9 (paper : alk. paper)
    1. Tarot. I. Title.
BF1879.T2K56 1996
133.3'2424--dc20   96-22675
                                                         CIP

ISBN 0-87728-873-9
BJ

Cover art is "The Fool's Paradise" by Ray Rue
Copyright © 1996 Ray Rue

Printed in the United States of America

02 01 00 99 98 97 96
10 9 8 7 6 5 4 3 2 1

The paper used in this publication meets or exceeds the minimum
requirements of the American National Standard for Permanence of
Paper for Printed Library Materials Z39.48-1984

This book is dedicated with gratitude and affection to all fellow students of the Tarot who have shared its pleasures and its mysteries with me, by correspondence or in workshops, and in particular to those who set me questions to ponder (some of the replies to which are contained in these pages), or who have contributed in other ways, namely:

Bill, Caryl, Chris, Christine, Christopher, Daphne, David, Dawn, Derek, Diana, Diane, Ernest, Fran, Gareth, Gaye, Gloria, Jacqueline, Janette, Janine, Jenny, Joan, Kalyani, Libby, Mally, Margaret, Marilyn, Maureen, Muriel, Nelson, Pat, Patrick, Peter, Rosemary, Sigurgrimur, Susan, Terence and Tom.

Thank you, and may you always play your cards right.

CONTENTS

INTRODUCTION TO THE TAROT

The Fourfold Magic Mirror

Five hundred years ago, northern Italy was the centre of the Western world. Florence, Venice and other towns were thriving city-states in which the famous Renaissance princes ruled. They bustled with artistic creation, international business and politics. For many this was a 'golden' age. Artistic creativity was encouraged, and great artists like Botticelli and his master Fra Lippo Lippi flourished. It was during this time and in this place that the Tarot first came into being.

Elsewhere the Western world was in chaos: The Wars of the Roses had broken out in England, and at the further end of Europe, the Turks were besieging Constantinople. They killed the Emperor and took the city and nothing was ever quite the same again. It was the end of the Middle Ages. The Renaissance had begun. With the desecration of the monasteries their great libraries were broken up, and priceless manuscripts released from hidden archives. The Renaissance princes, with their questing minds, bought them up eagerly. These manuscripts included the Hermetic scripts, believed to be the work of an ancient Egyptian priest called Hermes Trismegistus. They included the wisdom of the temples of ancient Egypt but also contained an ancient oral tradition that stemmed from many sources.

The Italian princes were intrigued by these scripts. They showed a new approach to the mind of man and its powers, powers that had been condemned by the medieval church as heretical and tainted with sorcery. These scripts showed that there could be a good and wholesome approach to the traditions of pagan spirituality. This newly-discovered wisdom also had a practical side. Today we might call it applied psychology. The princes learned to meditate upon symbolic pictures as an aid to health and healing. Some of the famous pictures of this time were probably commissioned for this purpose: Botticelli's *The Birth of Venus*, *Venus Overcoming Mars*, or *The Primavera*, which has the Three Graces of classical antiquity as part of its composition, identified by some as the beneficent powers of the Sun, Jupiter and Venus.

It was now that the Tarot first appeared as beautiful, handpainted works of art, encrusted with gold leaf. Highly suitable objects for meditation to bring down the powers of the higher spheres, or, as modern man might prefer to say, to contact the deeper reaches of the human mind. Whether we use the astrological symbolism of the fifteenth century or the psychological assumptions of the twentieth, the images of the Tarot are extremely powerful. They exercise a great fascination for many people to this day.

The Tarot cards became widely known, being linked with playing cards, which had made their appearance in Europe a few decades earlier. Whether by accident or design, the association of the images of the twenty-two Tarot Trumps with the four suits of the playing pack has deep implications, for the four suits of the playing cards mirror the Four Elements of the ancient world: Earth, Air, Fire, and Water. The four Elements also appear in the make-up of the mind of man. The psychologist C.G. Jung equated them with the functions of Intellect, Intuition, Feeling and Sensation. Indeed, he used this fourfold structure to bring healing through the contemplation of images that emerge from the unconscious mind. This leads to a balancing fourfold image of healing that he called a 'mandala'.

The fourfold structure of the playing card pack is an extended mandala – a healing figure of psychic balance. Add to this the twenty-two figures of the Tarot and we have a powerful tool indeed – the intriguing system of interlocking images that can reveal the inner workings of the mind and the world about us. This system requires no special clairvoyant gifts or other rare abilities, simply a knack for using the creative imagination – which is the common heritage of us all. By these means the Tarot becomes a symbolic language by which we can communicate with a level of consciousness that is different from the everyday mode. Thus the Tarot provides the key to a whole new range of human ability that is not limited by the perceptions of the five physical senses. It is not weird and cultish. It is not superstition. It is a way of evaluating those dynamics of a situation that may not be immediately available to the rational mind. It is a way of cultivating the intuition.

We can consult the Tarot as we would an old friend. We can choose to take its advice or ignore it. However, as with the advice of any old friend, its value can only be discovered by experience. And it is only by trying to work with the Tarot ourselves, in good faith, that we will ever come to that experience. By intelligent use of the system of higher apprehension revealed by the Tarot, we can discover more about ourselves. This equips us to meet the challenges of life more confidently and more surely. The Tarot is a system whereby we can learn to know the inner springs within ourselves and the circumstances in daily life that arise from them. Thus it is truly a fourfold mirror – not only of ourselves but of the Universe.

Let us examine this fourfold structure, which runs through the Trumps as well as the four numbered suits, for it is the basis upon which the whole Tarot functions in an instructive and self-balancing fashion. We commence with two key images. They are key images because they represent between them the principal inner and outer polarity that runs through the whole system. Together, and each in their individual way, they also represent the unified spirit that is at the back of all 78 cards. These two images are the Fool and the Magician (Figure 1).

The Fool is the direct representation of the Spirit of the Tarot itself – the unencumbered, wise and lowly innocent who ventures forth into the world, taking things as he finds them and people as they are, for better or for worse, but instilling within them, by his example, all that is best within themselves. Appropriately numbered 0, the Fool at this level represents the pure human spirit, and at another the divine

Figure 1: The Fool and the Magician *(Grimaud Tarot of Marseilles)*

breath 'that bloweth where it listeth', bringing new life and new vision to all things. The Fool is the first character we meet in our acquaintance with the Tarot, for he is its creative fount.

The Magician is another aspect of the same character, this time not wandering free, dancing among all the other images as he danced before they existed, but the controlling focus of them all. All the other cards range up about the Magician in due formation and order. They are all part of his box of tricks, or the balls he juggles in the air, according to the way in which he is depicted.

Fool and Magician therefore represent the principle of creative freedom and the principle of creative organization, both of which are to be found behind all that exists in the world. They are the alchemical principles of *Solve* and *Coagule* (dissolving into free-flowing liquid or organizing into crystalline structural form, yet being the same substance). In esoteric philosophies of the world they are the *yang* and *yin*, or the pillars *Jachin* and *Boaz*, one light and one dark, that stand before the entrance to the temple. However, they are to us no mere metaphysical abstractions. In the Tarot they are living entities that we may get to *know*.

In the pictorial wisdom of the Tarot they are both wandering mendicants, travellers across the cosmic landscape. The Fool, or beggar man, owns only what he carries in a knapsack at the end of his staff (and in one sense this is the brain and spinal column of all of us who came naked into the world and who in the same way will leave it). The Magician is by contrast a travelling showman, putting up his pitch in every town he comes to, to demonstrate his skills and wares. In cosmic terms the travelling show is to be seen in our own solar system and in all the other star systems that are revealed to us, at a distance, in the night sky.

Both figures are in transit. They have their origins and their goals elsewhere, but each is functioning wholeheartedly in the eternal ever, passing now. In this sense they are not only demonstrators, but teachers, messengers, and prophets, bringing enlightenment to us and news of realms beyond the limitations of our own habitual attitudes and mental walls.

The Four Suits of what is sometimes called the Lesser Arcanum are the building blocks of life, and we represent them here in the four Aces, which signify their root and foundation. They are Wands, Swords, Cups and Coins (Figure 2), to be found to this day as the suits on ordinary playing cards in Italy. (Our own playing cards follow a later French system of Clubs, Spades, Hearts and Diamonds, that is an adaptation of the Italian originals.)

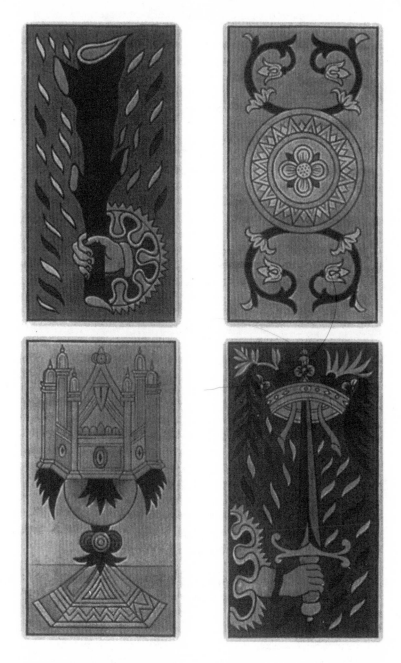

Figure 2: The Four Aces (*Grimaud Tarot of Marseilles*)

The fourfold division of the elements that make up the world is an ancient conception and shows how we may best organize our further studies as we proceed from the basic principles of pure polarity. In practical human terms they are allocated to the varied interests of:

> organizational activity, (Wands);
> justice and law, (Swords);
> love and pleasure, (Cups);
> finance and property, (Coins).

Each Ace is a fount of each particular aspect of human life, which may be developed into tenfold expression – according to the numerological and Qabalistic philosophy behind much of the Tarot – and into four human modes of expression, signified by Page, Knight, Queen and King.

The cards of the Lesser Arcanum all represent activities expressed in life. The twenty-two Trumps are major principles or archetypes that affect and control these activities from behind the scenes.

Four Trumps especially rule over the four Suits and also over the remaining sixteen Trumps. These especial four are those which represent the Cardinal Virtues, and their particular roles were indicated in one of the early packs of Tarot cards, (known as the Gringonneur), which gave them the angular haloes we see about their heads (Figure 3). They are Temperance (a); Strength (or Fortitude) (b); Justice (c); and Prudence (signified by the World) (d). Strength rules over the Wands, and in certain of the old packs the figure is depicted as Hercules with a club (Figure 4, taken from the Visconti-Sforza Tarot). Temperance rules over the Cups, and it will be seen on most cards that she holds two Cups. Justice rules over Swords, and it will be seen that she always carries a sword. And Prudence is signified by the World, nowadays usually represented as a figure balanced between four principles. She rules over Coins, seen in earlier designs of the card as two cherubs presenting a medallion upon which is depicted the world (Figure 5).

The first four Trumps represent principles of Power, and so fall under the presidency of Strength (Figure 6). The Hierophant or Pope, and the High Priestess or Female Pope, show forth spiritual or inner power, in male and female aspect respectively. The Emperor and the Empress similarly represent outer executive male or female power. We thus have two principles of interlocking polarity displayed; that of the spiritual and temporal, and that of masculine and feminine.

Figure 3: Temperance, Strength, Justice, the World *(Gringonneur Tarot)*

Figure 4: Strength *(Visconti-Sforza Tarot)*

Figure 5: The World *(Visconti-Sforza Tarot)*

Figure 6: Trumps in the Hall of Strength *(Grimaud Tarot of Marseilles)*

Figure 7: Trumps in the Hall of Justice *(Grimaud Tarot of Marseilles)*

Four Trumps fall under the presidency of Justice (Figure 7). Here we see the apparently malefic images of the Devil; the Lightning Struck Tower (once often called Hell's Gate or Mouth); also Death; and the Hanged Man, (formerly known as the Traitor). However, these images do have their positive and instructive side. The Devil represents our own shadow self that we can escape from by facing up to it instead of 'projecting' it in various pet hates onto other people. The Tower can also be a channel for spiritual realization – a 'bolt from the blue' that may upset us but which may also bring, if we receive it aright, enlightenment and transformation. Death represents radical change, but all endings bring new beginnings. And the Hanged Man, although he seems to be in a severe predicament, forms with his body a secret sign (that of inner activity, of alchemical sulphur), and is tranquil in his condition. He knows that however unfortunate outer circumstances may seem, he is in the right.

The four Trumps that fall under the wings of Temperance represent conditions of human life, and have slightly changed their imagery over the years (Figure 8). Now called the Hermit, the Chariot, the Lovers and the Wheel of Fortune, they were originally Father Time and the three goddesses of Victory, Love and Fortune. The Hermit's lantern was once an hourglass and, like Time, he went slowly on crutches, yet also had wings. The figure in the Chariot was once Winged Victory, familiar to the classical worlds of Greece and Rome. The Lovers showed a procession of lovers overshadowed by Cupid, the son of Venus, goddess of Love. And the Wheel had the figure of the goddess Fortuna, who turned it, whilst four figures about its rim rose or fell, or were at the height or depths of their respective fortunes (Figure 9).

The last four Trumps show different states into which the universe is divided, according to the ancient wisdom; hence they come under the presidency of the World (Figure 10). These are the Heavenly World, represented by an angel (and this card is sometimes called the Angel) announcing the Last Judgement. Next, the celestial world, represented by the Star. Then our own system, given warmth, light and life by our star, the Sun. And finally the lowest world, (anciently called the sub-lunary sphere), immediately about our physical Earth and encompassed by the orbit of the Moon.

This tiered vision of the universe was of fundamental importance to ancient philosophy and is still valid today. The discoveries of modern science have never overthrown it because they are concerned only with the structure of the outer world, not the states of being and consciousness within it.

Figure 8: Trumps in the Hall of Temperance *(Grimaud Tarot of Marseilles)*

Figure 9: The Chariot (Victory); The Lovers; The Wheel of Fortune; The Hermit
 (Visconti-Sforza Tarot)

Figure 10: Trumps in the Hall of the World *(Grimaud Tarot of Marseilles)*

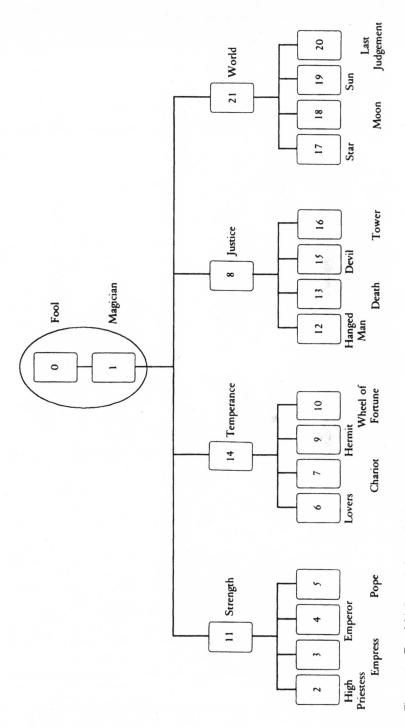

Figure 11: Fourfold Ground-plan of the Tarot

This then is the fourfold ground-plan of our study of the Tarot, and we can spread it out in a comprehensive diagram to clarify our minds. This diagram is laid out rather like a family tree. It is possible to represent it in other, three-dimensional ways, without losing the fourfold pattern. One method is in the various Halls of the Magician which we shall visit in our preparation for Tarot divination. Another is in the form of the Tower of the Fool which we may explore in our more advanced work. But now is the time to make the acquaintance of each and every one of the 78 faces of the Spirit of the Tarot, or to view the 78 facets of this wondrous mental crystal, one by one.

LESSON ONE

The Spirit of the Tarot

In my earlier book on the Tarot called *Tarot Magic* (Destiny Books, 1990, first published by The Aquarian Press as *The Treasure House of Images*, 1986) I acknowledged, in the usual way, all the people who had helped me in writing it, and said:

> *And finally my thanks to the spirit of the Tarot itself. Despite all the abuse it may have had from less than spotless hands and intentions in the past, it revealed itself to me as a very wise and gentle source of wisdom and encouragement, deserving much respect.*

If you have undertaken the study of the Tarot you have probably realized that there is more to it than meets the eye. There is in fact a hidden mystery behind the Tarot; this is why it has fascinated mankind for at least 500 years. Like all mysteries, this hidden power is not something that is obvious to everyone. Yet it is none the less real for all that, and the way to discover that hidden reality is to find the key that unlocks the door to the mystery. The key is in fact a very simple one. So simple indeed that most people overlook it. It is to approach the Tarot as if it were a real person. This may sound fantastic but the proof is there for anyone who will try it. If you treat the Tarot like a person, it will respond like a person – a very wise and friendly person, to whom you can turn for advice.

Now this requires an act of faith from you. We can show you the key, but it is up to you to put it into the lock of the door and turn it. The secrets of the Tarot will then be revealed. If you refuse to take this first step, for whatever reason, then the door to the companionship of the Spirit of the Tarot will remain closed, for only you can open it. It is no good trying to take a kind of superior, 'scientific' attitude and subject the Tarot to psychical or statistical experiments. The Tarot will not be put to the test in this way. It opens up, like a friend, only to human warmth and trust.

Yet you must still be careful as to how you approach it, for it will deal with you exactly as you deal with it. If you go to it just for a laugh or a lark, you will receive only misleading answers, for it will be having a laugh or a lark of its own at your expense. We have said you will find it to be a very wise person. This means it is not easily fooled. And what is more, it will deal with you for your own good if you approach it in the wrong kind of way!

What is the wrong kind of way? Well there are a number, besides the elementary mistakes we have already mentioned. The more serious offences are trying to pry into the affairs of other people without their consent, or seeking information for evil or malicious intent. If you are so foolish as to try anything like this you are likely to find that you are misled in a fashion that brings your own evil intentions right back on your own head. The Spirit of the Tarot will not allow itself to be abused for evil or selfish reasons and is likely to teach you a sharp lesson if you try to make it do so.

Another form of misuse is not so much evil as foolish. This is to begin to rely so much on the Tarot for advice that you are reluctant to do anything without asking its opinion first. This is not at all good for you. You are here on this good Earth to learn to stand on your own spiritual feet, and that is not done by relying for advice on every minor decision in your life. If you pester the Tarot too often in this way it is likely to respond by giving misleading answers, so that you are led in a circular dance of misdirections until you realize the necessity and wisdom of learning how to make up your mind for yourself. This may sound cruel but the Spirit of the Tarot has done you the good service, by this method, of making you self-reliant.

However, if you make up your mind to approach and consult the Tarot as you would approach a wise and trusted friend for advice and discussion, in a balanced and sensible way, you may rest assured that it will respond to you in similar good faith, and prove a friend and wise counsellor indeed.

How to Approach the Spirit of the Tarot

We make our first approach to the Spirit of the Tarot by making a picture of this person in our mind. The image we shall use is that of Trump 0, called the Fool. And we shall soon find that this figure is by no means as foolish as his name might suggest. Really he is extremely wise, but his wisdom is of the intuition, or higher mind, which is the kind of mentation we need to develop in order to become aware of inner and future trends. He will, in turn, introduce us to the other images of the Tarot that will form a special symbolic language of communication when later we learn to read the cards.

Take this Trump from the pack and prop it up on the table before you. It does not matter very much which set of designs you have. We will base our descriptions on the traditional Marseilles cards because, although they are crude, they are the direct descendants of the earliest handprinted designs and they have formed the basis for most of the later esoteric packs.

To begin with, make sure that you have the right conditions for doing the work. You need to be free from the likelihood of disturbance, the atmosphere should be calm and reasonably quiet and the room clean and tidy. Emotional turmoil, noise, dirt and muddle are not conditions under which psychic work can be properly conducted, at any rate until one is considerably experienced in creating an inner quietness and order that can overcome unsatisfactory surroundings.

If you are familiar with the practice of meditation then you have a head start. If not, it is never too late to learn, the rules are quite simple and you will soon find the results effective. Make sure you are sitting comfortably. A position of alert poise is best, sitting on a firm chair, with spine upright but not stiff or tensed, eyes looking straight ahead whether they are open or closed. The hands and forearms can rest along the top of the thighs, which should be parallel to the floor – a small footstool may well be found useful to achieve this.

Spend a little time relaxing your muscles and your mind, breathing gently and slowly. Then gradually forget about your breathing and your physical surroundings, and concentrate upon the images you are going to build in your imagination. You have already taken a good look at the card of The Fool in your Tarot pack. What you need to do now is to see the picture of the Fool in your mind. It need not be exactly the same as the one that is upon the card. In fact it may very well be different in many small ways. The Fool you will come to know in your mind is your own special friend, and although his general image is upon the card, he will appear slightly different to every individual who seeks him.

Begin by imagining that you are standing on a clifftop path. Be aware of the thinness and stillness of the air. Perhaps you can see snowcapped mountain peaks before you and wheeling eagles. On the other hand it may be that you are on a clifftop overlooking the sea, and can hear the sound of the breakers upon the rocks or the beach, and the cry of the sea birds. You may even find the wind gusty. The sun may perhaps be shining, but above all be aware of the expanse of cool clear air and sky. The idea is to let the images arise spontaneously before you, along the general lines described. Do not worry if at first you find it difficult to succeed. Just continue to sit there, and above all do not try too hard! Should wandering thoughts on other subjects come to mind, simply put them aside with the mental note that you will deal with them later, at the proper time. If nothing comes to you, simply build the picture and try to hold it there. Gradually it will take on greater reality and motion.

Now imagine that you hear a merry whistling, and perhaps the jingling of bells as in a jester's cap. See coming towards you along the path the figure of the Fool, dressed in his ragged or motley clothes, a bag and stick over his shoulder. He is accompanied by a barking and capering dog. See him come towards you as you stand by the path. Now the idea is to make contact with him. In fact as he is already in your mind you already have! But we seek to make that contact more conscious and formal. See him stand before you and smile. It is possible that you may hear him say something to you with the ear of your imagination. Although this may not come easily at first, you may well feel an idea come into your mind, and that idea may well come from the Fool rather than yourself! The important thing is whether it is a good idea or not, rather than who first thought of it.

Practise making this contact every day, because it is the first step to becoming an initiated Tarot reader. It is genuine contact with the Spirit of the Tarot that marks the difference between a genuine consultant and a casual fortune-teller who has only learned the 'meanings' of the cards by rote, or is relying on a natural psychic facility unconnected with the real source of wisdom that lies behind the Tarot.

When you have completed your period of meditation and contemplation give your farewell greetings to the Fool, and turning away from him in your imagination, feel yourself walk down the cliff path, whilst he turns and returns with his dog up the path to the heights from whence he came. When you have gone a little way down see a large boulder by the side of the path. Within it is a door in the rock. Pass through it, and find yourself sitting in your own room once again, in your normal physical surroundings, with the Tarot cards before you on the table. Open your eyes and draw your mind back to everyday reality. Be aware of being firmly in your own body, flex your muscles and move your feet and hands and head to establish this fact. Now stand and gather up the cards neatly and put them away. Think no more of your inner visions as you do so.

It is important that you make this firm break between outer and inner worlds, otherwise, especially if you have a natural psychic ability, impressions from the inner world may intrude when it is not convenient. By maintaining this simple routine, of only transferring consciousness to the inner worlds when you deliberately sit down before your Tarot cards, and deliberately transferring consciousness back when you have finished, you will always be in control of your developing psychic faculties.

Your cards should be kept in a specially chosen place, not simply thrown into an untidy cupboard or drawer or left lying around in the open. Traditionally they should be kept on a high place - at least above shoulder height. If you can find a nice wooden box for them, so much the better, and it is well worth the trouble of procuring a small piece of black silk in which to enfold the cards inside their box. It can also be helpful, when you work with the cards, to make something of an occasion of it by other small means. You could even have a special robe and light some incense. However, it is by no means necessary to go as far as this, and the same results can be achieved by methods that are less likely to excite unwanted attention from family or close neighbours.

Having a special ring, or other small piece of jewellery, that you wear only when you consult the Tarot, can be a help. Or you could have a particular piece of music on tape or disc that will put you into the appropriate mood. This is entirely a matter of personal choice. Perhaps most effective is to have a special cloth to put upon the table on which to lay the cards. And perhaps a candle or some other symbolic object might be added if it stimulates your imagination. The action of putting these things out carefully and methodically will serve to put you into the right frame of mind for successful divination. However, all are psychological devices, a means to an end, and should not become compulsive fetishes or objects of superstition.

Working Plan

In this first lesson you will only be working upon one image, that of the Fool. Give yourself at least three weeks of practical study before going on to the practical work of the next lesson. (This is an average time. If you are unused to this type of visualizing meditation you may need more time. On the other hand if you are in fact well practised at it *or* you find that the Fool comes alive for you readily because you have a naturally strong imaginative faculty then you could make do with less time. At any rate, try to get to know the Fool reasonably well before you go on to meet the other images.)

You will gain most from your study of the Tarot if you can arrange to work at regular times, preferably about the same time each day.

The time of day, or night, is up to you, according to personal circumstance and preference. However, ten-to-twenty minutes per day, every day, will bring more benefit than irregular work, even over longer periods. It is quite a good idea to take a day off from time to time, say once per week. It is another useful aid to keep a diary of your work, as you will find that this is a stimulus to regularity.

Diary Record
Take a ruled sheet of paper and divide it into headed colums as follows:

Date	Time	Total	Cards worked with
10th Oct.	9.00–9.15 pm	15 minutes	Fool
11th Oct.	9.00–9.15 pm	15 minutes	Fool
12th Oct.	10.15–10.40 pm	25 minutes	Fool
13th Oct.	8.15–8.20 pm	5 minutes	Fool
15th Oct.	8.20–9.05 pm	35 minutes	Fool

This brief example shows you the kind of thing to aim for. Another psychological aid will be to keep all your practical Tarot work neatly filed in a special loose-leaf folder that can be kept with your Tarot cards.

Knowledge Notes

These notes are not part of the actual practical lesson, but are added to help you to build up your knowledge of the history and most popular forms of the traditional Tarot images. In the last analysis, it is the forms that appeal most to you, or that come to your own mind's eye, that are really important for you. However, it is always best for your imagination to be founded on sound historical tradition, otherwise your work may become too personally biased and idiosyncratic. If this happens, the Tarot ceases to become a vehicle of communication of practical wisdom, but tends merely to reflect your own subjective opinions and fancies, presenting you with a mist of phantasms of your own subconscious instead of the clear mirror of inner perception.

Notes on the Fool

The Tarot Trump called The Fool is perhaps the most profound symbol of the whole Tarot. The Fool is a great archetype that has always played a major part in folk tradition. It is embedded in the collective unconscious of almost every race, whether it appears as the medieval Court Jester, the harlequinade of the *Commedia dell' Arte*, the puppet Punch and Judy, or the clowns of the modern circus. In the Arthurian cycle there is even a knightly fool, Sir Dagonet, the jester of King Arthur. Again, the Fool and tragedy, as for example in *Petrushka* or the perennially popular opera *I Pagliacci*, is something which strikes home deep in the subconscious mind. This is a quality which can be caught by comics of genius, such as Charlie Chaplin or Jacques Tati. Again, there were the Fool's Days of medieval times when the whole court was turned topsy-turvy, a tradition still carried out in some armed services at Christmas, where the officers serve the men their dinner. The idea even entered the Church, with the annual boy-bishop festivities, and attendant vulgarities and blasphemies. For such things to be tolerated and submitted to, a deep level of unconscious motivation must be in force.

The Fool is also an object of some respect – he is a creature of paradox, being at the same time wise as well as a fool. The highest example of this element of paradox and hidden mearnings and motivations is in the third Act of *King Lear*. Shakespeare created some marvellous fools in his plays but here he surpasses them all, in the situation of a foolish King (Lear) actually losing his wits; accompanied by his Fool, full of double-edged jokes and saws; protected by a disguised Duke of Kent whom Lear had banished and who is posing as an uncouth serving man; and meeting in a hut on a heath during a wild storm Edgar, heir to Gloucester, betrayed by his bastard brother on a false charge and posing as a madman. We have here the quintessence of the archetype and most of its possible combinations. The implications and undertones of this scene defy complete understanding – which is perhaps to be expected when great art is coupled with deep archetypal elements.

All this may help to show how difficult it is to make an adequate summary of this Tarot card. True to type it has frequently been misplaced in esoteric elucidations of the Tarot system, which throw out all or most of its attributions and so reduce comparative systems of occult correspondences to varying degrees of dispute and confusion. For example, some esoteric systems place the Fool at the beginning of the Trump sequence, some at the end, and others between Trumps XX and XXI. None of this need bother us on this course but it demonstrates how the Fool is capable of confusing the wise, or those who think themselves so.

In the game of Tarot The Fool has a special role, for with his Zero designation, he has no scoring capacity in the ranking of the Trumps. Rather, his function is that of being able to overturn all the rules. He is never 'played' in the usual sense. The player who holds him shows him at the appropriate moment, and this excuses the player from having to follow suit with a higher card that he may wish to reserve until later. For this reason The Fool is often called the *scusi* – the excuse.

It is natural to assume that The Fool is the last surviving Trump in the conventional pack of cards, where he now appears, with a similar kind of playing function, as the Joker. It appears however that there was no direct line of descent in this development. The ordinary pack never had a Joker or similar special card, it was a 19th-century American introduction. However, those who have some experience of the psychological power and persistence of the Tarot archetypes may be willing to concede that the Fool has willed his own re-invention or rediscovery and introduction into the ordinary pack of cards. He in particular, of all the Trumps, is too important to be ignored.

The realization of this especial role and significance carries over into the modern tradition of esoteric philosophy. Manly P. Hall makes the suggestion that the Fool contains all the other Trumps. In a full-page illustration to the Tarot section of his *Secret Teachings of All Ages* (Philosophical Research Society, 1962) he depicts this strikingly. The figure of the Fool has a pyramid of the other Trumps superimposed over his body.

In his novel *The Greater Trumps* (Eerdmans Publishing Co, 1976) Charles Williams emphasizes the central importance of the Fool in his description of the secret room where the original models of the images are kept. This is, of course, a very real inner condition, although for the conventions of the story it is described as if it were a physical location. Here, on a circular table, the Trump figures move about in a self-propelled endless dance, in a golden haze and humming with power. In this set-up the Fool is described as standing in the centre of all the moving Trumps, a stable focus and indeed Lord of the Dance. However, when someone inherently good, such as the character of Aunt Sybil, looks at the table, she can see that the Fool is in fact also dancing amongst the other cards. Aunt Sybil, in the story, is a remarkable person whose belief in the true and the good is firm and sure, and this is expressed in her daily life. To her the Fool is a living, active being, just as to the enlightened religious person God is not an abstraction somewhere out in the universe, a Cosmic Zero, but actively participating in the whole of his creation.

To put the meaning of the card in its simplest and most profound terms, it signifies the innocent and pure essence of the Spirit. This element was stressed in the A.E. Waite version of the card, and followed by Paul Case in his Builders of The Adytum pack, wherein the Fool is depicted with the innocence of youth, about to walk off a high precipice. In the esoteric version of the Hermetic Order of the Golden Dawn this is stressed even more by depicting the Fool as a naked child, stretching his hand to pluck a golden rose from a tree. These are welcome changes from the coarse and imbecilic appearance of, say, the Oswald Wirth version of the card, or some of the older packs that show the Fool with a half-witted or vacuous expression. He, is, however, considerably more than the complete and utter innocent. Although his actions might appear foolish or ill-considered to the average man of the world, he has a deeper wisdom that only appears as foolishness to those who are too stupid or insensitive to see it. Those who, in the tragic words of Jesus, 'know not what they do'. Most of the great geniuses of the world, in the arts or the sciences, to say nothing of the saints of God, would, by this token, at some time or another in their lives have been accounted foolish.

In our work on this course our first task is to make personal contact with this archetypal character known as the Fool. In a practical exercise given in another of my books on the Tarot, *Tarot Magic* (Destiny Books, 1990), I describe a contact with the Fool that may prove helpful here. In the exercise the situation is one of sitting in an upper attic room in a cottage, and the Fool appears, with his dog, up through the trap door. This can be slightly modified to the scenario of our course lesson where we see him on a clifftop. Apart from the location, the character of the Fool and his dog are the same.

> . . . we hear from the direction of the ladder beneath a scrambling sound, it sounds like a small animal scrabbling up the rungs. We look toward the opening and a hairy pointed face appears through it; it is a dapple-coated dog. It climbs into the room and gazes expectantly at us, its tongue lolling out of its mouth, and a mischievous look on its face.
>
> We have not time to speculate on how it got here or from whence it came for it is closely followed by someone else climbing the ladder. Through the trap door we see first the head and shoulders and then the rest of a merry looking young man, with yellow hair, and a coat and breeches of many colours. He carries a staff on the end of which hangs a knotted bag. He sits cross-legged between us and throws down his bag. It seems full of lumpy objects. His dog sits beside him. The young

man looks round at each of us in turn. We are very conscious of the personal contact he makes, with his light blue eyes that are full of merriment, yet which also seem able to see far within the deeps of each one of us.

He speaks: 'Welcome to my mother's house. This is the Cottage of Lost Play and I am the Poor Man who has nowhere to lay his head; the Beggerman who wanders the roads seeking love from strangers; the Fool, because no sensible person would do such a thing; even the Madman, because many would see no sense in what I have to tell them. To the worldly wise I am childish because of my faith in the true and the good, but that is because I am an innocent. And the innocent, the virgin and the pure are not well regarded in a world of corruption. When the sons and daughters of Earth are young they have innocence. That is why you must become as little children to enter the kingdom of heaven. I am like the pied piper who calls all who are young at heart to follow and join in my dance. For I am the Lord of the Dance and I am the Victor of all Games. Follow me, and I will show you a game that is outside your own space and time.'

So saying, he stands, and his dog scurries excitedly round him, jumping up and pawing at his back.

The adventure he is inviting the reader to embark upon is not quite the same as the one that we are exploring on this course, although it can lead in the end to much the same place as is described in our advanced work at the end of this volume. However, as an introduction to the person of the Fool it can serve us well in the beginning of our practical studies.

A Brief Review of Tarot Packs

We recommend for the purposes of this course the use of a standard traditional Marseilles pack. There are a number readily available to choose from these days. The principal traditional packs, produced mainly for the purpose of card playing, are made by the French cardmakers, Grimaud. Besides their full-size set they produce a very useful half-size version which is particularly useful for laying out larger spreads when working in confined spaces.

We would also recommend the Tarot Classic set, produced by the collector and authority Stuart Kaplan, of US Games Systems Inc., author of a book of the same name and of the three-volume *Encyclopaedia of Tarot* (U.S. Games Systems, 1978). We also find the Spanish Tarot very attractive. This is reproduced from a set in the Museo Fournier, Vitoria, Spain. Both these sets are standard traditional printed ones from the mid-eighteenth century, and have the slight advantage over the Grimaud that they have been marked to identify whether the cards are right way up or 'reversed'. However, this is a small task, and anyone who needs to can do it for themselves.

The IJJ Swiss Tarot is also traditional; although some find it attractive its style may not be to everybody's taste. It also has Jupiter and Juno in place of the Emperor and Empress. The Japanese have produced quite an attractive traditional pack called the Angel Tarot that aims to synthesize the best of many of the old designs.

For those with deep pockets there are also reproductions of early handpainted sets from the fifteenth century. These certainly look impressive but are perhaps not entirely suitable for starting with. The Visconti-Sforza is perhaps more readily appropriate for immediate practical use than the Cary Yale Visconti-Sforza, which is slightly variant from the main stream of tradition in that it has six extra cards (four Court and two Trump) and a suit of Arrows instead of Wands.

Many students will be attracted to more modern, 'esoteric' sets. They can certainly be more directly evocative in some of their designs, but have the disadvantage that the particular views of the designer have been impressed quite strongly upon the cards. This may be acceptable if one feels closely enough in sympathy with these ideas. There is also the question of the different numbering systems on the Trumps that different designers use, although this need not concern us in our immediate purposes. The original Trumps were not numbered anyway.

If an esoteric pack is preferred the Rider-Waite has certainly proved itself in general popularity and is used by many experienced readers. Its popularity is due largely to the suit cards being furnished with pictorial designs as well as the Trumps. (However, on this course, when we come to them, we do encourage you to formulate your own pictures.)

There are other sets that owe much to Waite designs in conception but which have been rendered in different styles. The attraction of these is largely one of personal taste, especially if the artistic conventions of the Waite cards do not especially appeal. Perhaps the most popular of these is the Morgan Greer Tarot, although there are many who find considerable appeal in the colourful stained-glass window effect of the Mystic Rose Tarot, the cozy images of the Hanson-Roberts Tarot, the Art Deco style of the Aquarian Tarot, or the muted traditionalism of the Royal Fez Moroccan.

The BOTA set by Paul Case should also be mentioned. The cards follow the Waite designs closely and to many minds are an improvement. However they are quite expensive for what they are, which is simple black-and-white outline, although this does enable you to colour them in yourself and so personalize the cards without any great artistic skill being necessary. Some students find this to be a suprisingly helpful exercise. The suit cards are geometrical, in the traditional style, rather than pictorial. This again has its advantages if the student seeks, as we recommend, to come up with personally-conceived pictorial images.

Other esoteric packs may be of historical or symbolical importance but are of limited value for our immediate purpose. They are generally too loaded with specific esoteric philosophical ideas of various individuals or schools of thought. Our own Gareth Knight Tarot might perhaps be a useful half-way house in this respect, based as it is on esoteric ideas, but on broadly traditional lines. Such packs are in general more suitable for specialist or advanced techniques of occult meditation than the day-to-day practicalities of Tarot reading. In the last analysis no Tarot images can be better than the ones you discover for yourself, and it is for this reason that we recommend the use of the old traditional designs. They may be crude but they do not intrude any particular line of modern occult theory and are sufficiently basic to allow you to formulate your own ideas.

Questions and Answers

Q. I have a vivid imagination, but after a while I have trouble holding on to the images. As I focus on the Fool or other aspects of the image the picture continually changes and flickers, producing either caricatures or totally unrelated, often bizarre images.

A. The visualization work should settle down with practice, and you are probably trying a bit too hard at the moment, perhaps expecting too much, or too much of yourself. Once you get into the swing of it in a more relaxed way you will indeed get good results, and ones that will probably surprise you. The Fool, I should say, does by his very nature tend to bob about a bit and be somewhat erratic.

Q. Will it be all right for me to use the IJJ Swiss Tarot to learn with?

A. This is quite a good traditional pack although it has Juno and Jupiter in place of the more usual Popess/High Priestess and Pope/Hierophant cards. The Tarot images are capable of carrying a great deal of meaning and also can present themselves in various forms. Juno and Jupiter as queen and king of the Roman gods are a logical and appropriate substitute for the Popess and Pope, and the imagery brings out quite well their role as the more spiritual equivalents of the more mundane Empress and Emperor.

Q. I possess the Mythic Tarot cards and now the Marseilles pack. I generally prefer the Mythic Tarot cards but I do like the image of the Fool within the Marseilles pack. Will this make things difficult?

A. The Mythic Tarot has much to recommend it and appeals to a number of people but it does suffer from a certain limitation in that it is designed and interpreted via Greek mythology. Let me hasten to say that there is nothing wrong with this, and the basic images of the Tarot are so universal that it is possible to construct various Tarot packs of different 'flavours' – Greek, Egyptian, Feminist, Tibetan, American Indian, etc. Whilst it would be quite possible to use any of these specialized packs to learn on I feel it would be better to go for a more general pack, either the traditional Marseilles designs or the Rider/Waite or one of its derivatives, such as the Morgan Greer.

Of course every pack has its bias and its strong and weak points. On this course my aim is to encourage each student to build flexible personal images around each archetype. These of course will vary in detail from student to student, and with each student may vary from time to time and context to context. But, within reasonable bounds, flexibility is the best way to allow the Tarot to work or to 'speak' to you. It is, after all, a species of language between one plane and another, and the more flexible a language is, the more sensitive and accurate a means of communication it is.

For my own reference I have a scrap book full of various designs that appeal to me, and from this comes a kind of amalgam for my own use. The images are variable to a certain extent in context. As a general guide use, in your own mind, whatever image most appeals to you.

Q. In the Marseilles pack Justice is No. 8 and Strength is No. 11. However in *Pictorial Key to the Tarot* by A.E. Waite (Weiser, 1973) and *The Complete Guide to the Tarot* (Bantam Books, 1971) by Eden Gray the opposite is given. Any comments?

A. The traditional Marseilles numbering is the correct one, insofar as there is a correct one, since the earliest cards had no names or numbers printed on them. And when there were, and before the Marseilles system began to be more or less accepted as a standard, there were some regional differences in the exact order. I have gone into this in some detail in my book *Tarot Magic* (Destiny Books, 1990).

These two numbers you ask about were changed around by the savants of the Hermetic Order of the Golden Dawn, of which Waite was a member, and you will find that a number of modern packs have followed suit. The reason for it was that they considered this more appropriate when one tried to make correspondences with the Qabalistic Tree of Life, which was the blueprint for their symbolic philosophy. There was also a move to transpose the numbers of the Star and the Emperor led by Aleister Crowley, but this never caught on. Most of the arguments for and against these changes are covered in the first book I ever wrote, *A Practical Guide to Qabalistic Symbolism* (Weiser, 1978). However, as we are studying the Tarot as a symbol system in its own right (as indeed it is), we do not need to try to fit it to the Procrustean bed of any other symbol system, so there is really no problem.

Q. Would you please tell me what exactly 'esoteric' means? And what is a Reversed Card? Does it mean upside-down?

A. 'Esoteric' means 'for the few' as opposed to 'Exoteric' – 'for the many'. It is therefore often used to refer to occult teaching of various kinds on the assumption that there are relatively few people capable of appreciating it, apart from clever and discerning people like you and me! A Reversed Card, as you surmise, simply means one that is upside-down.

Q. After meditating I feel refreshed mentally, yet drained and tired also. Is this normal? During meditation I could not feel my hands or feet and my heart beat slowed considerably. I felt a 'heightened awareness', the nearest thing I can liken to it is hypnosis (which I underwent once for an emotional/medical problem). After meditation I had a tingling sensation in my hands, and felt as though I had woken up after being alseep for 100 years! Is this normal? It was quite hard for me to come back to the physical world.

A. There is a certain similarity between the meditational state and light hypnosis, as you have observed. The breathing will usually become more stilled and regular as you have also noted. It is sometimes something of an effort to bring your attention back fully to the physical world. It is for this reason that it is useful to have a little set procedure of stamping your feet or clapping your hands at this point, and indeed the process of writing up a diary record is also a good 'earthing' procedure.

I am a little concerned about your feeling of depletion, which may be connected with the loss of feeling and the tingling sensation in your hands and feet. It could be that you are leaking etheric energy a bit, which might be a result of past hypnotic sessions which, although they can be helpful in some respects can also, like many healing methods, have side-effects that persist for a while. I suggest you try building in your imagination a sphere of golden light about yourself before each meditation. This should have a healing effect and also seal your aura from any slight leakages. I do not think it is likely to be too serious but let me know if you continue to have further trouble in this way. Psychic work of this nature should certainly not leave you feeling 'drained'. It could also help if you meditate in the morning rather than later in the day, but this may well be inconvenient for you, and in any case is an evasion of the problem rather than a cure.

Q. The Fool really came to life after a few sessions. He always whistles 'Yankee Doodle' as he approaches, and when he speaks to me in my mind he has an American accent. Is that all right? It seems to happen naturally.

A. It is good to see you have made a strong initial contact with the Fool, and don't worry about the American accent or his choice of tunes to whistle. He can be quite a surprising character, but very friendly and gentle, and a good teacher and guide.

Q. Sometimes I find my mind wandering to everyday subjects. What can I do about this?

A. Do not worry about the occasional mind wandering. This is only to be expected in the earlier stages, and affects everyone when they start meditating. With practice it will become less of a bother. Working in the same place at the same time every day can be a help in this respect as it establishes mental habit patterns, or what are sometimes called in some occult circles 'tracks in space'.

Q.   Sometimes when I was doing the practical work the muscles ached in my legs, neck, back and arms. When that happens it is hard to concentrate.

A.   I am a little puzzled about the aching muscles and I fancy you may be unconsciously tensing up during these periods. I suggest you spend a little while deliberately relaxing as a start to your exercise work, and make a habit of checking for a split second or so during your meditations that you are still in fact relaxed. It could be a problem related to your doing this kind of work late at night, and therefore tensing up as a means of avoiding dropping off to sleep after a hard day's work.

Q.   I've had Tarot cards for years but many books contradict one another. No two seem to agree, I find it totally confusing.

A.   The method I use is for you to teach yourself, or the Tarot itself to teach you (which are two sides of the same coin), and so you should soon find that you are able to work with it in a confident way, rather than being confused by the differing opinions that are to be found in mere book learning.

Q.   I've found it difficult to keep a visual image of the Fool. One minute he is the Crowley Fool doing cartwheels. Next minute he's the romantic Rider/Waite's, and then the blue-and-yellow diamonds of the Gareth Knight deck. A couple of times he's been a hippy with long hair, faded denim jeans and a guitar. And he was a Morris men's hobby horse. The dog, who has always been a black Labrador, turned in one meditation into a little white circus dog with a pink frill, dancing. In another I was standing waiting for the Fool and, bending down to pick up a pebble to throw into the sea, found myself holding a beautiful large diamond crystal. I don't know why but he always seems to be singing an old folk song 'I saw three ships a-sailing'. But the most puzzling thing is that every time I sit down and try to do the meditation, to think of the Fool and try to visualize him, I feel a surge of energy up the spine. I feel such a love for him and, well, no fantastic realizations, but surges of energy! If I wished, I could sit down and write all sorts about the Fool – being the pure spirit, innocent as a lamb, stepping through into manifestation, etc. – but I don't need to meditate to intellectualize about him.

A.   You do not need to be concerned too much about the antics of the Fool. Indeed he is often like that, particularly with students who he feels might otherwise think they know a lot about him through their study of esoteric symbolism and the Qabalah and so on. So your apparent failure in holding the images in accustomed fashion is in fact a success in that you have plainly succeeded in making a genuine contact with the Fool. As you say, you don't need to intellectualize about him. There is plenty of that in the various books. But the energy he is bringing you is probably what you mainly need at the moment in the light of your difficult personal circumstances.

Q. I have found that many interpretations of the cards conflict, therefore I find *The Definitive Tarot* (Rider, 1975) by Bill Butler most useful as it outlines the interpretations of the major contributors to the work of Tarot. It also allows one to note where they are in agreement.

A. The book you mention by Bill Butler is a useful compendium, I agree. However, the technique we use on this course should enable you to formulate your own interpretations without having to take recourse to analysis by other people, although I agree that there is no time wasted in studying custom and tradition in these matters. The main thing is not to let conflicting views confuse you.

Q. The Fool always seems to me to be flitting about, never still, sometimes beckoning, a truly free spirit; also, visualizing his face is difficult. Can you give me any hints to keep the images in my mind's eye?

A. The lack of stability of the images that you have found so far seems to me to be a characteristic of the Fool himself, and this is confirmed by the fact that you find things more stable once you go on to the images of Lesson 2. This seeming difficulty is in fact a good sign. It shows that you were getting on to the true characteristics behind this card, even if it showed up in this slightly disconcerting way.

Q. I used to practise yoga for long periods, sitting on the floor trying to keep my body still, later trying to keep any thought away from my mind. Working with images in contrast to excluding them is new to me. It is hard for me to keep the images in the field of vision, and to keep them whole and not as a collection of parts. It takes time to make a Fool out of legs and arms and a head and so on. Sometimes he comes alive although hardly having any parts – only a face, for instance.

A. I have no doubt that the meditation on specific images will seem very strange after the way of the absence of images that you have pursued in the past with yoga. Both ways are valid - one being traditionally called the Positive Way and the other the Negative Way. Needless to say I prefer the former, although in the end the Ways meet in a common goal. Which Way we use to reach that goal is largely a matter of personal temperament and contemporary culture. It also seems you are approaching the problem in a rather anatomical way. Why not try going for contact with the personality of the Fool, even if it is expressed only with a disembodied face?

Q. I have a Marseilles pack but the names are in French, which I find hard to interpret.

A. I am sorry to hear you find this a bit of a handicap. Here is a list of translations: *Le Mat* - the Fool; *Le Bateleur* - the Magician; *La Papesse* - the High Priestess; *L'Impératrice* - the Empress; *L'Empereur* - the Emperor; *Le Pape* - the Hierophant; *L'Amoreux* - the Lovers; *Le Chariot* - the Chariot; *La Justice* - Justice; *L'Hermite* - the Hermit; *La Roue de Fortune* - the Wheel of Fortune; *La Force* - Strength; *Le Pendu* - the Hanged Man; (*Un-named*) - Death; *Temperance* - Temperance; *Le Diable* - the Devil; *La Maison Dieu* - the Lightning-struck Tower; *L'Etoile* - the Star; *La Lune* - the Moon; *Le Soleil* - the Sun; *La Jugement* - the Last Judgement; *Le Monde* - the World.

I hope this is of some help. The method of the course is to make you familiar with the images themselves so this verbal difficulty should not be a problem for too long.

Q. The name Belzibub comes to mind when I think of the Fool. What does it mean?

A. This, I would fancy, is just a bit of mental lumber getting in the way, and is best ignored. Spelled slightly differently it is a name found in the Bible meaning Lord of the Flies, and is associated with a rather unpleasant character. As this has no possible connection with the Fool I would just ignore it and it should go away. (Unless it is some private joke of the Fool's connected with buzzing in and out as you contact him!) I note that you have formed a very good relationship with the character in your meditation work although at first you had a little bit of difficulty in the contact because you were trying to make him conform to a ready-made picture that you found pleasing to yourself. When you stopped doing this he appeared as himself, in an equally personable way. So it is possible the allusion has something to do with this.

Q. I was rather worried as the Fool said his name was 'Hex'. I felt quite disturbed at this as he was such a lovely person I couldn't imagine why he'd have such a name.

A. I would not worry about the Fool calling himself 'Hex'. He is rather a jokey character and I think is just drawing attention to the foolishness of some of your fears about the occult. 'Hex' can also be short for 'hexagram' which is the six-rayed star of esoteric achievement (the union of the higher and lower self), and you will no doubt be aware that all the 6 cards in the Tarot pack ('hex' means 'six' in Latin) are ones of good omen.

Q. I have read various sensationalized features and articles on Tarot which I find horrifying. Tarot does not get a serious press coverage, or at least one as serious as it deserves.

A. I am glad that you have not allowed horrendous stories about 'dabbling with the occult' to put you off the Tarot. It is indeed a very gentle and pleasant system which can be of very great help not only to those who use it for ourselves but also for others who may consult us. However, a number of popular newspapers, when hard up for something emotional to print, like to run some horror story featuring the occult in some way, because a lot of people who don't know much about it are frightened of it.

Q. I found it fairly easy to visualize the Fool, although the Hermit crept in occasionally. I found the image of a jester-type fool rather distracting in that it was hard to take seriously. Perhaps that is why I kept turning him into the Hermit.

A. I note your slight difficulty with the jester image of the Fool. This is however an important part of the character of this card, and with some students he capers wildly and goes through all kinds of unlikely transformations as a means of teaching. All the tomfoollery has a deep wisdom behind it though. In your case he seems prepared to meet you halfway and take on the more serious mien of the Hermit now and again so as not to put you off too much, and to confirm that he does have a more serious side.

Q. I've not done any meditation or visualization before and I must say I find it difficult. I can picture the clifftop path and meeting the Fool but cannot hold the image for too long. My mind tends to wander, but I do try. Presumably practice makes perfect. The only thing is I cannot manage to give my Fool a face. The feeling I get back from my friend (the Fool) is positive but also 'to be patient'.

A. I note your slight problem in building the image of the Fool but if you are not experienced in meditation work this is to be expected, and your abilities in this direction will certainly improve with practice. In fact there are some people who never do visualize with vivid detail but who nevertheless work very efficiently on an intuitive or feeling level. Indeed it is possible to be aware of people or things in everyday life without examining them in minute detail. You are simply 'aware' that they are there, and of their general qualities. Much the same can occur at the imaginative level.

   Despite the fact that you are unable to formulate a face for the Fool you have evidently established a mental rapport and this is what we are after. His advice to have patience and keep working away is exactly what I would expect him to say, and would also advise myself. In any event, whether working in vivid visual detail, or at less defined intuitional levels, all these methods are superior to a mere intellectual book learning.

Q. I don't believe that I did very well on the practical side of the lesson. To be honest I'm very disappointed with myself about it. I only managed to see in a visual sense twice. I don't seem to be able to visualize although I know I have a fairly good imagination. But why can't I visualize? Please help on this.

A. Sorry to hear about the visualization difficulties. Actually it is not an uncommon problem so you should not feel too discouraged, and it need not be a real bar to working with the Tarot or any other inner images. It is largely a matter of personality type. There are some people who concentrate strongly upon physical details in their daily lives, who could tell you exactly what they have seen and details of how someone they spoke to was dressed, the colour of his hair, eyes, and all the rest of it. Others do not perceive in this detailed way but have a more general, intuitive perception of what is going on around them. It does not mean to say that they are vague or woolly-minded, it is simply another level of registering the environment.

The same thing occurs with inner work. You do not *have* to be able to describe any of the figures in minute detail - but you should be capable of an awareness that they are there. It is this feeling of a real presence that we are after. And if you do this you may then find that ideas are coming into your head. These are not necessarily idle fancies of your own, but an actual intuitive communication between you and the forces behind the card. In some respects this is a superior way of working than out-and-out visualization, which can result in just a mass of inconsequential detail. A number of clairvoyants have examples of this, picking up largely trivial material as opposed to getting a grasp of any wisdom principles.

LESSON TWO

The Next Step

We have now made contact with the Spirit of the Tarot through the most important image of its master card, the Fool. However, the Tarot has many faces to present to us, and we may now start to meet them.

As we have said, it is not sufficient simply to learn the 'meanings' of the cards from a fortune-telling book or instruction booklet that is sold with each pack of cards. We have to meet each face of the Tarot, and make it part of our own experience, just like cultivating a host of friends. This may seem a tall order. How is one to meet a crowd of 78 people and remember them all individually? It is, however, easier than it may at first appear. The Tarot has a special structure built into it by the wise men who designed it, for they were also expert at the working of memory systems. There is no need for lengthy attempts at learning lists of meanings off by heart, or to adopt crude methods such as writing potted meanings or key-words on each card. All that is needed is a proper use of the creative imagination. The true use of your imagination is indeed the royal road to successful divination.

After you have built a good relationship with the Fool by the method already described, you may take the next step. Ask him, mentally or by hearing yourself say the words to him, if he will introduce you to the other powers of the Tarot. Now see him beckon to you, and follow him, along with his faithful dog, as he passes on down the path. When he gets opposite the rock which holds the doorway to your room, however, you find that he turns away from it, and walks over the edge of the cliff into the air! You see that his dog follows him safely. So, taking your courage and faith in your hands you follow too, and find that you are walking close behind him, high in the air.

After a short while he looks over his shoulder and smiles at you knowingly, and with a gesture of his hand points beside him. And there, in the air, appears a doorway. It is in the form of two pillars supporting an arch, with a veil between them. He smiles again and draws aside the veil, inviting you to enter. As you do so, he follows on behind you, but your attention is drawn to the details of the room you have entered. It is dimly lit by an unseen source, and is humming with tremendous power. The room is circular, with a floor of small black-and-white squares. Tall figures can just be discerned at the four quarters of its perimeter. The walls seem to rise to a great height, to what seems to be a pyramidal roof, beneath which, in the centre, is a waist-high square stone table, behind which there stands the figure of the Magician.

He is an impressive presence, with his right hand held high, holding a wand, and his left hand pointing towards the top of the table. Upon the table is a pack of Tarot cards, spread out, face upwards, in a spiral formation. They seem to circulate of their own volition, by a great current of power that comes from the high pyramidal ceiling, down through his wand and thence, directed by his pointing hand, to the cards that swirl and turn upon the table. He sees us standing before him, accompanied by the Fool, and smiles gravely in welcome. Then, rather like a stage magician, he ceremoniously indicates, in turn, the four figures that stand at four points of the circular room around us. As he does so, and points to them, the figures are illuminated clearly to our vision.

Behind him, and immediately before us, the figure is of a young woman holding and caressing a great lion. It is the Tarot image usually called *Strength*.

To our right, as he points toward it, there appears the figure of a stern-looking maiden, enthroned and holding a drawn sword in her right hand and a balance in her left. It is the image known as *Justice*.

The Magician points behind us, and turning we see not the door through which we have just come, but the radiant figure of an angel, a cup in each hand, pouring liquid from one to the other. This is the image known as *Temperance*.

And to our left, as the Magician points in that direction, is to be seen a naked dancing figure within a laurel wreath that is surrounded by heraldic images, as vivid as if they were alive, of a lion, a bull, a man and an eagle. It is the Tarot image of *The World*.

We realize that we are in the Hall of the Magician, which is the central powerhouse for all the images of the Tarot. The four images at each quarter guard the doorways to four other halls, beyond which are to be found the other images of the Trumps and also the so-called Lesser Arcanum of the suit cards. Our first task is to become familiar with the images within this hall. First of all the Magician himself, and then Strength, Justice, Temperance and the World.

In one of the oldest Tarot packs that survives, the Gringonneur in the Bibliothèque Nationale in Paris, the four latter cards are distinguished from the others by an angular aureole or halo about their heads. This indicates that they are special gateways, and this is further indicated by related symbols to be found on these cards. An alternative representation of Strength (to be found, for example, on the early Visconti-Sforza handpainted Tarot) is that of a man with a club standing with the lion. Strength is therefore associated with the suit of Wands, (the Clubs of the modern playing card pack). Justice holds a sword and is associated with those forces in life that are represented by the suit of Swords. Temperance has two cups, and is associated with those forces in life that are represented by the suit of Cups. The figure in The World stands within a medallion shape, and this is even more evident in some of the older handpainted cards where, as in the Visconti-Sforza, the world is plainly an image on a medallion held up by two cherubs. It is thus associated with those forces in life that are represented by the suit of Coins or Pentacles.

At this point it is enough to say that:

> Wands are associated with executive power,
> Swords with external competing forces, lessons to be learned,
> Cups with social affairs and matters of the heart,
> Coins with material wealth and well-being.

For the present it is sufficient that we concern ourselves with the basis of all this, to be found in the four Trumps that surround the Magician in his hall of power. By using your imagination to approach these images as living beings they will become fixed firmly within your mind and memory. This will lead on naturally to further revelation of the Trumps and suit cards beyond them in a structured and logical way. This is the practical application of an ancient memory system that was well known to the Renaissance savants who designed the Tarot system of images.

We have before us all the material for the next step in our work. Spend the next few meditation sessions in approaching each of the images we have met in turn. Keep a notebook in which to record your realizations about each of them. The way to go about this is exactly as we got to know the Fool. Approach each image as a person, and try to make conscious contact with it, as you would a friend. From this contact you will find ideas coming to you about the deeper meanings of the symbols associated with each figure, and also the core divinatory meanings for when you later use the Tarot for this purpose.

Thus we have found the Fool to be a friend, and one who has knowledge of deep places and things that are belied by his outer appearance. He has the seemingly completely foolish propensity for walking off the edge of cliffs, but he does so without harm because he is aware of the existence and operation of higher powers beyond those of a physical nature. In divination therefore he may well represent intuition, or ideas of the higher mind, bright ideas that others ignore or have never thought of, ideas that might well seem foolish to the commonsense criteria of the daily round. And indeed these ideas may well not work out in practical terms or may not have obvious material value. They may reflect instead the values of the creative artist, or of the mystic or of the moral reformer. The Fool is, therefore, a much more important figure than he looks.

The Magician, on the other hand, is more a figure of obvious power, although to those who are not familiar with the inner forces that he commands this power may appear more like trickery or legerdemain. However, he is basically one who controls things from the centre, and thus may represent this principle in any divination – of control, balance, demonstration, power in action.

In a similar way we approach the ideas embodied by the other four figures.

Variations in the Tarot Images

There are nowadays very many packs of Tarot cards on the market from which to choose – each one having its own variations on the basic imagery. Do not let this confuse you. There is no 'one and only true' version. Each Tarot image is like a magnet that attracts to it various other minor images and ideas, and people will differ as to which is more significant for them. This also acts more generally in the course of time, so that a Tarot image can, even in its major presentation, undergo a certain change. Examples of this are the Hermit, which was originally Old Father Time with an hourglass rather than a lantern; or the Chariot, which was earlier driven by a female figure, (the Winged Victory); and the Hanged Man, which was at first known as the Traitor.

For practical purposes we have to settle upon a specific pack to work with – although some diviners may prefer to have more than one, for different occasions or types of work. The principle we recommend is to settle upon one of the older printed sets issued for game-playing purposes. The various esoteric packs have their advantages, and no time is wasted in studying the ideas of their different designers, but they have the drawback of sometimes making a particular interpretation too specific. It is for this reason that I personally prefer to use a traditional Marseilles pack. The old crude cards give greater play to the imagination, although with experience one develops one's own inner relationship to the images that hold good irrespective of the pasteboard pictures that one may happen to be using at any particular time. None the less it is appreciated that to many readers, an esoterically-designed pack can be very evocative and a positive stimulus to the imagination.

As an example of how images change we can take various representations of the Fool. The earliest representation we have, the Visconti-Sforza handpainted one, shows him clad in rags and bereft of wits, with feathers in his hair and a long staff over his shoulder. In the later printed cards he has become a jester, dressed in motley and cap and bells, with a traveller's bag at the end of his staff and accompanied by a dog. It is often not clear whether the dog is gambolling beside him or attacking him, driving him out of town.

Musical instruments are given to him in various versions – lute, guitar, trumpet, pipe, flute, zither – and the dog can become a showman's performing dog. The Fool may sometimes appear blindfold, sometimes scattering money. His staff may become a corn stalk,or a magic wand, or a whirligig. An esoteric tendency, probably starting with A.E. Waite, is to show him as a fair innocent holding a rose. The Hermetic Order of the Golden Dawn's version depicted him as a young child. He may be about to walk over a cliff. He may be accompanied by a butterfly. Others introduce a crocodile or a leopard in place of or in addition to the dog, the former being a favourite of those who prefer an Egyptian ambiance to their cards.

The old handpainted Gringonneur Tarot shows him as a carnival figure with bauble-like beads, wearing ass's ears and a prominent codpiece, attributable to fertility, while children gather stones to ritually do him to death at the end of the festival. This opens up a deeper aspect to the dynamics of this figure, which in Charles Williams' novel *The Greater Trumps* (Eerdmans Publishing Co, 1976) is extended into a role similar to that of the creator of the world, who to the person without direct religious experience seems a static, remote and unmoving figure but who, to those who have faith and belief, is to be seen dancing everywhere within and throughout the whole of his creation.

The Magician too has varying aspects. In the Visconti-Sforza version he has the appearance of a rich merchant from far places displaying his wares, and this tradition is carried over into printed cards which depict him as a tradesman or artisan – often a cobbler, but sometimes a metal smith, alchemist or conjuror, at least a thimble-rigger gulling the naïve and stupid of their money. In later esoteric packs he becomes much more the magician, his table an altar upon which appear emblems of the four Tarot suits, representative of the four elements, and upon which he directs forces from a higher level.

Working Plan

Diary Record
Continue as before but this time you will be able to record the other images besides the Fool with which you worked, as we have now proceeded to the Magician and the four other figures within his Hall; Strength, Justice, Temperance and the World.

Exercise 1
Record your impressions of your meetings with each of the five new images you have met.

Exercise 2
As a result of these meetings list out for each one the general meaning you might expect each one to represent if you came across it in a Tarot reading. Do this also for the Fool.

Knowledge Notes

The Magician

The Magician, or Mountebank or Juggler as he has sometimes been called, is a figure who carries a certain charisma or glamour about himself, whether he is conceived as a rich merchant from far-away places setting out his wares in a marketplace, or a master of conjuring tricks and legerdemain entertaining passersby at a fairground. To an extent, all actors, performers, showmen, even market traders share in this archetypal role. In a sense he is therefore an extension of the Fool – or is perhaps his polar complement. He is one who demonstrates a wisdom and skill superior to the knowledge and understanding of those who make up his audience. This applies whether he is tricking them, entertaining them, or selling his wares to them. Perhaps all three!

As a wanderer, whose home is always somewhere else, or in another sense everywhere, he carries with him the ambience of another world, or of another dimension of existence. This is the attraction of the unknown, of the adventurer and the explorer. He is full of traveller's tales, a repository of unusual knowledge. In more esoteric renderings of the card he appears as a priest or magician, bringing down power from the heights of wisdom to the altar top before him, where lie the representations of the material world in the form of the symbolic emblems of the Tarot suits. He can thus stand very much for the true pattern of the Tarot card reader, who is, or should be, a source of higher wisdom and knowledge for whoever comes for consultation.

This is the sense in which he should be approached in our current work. He should come across as a kind of elder brother: wise and well-intentioned, and friendly towards us; very much a guide, philosopher and friend.

Strength

In the Visconti-Sforza handpainted card this was represented by a male figure with a club and a lion at his feet, no doubt being a form of Hercules, the strongman and hero of classical mythology. We feel it is best to stick with the broader stream of Tarot tradition that sees the figure as female.

In some old cards the maiden sat beside a pillar (which in some versions was broken), and in others she was shown holding open the jaws of a lion. The maiden and the pillar is perhaps the more conventional image, and was depicted by many artists, including Botticelli, as one of the Cardinal Virtues of Catholic religious tradition. Although the pillar may be broken, or show the maiden apparently breaking it, the image more consistent with the spirit of the card is really an unbroken pillar, for the sense of the image is strength and support. Indeed the maiden could well be depicted as a pillar herself, a caryatid, although this idea does not appear in any of the known Tarot versions.

The maiden with the lion, is, however, a more appealing image perhaps, with its associations of beauty and the beast, or spiritual will gently but indominatably controlling brute force. This ambience should come across to you from the figure. You may see her smiling at you, encouragingly and compassionately, as she demonstrates how, by right intention and the proper application of the right kind of force in the right place at the right time, we could so easily control the world in which we live – and make it a much more pleasant place. Thus she is very much the archetype behind all kinds of expression of power – whether this be in the Trumps of Emperor, Empress,

Hierophant and High Priestess, or the activities and conditions represented by the suit of Wands, all of which we shall examine later.

Justice

This figure is very close to the traditional figure of Justice. She is shown in the Tarot as clear-sighted, as opposed to some conventional forms that show her with a blindfold, to indicate impartiality. However, the intended meaning is much the same. Some old designs had a knight on horseback in the background, which has resonances with the law-keeping traditions of a true knight errant. But she also represents natural law, upon which the right working of the whole world is based.

A stern figure then, in some respects, but one who threatens only the wrongdoer and the deceitful. Of course this includes all of us to some degree! But rather than seeing her as a condemning or accusing figure, we do better to come to terms with her as a just upholder of what is good and fair and right; a protector of the weak who corrects whatever is out of time or out of balance. In this respect she is very much in control of the somewhat negative aspects of the Trumps of the Devil, the Tower, the Hanged Man and Death, and also of the suit of Swords. By recourse to this strict and firm but ultimately merciful figure we have nothing to fear. She seals the door where evil dwells, and is, indeed, a great protectress.

Temperance

This figure is another standard form for one of the Cardinal Virtues, and is found in many works of art. It also has strong associations with the symbolic teachings of alchemy concerning the purification and tempering of metals. In spiritual alchemy this purification and tempering process is concerned with aspects within ourselves that correspond symbolically with the various planetary powers and the metals traditionally associated with them.

In another sense that is not so readily obvious, this figure represents the servant who, in the days before piped running water, poured water from one bowl to another so his master and mistress could wash their hands. Service is therefore an important aspect of this image, and you may well find it helps a personal contact and appreciation of the card to imagine the figure, whether as angel or serving maid, pouring the waters to make your own hands clean – in a figurative as well as literal sense.

This spirit of service and of good living, in all senses of the word, is most appropriate as a guardian and overseer of the Trumps the Hermit, the Wheel, the Chariot and the Lovers, which represent amongst other things the general conditions of life represented by Time, Space, Triumphal Progress and Love, as well as all that is embraced by the suit of Cups.

The World

The Marseilles Tarot shows a female figure, naked except for a scarf, dancing in a wreathed oval, and surrounded by emblems of the head of a bull, a lion, an eagle and a man. It is very much a universal symbol, and indeed the card is sometimes called the Universe. The central figure could, for example, be regarded as similar to the dancing Shiva of oriental mythology, whose dancing creates the worlds. A similar ancient Western conception is of the goddess Isis, who is the feminine principle behind all goddesses and the inner powers of nature.

The four emblems about the wreath of victory have their origin in the Old Testament vision of Ezekiel, although their roots may be older than that in the corresponding signs of the zodiac – Taurus the Bull, Leo the Lion, Scorpio the Scorpion (sometimes replaced by an eagle), and Aquarius the Water-bearer. These were particularly important signs to the early astronomers because they each held an important bright star, one of the Rulers or Watchers of the Heavens, that are almost exactly at right angles to one another. Aldebaran, the 'eye of the bull' in Taurus; Regulus, the 'little king' in Leo; Antares, 'the opposite of Ares or Mars' in Scorpio; and Fomalhaut, the 'mouth of the fish' into which the waters of Aquarius flow. In later symbology they have been used to signify the Four Evangelists, Luke the bull, Mark the lion, John the eagle, and Matthew the man. They are also held to represent the principles of the Four Elements that make up the created world – Earth, Air, Fire and Water – in their cosmic or spiritual aspect. The detail of this need not bother us for the purposes of this course, so long as the general intention, that this represents the creation of a completed world, is quite clear.

Other old versions of the card carry the same significance. The Visconti-Sforza, for instance, shows two winged cherubs, each draped with a scarf, indicating a sphere above them in which there is a fair turretted castle, with golden stars above it, upon an island in the middle of the sea. There is a strong impression that it is an ideal world that is being presented, the New Jerusalem yet to come. The card therefore seems the summation of achievement, as befits, in the game, the highest scoring Trump. The Cary Yale Visconti-Sforza card shows a woman in the top half of the card bearing a trumpet in her right hand and a crown in her left. Below is a large crown beneath which, under an arch, is a scene of various castles and buildings, with sea and a river. Ships embark on the sea, and there is a boat being rowed in the river, between a fisherman on one bank and an approaching knight on horseback on the other.

We suggest that in your approach to this card you see the central figure as a welcoming guide and messenger who is willing to take you upon a tour of the other worlds over which she is custodian, represented by the Trumps of the Star, the Sun, the Moon and the Last Judgement (or angelic world, this card being sometimes called The Angel), as well as the worldly powers and activities that are signified by the suit of Coins. Money, it might be remembered, is concentrated energy, a token of what has been worked for, or at any rate manipulated, by human endeavour.

Divinatory Meanings of the Cards Described So Far

It is not part of our method of teaching the Tarot to give lists of meanings to learn by heart. By learning to approach the images on the cards themselves in a creative and sympathetic way, their significance should make itself very plain to you by your own realization and imaginative experience. This will enable you to be a much better reader and to gain a far greater subtlety and complexity of meanings from the cards. However, if you find this a little difficult in the early stages, it may not be amiss for us to provide a few indicators and pointers to the general significance of the cards when found in a divinatory reading.

The Fool, as you may discover from your personal contact with the figure, is full of vision, enthusiasm, and great expectations. He represents intuitions to follow, new roads to tread, adventurous attitudes, ideals to be expressed. (If reversed or badly aspected, in real life he could signify an unrealistic approach to life, blinded by glamour or immature dreams of never-never land.)

The Magician, however, is one who is very much in control, yet not a mere organizer or administrator. He can create new situations from his ability to envision what is practicable and possible, allied to his skill and knowledge in how to convert visions to reality. (Reversed or badly aspected this can indicate cunning or trickery, and the manipulation of others in a high-handed or selfish way.)

Strength shows forth confidence and effortless control, that comes from high skill and right intentions. (If reversed or badly aspected by other cards it could indicate repression or an abuse of higher intelligence or ability in pursuit of power or in the assumption of knowing what's good for other people.)

Justice means right balance and control and the expression of evenhanded fairness. (It could also indicate legal matters per se, or if reversed or badly aspected tyranny, accusations – possibly false – bigotry or intolerance, the worst that can come from a closed, legalistic mind.)

Temperance indicates a harmonious blending of forces or energies and the opportunity for growth. (If reversed or ill-aspected then there could be sparks flying from lack of harmony in some partnership or merger. Such problems might, however, be only temporary until the situation settles down to one of smooth cooperation. Few new partnerships are utterly smooth unless both parties are particularly bland or characterless.)

The World generally signifies completeness or the whole of the affair in question. It represents a kind of overview or encapsulation of the entire situation. This may well be success and movement to a new level of expression following a previous achievement. (If reversed or badly aspected it can indicate restriction to the same dreary round, confinement to stereotyped reactions rather than full expressions of achievement about to break to yet new bounds. Perhaps lessons poorly assimilated, or a refusal to look at what needs to be learned from the circumstances of life.)

Recommended Books

You should have all you need to learn to read the Tarot effectively and well from this course alone, for it directs you towards how to learn from the Tarot itself. However, reading around the subject does no harm if you are so inclined, particularly books by experienced Tarot readers. There is a plethora of books on the subject available now, some frankly hardly worth reading, let alone the cost of purchase. And others are of a highly esoteric or philosophical nature that really does not concern us at this stage of our studies, which should be concerned with practicalities rather than metaphysical theories. Here are a few I *can* recommend:

A Complete Guide to the Tarot by Eden Gray (Bantam Books, 1971) is a well-established text, indeed almost a classic, by a very experienced author and card reader. She covers a wide ground, giving lots of useful information on the generally accepted meaning behind the cards as well as practicalities of actual spreads.

Rachel Pollack is an author worth reading. *The Seventy-eight Degrees of Wisdom* in two volumes (Aquarian, 1980 and 1983) describes the Major Arcana and the Minor Arcana in a sensible fashion, and includes sample readings, which are always useful study for the beginner. A third book, *Tarot Readings and Meditations* (Aquarian, 1990) first published as *The Open Labyrinth*, 1986 is a collection of readings, and this opportunity to look over a cartomancer's shoulder in the analysis of a reading is excellent training, even if one may not agree with all that is said. Indeed, the exercise of evaluating the merits of an interpretation differing from your own is a very effective way of becoming a good reader.

Another eminently practical book that students have recommended to me is *Easy Tarot Guide* by Marcia Masino (A C S Publications, Inc., 1988), who had a very rigorous apprenticeship as a practical Tarot reader working for a commercial organization that demanded accuracy sufficient to satisfy its clients but limiting the length of any reading to no more than ten minutes! She was good enough to have a number of customers always waiting, so quite sensibly quickly set up business on her own in a small partnership.

We will talk about other books at a later stage, but these few are more than enough to get any reader well grounded in practicalities by providing detailed results of cartomantic experience rather than delving into the depths of esoteric philosophising. Such books do indeed have their place but we do best to reserve consideration of them until a later stage.

Questions and Answers

Q. In my meditation impressions I sometimes receive personal advice related to my problems. Sometimes I've asked for it, sometimes I have not. Have others reported this?

A. You may well indeed find personal advice coming to you when working with the Tarot, sometimes asked for and sometimes not. It is almost as if one is tapping into a kind of personal help organism, so to speak, and on occasion one does not even have to lay out the cards if one has the required sensitivity and experience. More usually, I think one tends to pick up on this level when reading a specific spread, in the form of intuitional insights about the cards, the spread, the querent, or the question being asked, that would not normally be found in the published textbooks.

Q. Is it all right to put myself in the place of the archetypes to experience what they do, like putting myself in the picture on the card?

A. Putting yourself in the position of any of the archetypes is a very good method of learning about the Tarot images, and is also first-class training in the mediation of archetypal principles, which is magic in the truest and purest sense of the word.

Q. Does it matter if meditation is interrupted by a phone call or the doorbell or people visiting, etc., and I have to come out of it suddenly without 'closing down' properly?

A. It is not a matter of dire consequence if you are interrupted during meditation but it can be a bit of a shock to the system, although no more so than being awakened suddenly from sleep. But as it also pulls you out of a level of awareness that may have taken you some time and effort to get into, it is obviously best to avoid interruption if you can. This is obviously not possible in most peoples' daily circumstances and we have to do the best we can. In fact when you become an old hand at this game it will not matter too much as you will find you can meditate in the middle of a railway station if you have a mind to it, and be able to change levels of consciousness easily and at will. However, for the first few months at least, the best counsel is to try to have a special place, a special time, together with peace and quiet and a reasonable chance of being free from interruption.

Q. I find Bible quotations often come into my mind whilst talking with the images. Is this all right?

A. Bible quotations coming up in meditation are quite in order, and show that you are tuning in to the more positive and mystical side of the images concerned.

Q. Do all the Tarot Major Arcarnum cards relate to a sign of the Zodiac? If so, would you please tell me which ones are which? I have worked out three or four for myself but am not sure of the rest.

A. With regard to Tarot Trump correspondences with the zodiac, there are of course twenty-two Trumps and only twelve zodiacal signs. There are certain traditional attributions that some people find helpful, although they are by no means necessary, and opinion differs as to which are the best ones to use. Therefore I make no reference to them in this course, as the Tarot is quite capable of being used without reference to other systems of symbols. However, you do sometimes find them featured on some modern packs of cards, and the most generally favoured attributions are as follows. (However, it is what *you* feel to be correct that is the keynote of all of this, not anyone else's ideas. In this system twelve Trumps are allocated to the twelve zodiacal signs, seven to traditional planets, and three to the elements. If you want any more detailed information you had better consult my book *A Practical Guide to Qabalistic Symbolism* (Weiser, 1978), where all this is covered in considerable detail.)

The Fool – Air; *The Magician* – Mercury; *The High Priestess* – Moon; *The Empress* – Venus; *The Emperor* – Aries; *The Hierophant* – Taurus; *The Lovers* – Gemini; *The Chariot* – Cancer; *Justice* – Libra; *The Hermit* – Virgo; *The Wheel of Fortune* – Jupiter; *Strength* – Leo; *The Hanged Man* – Water; *Death* – Scorpio; *Temperance* – Sagittarius; *The Devil* – Capricorn; *The Tower* – Mars; *The Star* – Aquarius; *The Moon* – Pisces; *The Last Judgement* – Fire; *The Universe* – Saturn.

I wonder if any of this accords with what you felt to be right? There is room for considerable argument and discussion over all of this. And many people spend so much time doing that that they never seem to get down to any practical work! They are what is known as 'armchair occultists'.

Q. This is a wonderful course and I look forward to the meditations. However, it seems to me that I will always be a better meditator than reader.

A. You are obviously a pretty good meditator and getting quite a bit out of the meditations on the images. This brings rewards in its own right and at its own level by virtue of the fact that the Tarot images are symbolic figures that lead to the development of higher consciousness. However, with the Tarot there is the added bonus that one can develop a more live astral consciousness by coming to terms with the figures as characters – and of course particularly with the Fool and the Magician, who might even be regarded as two sides of the same character, able to undergo a series of transformations that are demonstrated in the other images.

As to divination, a number of formally-trained occultists have reservations about it, and it is true that if one has one's intuitive powers well tuned one can get along pretty well without it.

However, it can be a valuable discipline in getting some of the (occasionally rather stilted) Hermetic philosophical conceptions down to earth, thus bridging the gap between the meditation shrine and life as it is lived – which is really a profound magical act and a way of life of course.

Q. You advised me that on this course I should try to look at the Tarot as separate from the Qabalistic Tree of Life. I am trying to do this but how successfully I do not know.

A. Your work shows that you have indeed taken a great step forward in heeding my words about not being tied to the formal concepts of the Tarot as applied to another system. Of course you can always go back to the Tree of Life attributions at a later date and I think you will find that your appreciation of both the Tree of Life and Tarot will have expanded through working upon them separately for a time. Both indeed are free-standing systems, sufficient unto themselves, and do not in any sense have to rely on each other. They can of course be 'worked' together but there are many ways in which this can be done. We should not be tied to Golden Dawn or other traditional formulations. The inner world is a free country! You can let your imagination wander, within reasonable limits.

Q. When introduced to the Strength card, try as hard as I could, it always came in the image of a man.

A. Interesting. Although many versions of the card show a girl, either with a lion or alternatively sitting beside a pillar, there are early designs that show a man, generally accompanied by a lion or else wearing a lion skin, and also bearing a club. Some say that he represents Hercules, the strong hero who represents humanity as a whole. At any rate it is a very protective card and one that shows higher impulses and intentions ruling over brute strength.

Q. After my meetings with the cards in the Hall of the Magician I have made a most startling discovery. On meeting them as real people I realize that I actually know some of them in my circle of friends. This seems unbelievable but true. Does anyone else have this experience?

A. You need to treat this with some caution. It is caused by certain psychological characteristics in the people concerned having something particularly in common with one or other of the Tarot archetypes. This you are picking up psychically or subconsciously. Whilst this is an interesting phenomenon you should avoid doing too much work identifying any particular person with any of the images in your meditative work. This is because the power of creative visualization used on a systematic basis and connected up with archetypal figures is far greater than most people realize, and it could happen that you start to affect or intrude upon the consciousness of your friends or acquaintances in this manner. This of course is hardly occult good manners, and if deliberately entered upon with personal or selfish intent in order to subtly influence people becomes, in effect, 'black magic'.

This phenomenon was for many years kept secret by occultists because it was felt that if generally known, the knowledge could be abused. However it is quite possible to stumble upon it accidentally, as you have done, and in the modern climate of opinion there would seem to be more possible dangers and difficulties in withholding information than in making it freely available. What people do with the facts must be their own responsibility. I am sure any misuse of the power of the images was far from your intentions, and I am also sure that no great harm has been done in your discovering this phenomenon. If in future any of the figures take on the appearance of actual people you know, gently dissolve the image and let it build up again slightly differently, without that personal identification. This they will readily do for you.

Q. I have experienced some difficulties with the meditations. One of these is a reluctance within me, suprisingly, to get down to meditation. But I have also had dizziness and nausea during meditation, forcing me to pull out. This could of course be an extension of the reluctance manifesting itself, but I wonder if other people have come across this too?

A. Dizziness and nausea are not symptomatic of meditation generally, in fact rather the opposite, it having more often a quietening and calming effect. However, if you have a lot going on around you in your personal life it could well be that you have a bit of repressed tension coming out at this time. I suggest you try relaxing mentally and physically for two or three minutes before you start in onto the visualizations.

The feeling of reluctance to start is not uncommon, and is also to be found with many artists and others before commencing creative work. It is on a par with the writer's finding any excuse to avoid sitting down before a blank sheet of paper, or a painter putting off facing an empty canvas. I'm afraid discipline is the only cure here, at any rate in the early stages, which is why we have the device of keeping a meditation diary, which can be of great help in this respect. As you get into the swing of things though, and meditation becomes a productive pleasure, these problems pass. There may well be occasional 'dry' periods, when we are 'off form', so to speak, but a regular discipline prevents us from petering out into inactivity or unproductive stops and starts.

LESSON THREE

In this lesson we continue our encounter with the images we have met thus far. After the usual preliminaries of meditating on the Fool and following him to the Hall of the Magician you are ready to meet formally and interact with the four Trumps that surround the Magician.

Strength

Go first to the figure of Strength. As you stand before this image see her as the gateway to all that stands for control and power, whether it be of mind over matter, or by way of organization or invention, whereby the higher elements of consciousness reign over the lower forces of life. Now see her rise, and with the lion following docilely behind her, she turns and invites you to follow her through a doorway behind her. There we find another circular room similar to the one that we have left, but with different figures at the four quarters. The maiden who controls the lion indicates each one in turn, and as she does so, each is illuminated to our vision.

Each of the four figures represents executive power. The figure before us, opposite the door from which we have entered, is that of the *Pope*, who represents spiritual or moral power and authority. To our right is the *Emperor*, representing physical power and authority. Behind us, at the door by which we entered, is the *High Priestess*, who represents the feminine aspect of spiritual or moral power, which is higher wisdom or intuition. And to our left, opposite the Emperor, is the *Empress*, representing the feminine aspect of material power – the maternal principle, whether it be exercised over a home, a social group, or a nation.

The way to become familiar with the principles of each of these four cards is to come to this place, which we may call the Hall of Strength, and stand before each of the figures in turn. Choose a different one each day, recording ideas and impressions in your notebook, which should have a different page or section for each Tarot image. Obviously in the course of divination one will not meet many enquirers who have directly to do with emperors, empresses, popes or high priestesses! So it is a matter of realizing what each of these images signifies in terms of daily life. Every home, business, office, workshop and social group has these elements of power within it, exercised either individually or as a group, or representing some controlling person or group. So the Emperor might well represent a managing director, headmaster, foreman, father, or the kind of power or authority exercised by anyone in these kinds of roles.

The Pope represents a rather different kind of authority, less direct but none the less powerful. It is not necessarily that of a vicar or other kind of churchman, but will represent a moral code or pattern of acceptable conduct in a particular environment. It might well represent the conscience of the enquirer or of another person closely associated with the situation under review. The corresponding female cards of Empress and High Priestess have the same kind of application, except that being female they have a different general effect or approach. A mother obviously has a different relationship to her family than a father, despite the current vogue (however laudable in many respects) for trying to avoid sexual stereotyping.

Justice

When we have completed our work in the Hall of Strength, we can investigate the three other halls that adjoin the Hall of the Magician. The next one is called the Hall of Justice, for it is the figure of Justice that guards its door. *Important Note: The figures in this Hall tend to have a negative aspect. Do not let this make you feel nervous. Remember that they are in the charge of the powerful figures for good of the Fool and the Magician, and also of Justice herself, in whose Hall they appear, as subordinates of her function. Also you are in control of all the work that you undertake by virtue of the techniques for opening and closing that we have followed. Should you ever feel dominated or overshadowed by any imaginative figures, whether good or evil in appearance, then practical occult work is really not for you until such time as you have built a more positive spiritual intention and personal integrity. This kind of problem is however, rare, and generally encountered only in cases of drug abuse, or the deliberate encouragement of negative or morbidly passive psychic states, as in some types of hypnosis, regressional analysis or trance mediumship.*

Let us therefore stand before Justice and make contact with this stern figure who sees all within us, right or wrong, and is not only a judge but a great healer, for it is she who holds the balance and makes things right, even if that process may not always be enjoyable to us. When you have spent some time communing with this figure, see her rise and invite you to follow her into her hall. You will have realized that in a divination the card she represents will signify justice, things coming up for review or correction, and a dispassionate, objective assessment of how things really are.

Immediately before us as we enter the hall is the figure of the *Devil*. This should not cause us alarm. The devil is not an all-powerful figure. He can only influence those who are willingly tempted by him. In a number of packs the figures chained to the stone block at his feet have iron collars that they could easily remove for themselves. The irony is that when we do wrong, even though it causes us misery in the end, we do so voluntarily. Thus this image of the Tarot represents our own folly. Although it seems a figure of power it is really one of foolishness, an interesting counterpart to the Fool who, although he appears foolish, wields great power. So in a divination the Devil is likely to indicate pig-headed obstinacy, pride or stubbornness, which in the end is self-defeating.

If we turn to our right we see as the figure of Justice who stands with us points her sword in that direction, the image of *Death*, a skeleton with a scythe. He does not necessarily represent physical death, but rather any complete change; the end of something. And even though this may be painful when it occurs, it may also be a merciful release, or a natural conclusion to a matter whose time is now well past, and it should make room for new life and new beginnings. Therefore this is not entirely a morbid image.

Now if we turn to look back toward the door by which we entered we will see the figure of a mighty *Lightning Struck Tower*. This differs from the images we have so far contemplated in that it is an object rather than a person, although it does have two figures falling from it. We may see the Tower in constant motion; it rises continually only to fall again when struck by a bolt from on high. Like the figure of Death this image demonstrates sudden change, but it is also allied to the foolish will of the Devil, in that it may well be an edifice of pride, like the Tower of Babel. However, we should reflect that it is an act of God that strikes it down, an element of the justice and re-establishment of the right balance of all things. So it should be regarded, not simply as catastrophe for those who falsely believe in this proud edifice, but as the possible beginning of wisdom if they can learn from hard experience.

To the left we see the figure of the *Hanged Man*. This is someone who is being punished, or who is the victim of circumstances or of the actions of others. In many versions of the card he seems to have nevertheless a great calmness, even happiness, about him. An old title of the card was the *Traitor*, and it was ancient practice to hang the effigies of traitors upside-down in public places. A traitor is someone who follows moral values that do not coincide with those of his or her social group or nation, so there is an aspect of this card which denotes someone who lives according to perhaps higher principles than those amongst whom he lives. So the Hanged Man could be a hero – someone who defies a mob for example, or espouses an unpopular cause. On the other hand it may simply denote someone who is individualistic or eccentric. Any of these aspects may be indicated when this card appears in a divination. Meditation upon this image and communion with the Hanged Man will help to fathom its many implications.

Temperance

When you have become thoroughly familiar with the images in the Hall of Justice it is time to pass on to the Hall of Temperance, which is guarded by the image of that name. The mighty angel at its doorway pours liquid from one cup to another, signifying the blending of life forces found in all social life. If this card appears in a divination it signifies a mature control of people and events. It is a very healing image, as personal contemplation with it will reveal.

The angel invites you within the doorway it guards, and you find yourself in a circular chamber similar to the others. This chamber contains images that represent particular conditions and circumstances of life. Before you, as you enter, you will find the figure of the *Hermit*, an old man who holds aloft a lantern. He represents prudent wisdom, and is a guide, philosopher and friend who has much to teach those who are willing to follow him. In the earliest cards he held not a lantern but an hourglass, for he is also a form of Old Father Time, and it is indeed time that brings the wisdom of experience to us.

Now the angel will indicate the figure to our right, and this you will see to be the *Chariot*. Although most cards now show a male figure within it, originally it was female, the famous classical figure of Winged Victory. On some early handpainted cards either she or the horses were winged. By becoming familiar with this figure you will learn that when it turns up in a divination it represents successful progress over circumstances and contending forces, though perhaps not without struggle.

Behind you at the entrance door there is to be seen another image, one that is depicted as impersonal on most modern designs, the *Wheel of Fortune*. However, older cards clearly showed a woman standing before the wheel rotating it. She was Fortuna, the goddess of fortune. It is this figure that you may communicate with in your meditation, and the wheel over which she presides is the turning of fate and fortune, often denoting a change of circumstance.

Finally, the angel will indicate another multi-personal image on your left, that of the *Lovers*. The key figure on this card is Cupid, the son of Venus (the goddess of love). The oldest versions of this card show a procession of loving couples, with Cupid shooting his arrows at them. This is the basis of the modern card, although most show only one couple, with an officiating priest or master or mistress of ceremonies. We would recommend that with this card you try communication with all the individual elements of the card; with the young god, with the master or mistress of ceremonies, and with the two young lovers themselves. The meaning of the card in divination will obviously have to do with love, possibly betrothal, and the sometimes-difficult decisions that go along with making a close personal commitment.

The World

Having assimilated the contents of the Hall of Temperance we now seek entry to the Hall of the Worlds or of the Universe. The dancing figure within the oval wreath is the one who controls entry to it. This figure is one who knows much and is a messenger from far-off places, and when appearing in a Tarot spread signifies generally the fullness of knowledge and completion, which of course may be the prelude to things new.

When the figure bids us enter the Hall of the Worlds we find that on the far side of the circular hall is a mighty angel leaning down from the Heavenly World blowing a trumpet to awaken the dead, the image of the *Last Judgement*. He is a great herald angel who is not always dramatic in his annunciation of what is to be; his intimations may well come gently or silently to us, but when found in a Tarot reading, they are still likely to signify a great awakening or re-awakening to possibilities or opportunities.

To our right we find the mighty golden orb of *The Sun* shining upon two children playing happily in an enclosed garden. In contemplating this card simply be aware of standing within the sun's rays soaking up the general health and well-being that radiates from it. It is a fortunate card to find in a divination spread.

Behind us, at the doorway by which we entered, we find a landscape wherein a naked maiden pours waters into a lake under the presidency of *The Star* which shines large and bright in the sky against a background of other stars. By communing with this figure you will find that she is one who represents hope and far-sighted wisdom.

Lastly, to our left, we find that there is a stream, beyond which are two towers. A large craw-fish is to be seen in the waters, and beyond two dogs bay at *The Moon*. Again, as with the Sun, when contemplating this scene simply be aware of standing within the moon's rays, soaking up the influence that they bring. This should also bring realizations as to the meaning of the card. Its general principle, like the moon that orbits our Earth, is one of hidden forces that are yet strong enough to cause the tides of the sea and the growing patterns of biological and botanic life.

Working Plan

Diary Record
Continue as before. Note that there is a lot of work to get through in this Lesson - no less than sixteen new images - so take all the time that you need over it. It is important not to skimp your work at this crucial formative stage.

Exercise 1
Write a summary of your experiences in the Hall of Strength.

Exercise 2
Write a summary of your experiences in the Hall of Justice.

Exercise 3
Write a summary of your experiences in the Hall of Temperance.

Exercise 4
Write a summary of your experiences in the Hall of the Worlds.

Exercise 5
As a result of your meetings with the sixteen further Trump images list out for each one the general meaning you might expect it to represent if you came across it in a Tarot reading.

Knowledge Notes

Trump Images in the Hall of Strength

The Pope

The Pope card represents the principle of spiritual or moral authority, and although depicted in priestly robes its function is not limited to ecclesiastical associations. Every group, however large or small, however transient or long-lasting, has its code of expected practice or behaviour from its members, even though this may not be a written code or one that has been formally discussed and decided upon. Your own feelings for or against organized or ritualized religious practice should not influence your approach to this image. He can be a guide, philosopher and friend just as much as can the Fool, the Magician or any other expression of the Spirit of the Tarot. In this aspect, however, there certainly is that of the wise counsellor, the confessor, and the shepherd of souls.

The Emperor

Here we have a similar figure, although the authority expressed is more secular than spiritual. Again the fact that he is traditionally in the robes and regalia of an emperor does not mean that the principle does not exist in democratic societies. Some person or people within any group has to make decisions and provide stable organization and leadership. Once again, do not be thrown by any personal hang-ups about 'authority'. This image can be guide, philosopher and friend, in the way of an experienced man of affairs.

The High Priestess

What we have said about the Pope applies to this image also, except that feminine wisdom has an ambience all its own. This is of the more spiritual and perhaps austere kind, very much akin to the associations made with Pallas Athene, the Greek goddess of wisdom. Holy wisdom has indeed often been depicted as a feminine image. The contact with this figure is an inspirational one, and Pallas Athene was very much the ruler over heroes, bringing out the best in them. In Charles Kingsley's *The Heroes* she says, '. . . . I know the thoughts of all men's hearts, and discern their manhood or their baseness.' The card can therefore represent ideals and their fruition.

The Empress

Again, in some respects this image is a female counterpart to the Emperor, but is no less a figure for that. Indeed the ruling principle in its feminine aspect is a very powerful one, embracing motherhood in all its forms and expressions. This aspect is helped in the Waite version of the card, and those that derive from it, where she is shown out-of-doors on a green mound, with wheat and other forms of vegetation growing luxuriantly about her. In Greek mythology she would be represented by Demeter the great Earth Mother, and by an equivalent image in any other pantheon. This gives the key to the way to approach her. She should be a help to any who have problems coming to terms with the mother image – just as the Emperor can help with regard to the father figure. Both these figures can, in a spread, represent therefore a mother or father, or an older individual, perhaps an employer, who performs a similar beneficent/authoritarian role.

Trump Images in the Hall of Justice

The Devil
The figures at the feet of the Devil plainly indicate bondage, and most evil could be described as a form of bondage – or compulsive behaviour. Compulsion is a hallmark of a lack of personal balance or spiritual will, whether it is expressed in serious ways or trivial. Compulsive behaviour is to be found in all of us in many ways, be it simply a tendency to eat or drink more than is good for us, or perhaps to indulge in malicious gossip. We do not have to fear raising the Devil by 'dabbling in the occult' – he is very much with us all the time. So we should not approach this rather unpleasant-looking figure in any great fear and trepidation. He is a very familiar figure to whom we play host for much of the time. To that extent he is a reflection of the worst aspects of ourselves. Accordingly, in occult teaching this image is sometimes called the *Dweller on the Threshold*. Or in psychological terms, our 'shadow'. This shadow side of ourselves is often projected on to other people for whom we have an irrational disliking. It means they mirror something in ourselves that we do not like or cannot readily accept. The appearance in a reading of this card therefore usually indicates pet-hates and self-delusions rather than the onset of terrible or evil happenings.

Death
This is another traditional image that should not be interpreted at face value in any reading. It does not portend the physical death of the querent or of other persons closely concerned. It does however signify the end of a phase, for every sequence of events has its beginning (or coming to birth), its growth (or coming to maturity), and its eventual

decline (or death). So we are looking at the principle of the ending and beginnings of things, because every ending heralds a new beginning. This may be looked upon with great regret and sadness or alternatively it may be welcomed; much depends on what is passing out of expression and who gains or loses by it.

The Lightning Struck Tower

An immediate association with this picture is the Tower of Babel, the Biblical story exemplifying how pride comes before a fall. There can however be a more positive side to it, and some cards show the top of the tower as a crown, gently raised to receive the shaft of lightning as if it were a welcome revelation or flash of inspiration. Although an alternative early title for this card was *Hell's Gate*, this image came from medieval Miracle Plays, wherein the risen Christ was shown opening the gate to release sinners in bondage and allowing them to enter heavenly life. In some practical workshops for personal spiritual development it has been used to signify a sudden revelation of the truth about oneself. This can be a pleasant or unpleasant experience, but should prove to be a salutary one.

The Hanged Man

Originally this card was called the *Traitor*, as it was common custom to display the effigy of a traitor upside-down. No less an artist than Botticelli was commissioned to produce effigies for this purpose. In modern times, the corpse of the dictator Mussolini was treated in this way by a vengeful mob. The bags of money shown on some cards could be an allusion to Judas Iscariot, the archetypal traitor, on the assumption that he betrayed Jesus for money. However, at a deeper level, a traitor represents the inversion of commonly-held values. This is inferred by the serene expression seen on the hanged man's face on many cards, or even the addition of a halo, indicating his is a willing sacrifice for a valued principle. This may well be the meaning to be read from its appearance in a spread, rather than any literal martyrdom, (although some self-sacrifice might be implied). Once again, as with the other images to be found in the Hall of Justice, there is a possible dual interpretation – which perhaps is why the figure of Justice is equipped with a set of scales!

Trump Images in the Hall of Temperance

The Hermit

This figure has undergone a sea change. Originally he was *Father Time*, carrying an hourglass and sometimes seen with wings or crutches; for time can crawl or fly according to circumstances. As soon as the hourglass became a lantern the basis was laid for an additional range of meaning that seems to have gone far to oust the original conception. Nowadays this image tends to be seen as someone showing the way, or as a keeper of secret wisdom. The image can in fact carry all the attributes conventionally associated with age, whether they be the wisdom of experience or a difficulty in accepting change. The snowy heights introduced on some modern cards indicate lofty wisdom, but in practical terms one should not forget the alternative range of original meanings concerning time and age.

The Chariot
Another changed image, the original handpainted cards showed Winged Victory, a familiar image from classical times, riding in her chariot, which was also a triumphal processional float. Somewhere along the line the sex of the charioteer changed. However, the meaning has remained much the same, and this image can prove a very positive and confidence-building one; perhaps the more so if one reverts to the more traditional female figure.

The Wheel of Fortune
It is surprising that the figure of Fortuna should have been dropped from this card and we recommend that you reinstate her in your visualization for it is she who turns the wheel whereby men and women suffer the vagaries of 'those two imposters – triumph and disaster' as Kipling described them. Those of an esoteric turn of mind may see cycles of karma or destiny depicted here, but in the short-term view of a Tarot reading it is perhaps best simply to regard it as a sign of a sequence of events taking their natural course either for better or worse, although, as the figures around the card indicate, one person's rise implies another person's fall.

The Lovers
The original principle of this image was Love, the key figure being Cupid hovering over a procession of lovers. In the course of time the centre of interest subtly changed, which has caused certain differences of interpretation and even confusion as to what the card depicts. Some see it as a young man standing at the crossroads of vice and virtue, or facing some other dilemma. However, if we bear in mind the fact that all expressions of love imply decisions of one kind or another we shall be able to interpret the card in the broadest possible manner.

Trump Images in the Hall of the Worlds

The Angel or Last Judgement
This is obviously an image of rebirth, new opportunities, and good news. It is couched in terms of Christian iconography but does not necessarily have a religious connotation in interpretation. For the purposes of illustrating a divinatory meaning, the rescue of the beleaguered could just as easily be conceived of as the United States cavalry in a Wild West film as an Archangel sounding the Last Trump! No corresponding event in daily life is likely to have quite so dramatic a scenario, but picking up on the principle of rescue and identifying with the emotions of the saved is perhaps the best way to form a rapport with this card. In another sense it could be regarded as akin to an alarm clock: something that awakens sleepers.

The Sun
This is one of the most direct and positive images of the Tarot – a life-giving, loving fount of creative energy. Some old cards depicted a maiden seated in a meadow combing her hair, as an alternative to the two dancing children, and this image may appeal to you. Another version showed a young boy running across the sky with the sun upheld in his hand. And A.E. Waite popularized the image of a young boy riding a horse. All these are images worth contemplating since they reveal various aspects of this image, which can also represent the true self of the Querent, or the heart of any situation.

The Star
Earlier versions of the card emphasized the star or stars rather than the figure below. As the star maiden bringing the dew of the stars, an ancient symbol for higher wisdom and healing, and also for the hope of being released from constricting circumstances, she is very important.

The Moon
This card hints at mysteries just beyond the range of intellectual consciousness and has (not inappropriately) also been called *The Twilight*. In Renaissance and early philosophy there was a great deal of difference between the world of the stars and that of the moon, even though they were both up in the sky. Whereas the stars represented a higher angelic world, the sub-lunary sphere was the province of various spirits, from higher guides to beguiling deceivers. This is very much the psychic world therefore, or, if one prefers modern psychological terms, the subconscious. Perhaps the best way to regard it when it appears in divination, is as representing things that are not quite clearly and logically resolved.

Divinatory Meanings

You will benefit most by working out your own meanings as best you may, so we will leave any of our own hints and ideas until the next Lesson.

Questions and Answers

Q. Do you consider the 'gate cards' (the Fool, Magician, Strength, Justice, Temperance and the World) more important than the other Major Arcana cards? If these cards should appear in a reading, do you give them special importance?

A. Yes, I do think that the 'gate' cards have a greater significance in the general structure of the Tarot, although I do not think that this necessarily applies to their divinatory interpretation in a spread. Their importance comes to the fore, I think, when one is using the Tarot as a means of spiritual self-development and inner exploration. Any possible greater significance in an actual spread would relate to their role as representatives of moral virtues – those traditional Cardinal Virtues of medieval Christendom of which any old-time reader of the cards would have been aware. In our own day this particular ambience has rather dropped out of general consciousness, perhaps to our detriment.

Q. As most books and classes use the Rider deck, and sometimes the BOTA deck, in my meditations I tend to get imagery from these versions mixed up with those of my own Hanson-Roberts deck. I don't think it matters much as the decks are just saying the same thing in slightly different ways. Do you agree?

A. I see no problem in a mixture of imagery from various decks and think it all to the good. Most decks on the market are based on pretty standard traditional ideas, and the individual extras or varieties of interpretation they bring seem to me to make the field so much the richer. It is my hope that students of mine will be able to use any deck (within reason), and that their inner perception of the various images will have access to a wide symbolic database, so to speak, with a fair degree of their own interpretation and pictorial ideas thrown in.

Q. I have some trouble with the Devil. Most cards, when dignified, present the best aspect of the card. But there isn't much of a 'best' aspect to the Devil except that you can finally see that the situation you're in isn't a good one and realize that you could be doing something else. But where do you assign the 'best' aspect of a 'bad' card? When a difficult card is ill-dignified, does it get better or worse?

A. When it comes to reversed meanings of 'difficult' cards such as the Devil, these often indicate what happens in real life, where evil or illusion overstep the mark, because of their inherent self-contradictions or imbalance, and become obviously false, or at any rate due for their 'come-uppance'!

Q. The only reference to time that I have come across is in the book *Tarot* by Eileen Connolly (Aquarian, 1990), yet I would have expected much more to be written about this aspect of the subject. 'When?' questions are very common and will, no doubt, be asked time and time again. I would appreciate your comments on this.

A. You raise quite a problem with this question of time and I regret that there is no easy answer. In my experience inner-plane sources have never been too reliable on timing. It would seem that time exists in a very different way within the physical world and out of it. Apart from reliance on personal intuition I would think that one possible way through this problem might be by recourse to astrology, if one has the knowledge and the time to devote to this avenue. Any major event ought to show up in forthcoming transits or progressions.

Apart from Eileen Connolly the nettle has been grasped by Emily Peach in her book *Tarot Prediction* (Aquarian, 1991, first published as *Tarot for Tomorrow* 1988), and she has a lot of experience as well as quite a deep theoretical knowledge. She describes questions that begin 'When shall I . . .' as 'a snare for the unfortunate reader's feet' because they are not only riddled with assumptions but also require an extremely complex spread. She goes on to suggest the type of spreads that might be used, but they are too detailed to quote and so I can only refer you to a copy of the book.

She also mentions timing devices that can be built into spreads. One that was devised by Jean Goode, and which also appears in Sasha Fenton's *Fortune Telling by Tarot Cards* (Aquarian, 1985) is based on years, months, weeks or days being indicated by certain small value Coin, Sword, Wand or Cup cards. Emily Peach reports that she has found this to work well. Mary K.

Greer cites a similar method in her book *Tarot Transformation* (Aquarian, 1987) (known as *Tarot for Yourself* in the original American version). She recommends specifically taking a card from the pack to represent time. If a suit card is drawn then according to its number it represents so many days for Wands, weeks for Cups, months for Swords, and years for Coins. Court cards refer to stages of development, Pages for beginnings, Knights for the process itself, Queens for maturity and fruition, and Kings for completion, whilst Trumps refer to the month indicated by the astrological correspondence, for which she used the old Golden Dawn system (see pages 50–51).

Obviously this is a complex area with many differences in points of detail. However it is pretty well established that anything that one decides to believe in will tend to work. 'What I tell you three times is true' declares the Bellman in Lewis Carroll's *The Hunting of the Snark*, and this is a valid remark on certain levels. So I trust that all this will give you a sound base upon which to work out your own investigations and see what works best for you. In more general terms there is a popular method of gauging whether the important part of a reading is going to concern past, present or future by noting whether the querent puts the left-hand, central or right-hand packet respectively on the top of the pack immediately after the traditional three-way cut after shuffling.

Q.   I found it hard to communicate with the Tower because it is an object rather than a person. How should I tackle it?

A.   The Tower does have its problems of communication because of its configuration. Quite a good way is to see it as a moving picture, continually falling and then building itself up again. It may then stop at various points during this cycle, according to circumstance, and so convey something of its meaning in that way. Alternatively you could try talking to the two figures when they have reached the ground and recovered themselves a bit. Or yet again, try formulating an angelic figure above the lightning flash, somewhat after the fashion of the one behind the trumpet in the card of the Last Judgement.

A.   (To a student whose work ran closely to published sources.) Your close reliance on the ideas of Paul Case and the traditional Golden Dawn ancillary attributions comes over strongly. There is nothing wrong in this, as it is all fairly sound, reliable stuff, but to get the most out of the Tarot you will need to free yourself from these intellectual aids. Let your imagination and intuition run free. This is beginning to happen, for instance in your questioning some of the attributions and adding in bits of realization of your own.

Q. How do other students approach the Tarot images?

A. This varies enormously. Some people have great difficulty in releasing their imaginative faculty and thus have rather stilted, formalized responses, often leaning heavily on what they have read. Others have an almost reverential approach to the images, as if they were god-forms or saints. Others yet again will respond to various images according to their own particular personal hang-ups, and of course this is good therapy in itself, although I consider the Tarot and its dynamics to have an inner objectivity that goes beyond psychotherapy. One young lady felt positively bullied by the Emperor – who acted like a very overbearing chauvinist pig. However, she overcame the problem by talking to the figure of Strength, who lent her her lion, which she took back to confront the Emperor, who as a result soon modified his behaviour.

People seem to have confrontation problems mostly in the Hall of Strength, perhaps because they are all 'power' figures, and we tend to have more problems on this front than even with sex (maybe Adler was nearer the truth than Freud!). If there is any problem of this kind the solution is to call upon the relevant guide – Strength, Justice, Temperance or the World. Each of them, being Cardinal Virtues, exercises a controlling and balancing influence. The same function applies overall, each in their way, with the Magician and the Fool. The whole Tarot system is thus self-balancing and protective through its fourfold structure, based as it is on the free powers of the Spirit (in its dual aspect) and the Cardinal Virtues.

Q. The Fool often seems to enjoy himself. When I went to visit the Chariot, the Fool came down the path on a skateboard. For the next card, the Wheel of Fortune, he had a unicycle, like clowns have. I am afraid of appearing frivolous but the things really do seem to be there.

A. It is certainly not frivolous to see the Fool appearing according to his nature, and the objects were not entirely inappropriate in each case. I would say he is introducing an element of freedom and humanity into what might otherwise become an area of considerable portentousness and quasi-spiritual pomposity.

Q.   I found it difficult at first to get a clear image of the Emperor and Empress cards. I can't understand why these two cards were a problem.

A.   It does happen from time to time that people find an initial difficulty with certain of the Trump images. I had expected that this might be the case with those in the Hall of Justice because they are rather negative and awesome-looking pictures, although there has been singularly little bother with them. Rather is it the comparatively benign figures in the Hall of Strength that seem to cause difficulty.
     It would seem that this is because each one represents a source or focus of power and authority, each in its own way. It is possible that some unconscious kind of parental hang-up may have caused this slight difficulty for you with these two cards, but you appear to have worked your way through it quite satisfactorily. In cases of more prolonged difficulty the summoning of the balancing powers of the figure of Strength has proved an effective remedy, as this Cardinal Virtue rules over this particular Hall of images.

Q.   Whilst standing in the middle of the Hall of Strength I found I had a three-branched candlestick in my hand. I still don't know why, despite asking.

A.   The meaning of symbols that come to hand or to mind is not always readily apparent but you did well in taking it into account and recognizing its existence, and not dismissing it just because you did not readily understand it at the time. This is a way that wisdom can come to us from superconscious levels. I fancy that it represented in symbolic form some of the realizations that came to you later in the Hall of Justice, namely 'a meditation on trilogies, everybody being made up of three psychological aspects, areas of consciousness: mind, body, spirit.'

Q.   I asked the Empress to *show* me the hidden meaning of the cards, rather than tell me. She then handed me a knife. Over the next few days I continued to ask for pictures not words. These are the pictures I received. *Magician*: the world being turned by a huge hand. *Strength*: cupped hands with sunlight pouring out of them. *Empress*: huge pillar with background of blue sky and clouds.

Priestess: delicate hand effortlessly breaking sturdy chain. Are these images the hidden meaning of the cards or is my mind playing tricks, because I don't understand the pictures I see.

A. I was quite intrigued by your asking for the inner meanings of the cards to be given in pictures and not words. This is an entirely valid way of working and a very effective one, although it does mean that at some stage or another you will need to sit back and try to sort out in your logical mind just what the pictures mean. You can do this either formally or by meditating upon them for set periods. That is, sit down for ten minutes or so, hold the image before your mind's eye and see what meanings come to mind. Jot them down in a diary record and you will in time build up quite a bank of descriptive material. Or you can do it more informally, by deciding to think about a particular image at various times in the day; or you may find that ideas about it come to you at quite unexpected moments. Again it is best if you have a notepad nearby so that you can jot down such ideas before you forget them.

The images you are getting are not so much 'hidden' meanings of the cards but rather 'alternative' meanings or images. And the fact that you do not immediately understand them does not mean that they are worthless. On the contrary, like images from important dreams, they contain valuable information in an encapsulated form – rather like a golden nut you have to open up, which is, I would suggest, why the Empress gave you a knife. You have to learn to 'open up' or 'cut open' the images for the teaching they contain. It is, in a sense, your mind 'playing tricks', (or the Tarot 'playing the Fool'!), but the tricks are very worthwhile and clever ones. I leave you to work out what the images mean, although I would say that each of the four you have described gives a beautiful visual example of spiritual strength in action.

Q. Working with the Moon had a deeply soothing quality and it seemed to stimulate a lot of dream activity. Am I correct in seeing the Moon as symbolic of the 'borderland' between death and other planetary dimensions? The idea of its being the astral realm has become clearer to me since working with the Tarot, but until now I have tended to be quite psychologically based and have always thought in terms of the subconscious and the unconscious rather than the astral.

A. I agree that the Moon is, or can be, a gateway to the astral realms, whether in a psychic or after-death condition. Psychological terminology, particularly the Jungian variety, has its usefulness, although I tend to regard it as something of a double-edged weapon, as it can lead to a rather restrictive 'psychologizing' of the inner worlds, so that they are regarded as subjective happenings inside one's head instead of perceptions of a wider and more wonderful series of worlds beyond the focus of our own physical limits. Thus one has to use the terms with some caution, as they are not always entirely synonymous when used by a psychologist on the one hand and an occultist on the other.

Q, I had trouble talking to the Skeleton and didn't even try talking to the Tower. And I don't quite know how to talk to a Wheel. I can't make the Fool act serious, though notwithstanding his fooling around I get a serious message from him and a sense of power, as well as the proviso not to take life too seriously. I enjoy his dog and its crazy capers.

A. The Wheel, as originally conceived in the old designs, had the goddess of Fortuna turning its handle – so you do not have to feel a complete lemon trying to talk to the spokes. A passing acquaintance with the characters revolving round it might also be worth cultivating. Originally these were not the strange monsters we see on the modern esoteric decks, which are mutations of human characters, one 'on the up', one at the top, one with the skids under him, and the fourth crawling about on the floor at the bottom, and each with a balloon coming from his head, saying respectively 'I shall take over!', 'I'm in charge!', 'I was boss once!', and 'I rule nothing!' So there is plenty of opportunity for philosophical chat with these characters.

Similarly one could make the acquaintance of the two characters who inhabited the Tower while it was standing, and who may well be those who were concerned with building it, as well as those suffering the catastrophe. Will they learn from their experience? Will they build another tower? Or maybe seek refuge in a bunker? In a sense the continual rising and falling of the Tower has resonances with the Wheel of Fortune: Tower of Babel in one epoch, big-city tower blocks in another.

I'm surprised you got nothing from the Skeleton. Never mind the absence of a tongue or a larynx, which is a minor problem for this ancient and philosophical chessplaying gentleman. At least he is down to bare bones, which is a refreshing change from much human duplicity and fabrication, which I would think you would appreciate as a lawyer. You don't mention the Devil. Any trouble there? Or did you find him a congenial member of your own profession? As for the Fool, I am glad to hear he continues to frolic. There's much wisdom and healing in that.

The World, also, can be used as a meditative healing symbol, as it is, in effect, a complete mandala in Jungian fashion.

LESSON FOUR

The Basics of Divination

We have now become acquainted with the images of the Tarot Trumps and by our sustained work in visiting their five Halls have made contact with the powers of each one of them. This means that we can start to work with their cards in a meaningful manner. They are no longer pieces of paste-board but the talismanic links with the forces that operate behind daily life in the world.

To work fully with the Tarot there are also the fifty-six suit cards to take into consideration, but we can make a start in practical divination simply by use of the twenty-two trump cards. Indeed some Tarot diviners work only with the Trumps. However, although the Trumps do indeed represent the more powerful archetypal forces of life, the suit cards provide a full and useful complement to show how these basic forces are likely to work through our daily circumstances.

We will start simply, with the most basic of Tarot spreads, from which through developing experience we will be able to build up to readings of considerable complexity. No Tarot consultation that is worthy of the name should be done casually. Therefore make due preparation by laying out a space for putting out the cards, preferably on a cloth or table dedicated for this purpose. Prepare yourself and the immediate surroundings by ensuring that all is neat and tidy and that you are in a calm and poised state of mind.

Select the Trump cards from your pack and return the other cards to their box. Place the cards face down in a pack on the table before you. Establish mental contact with the Fool. When you feel that you have made this contact, formulate a question that you would like to have advice upon. (If you have not already formulated a question, or are undecided, it may be that you find the Fool suggests some topic for you to enquire about.)

Having formulated your question pick up the cards, and keeping the question or topic in mind begin to shuffle them. During the course of shuffling, try to feel in rapport with the cards and with the Fool, whose means of communication they are, and follow any inclination that comes to turn some of the cards so that they are reversed. You may not have such an inclination. On the other hand you may be inclined to reverse several, or perhaps just one or two. If you should inadvertently drop any of the cards it is no bad idea to put them back into your pack reversed. When you are shuffling, be aware also of the type of spread that you intend to use. In this case we will simply use a three-card spread, consisting of a central card giving the main drift of the answer with the card on each side of it giving supporting amplification of its meaning.

When you feel it is time to finish shuffling place the pack face down on the table. Then cut the pack into three piles, using your left hand to lift a section of the pack and place it to the left, and then a section of this second pack to be placed to the far left. (If you are left-handed then use your right hand for this operation and place the packets from left to right. If you are ambidextrous then use the hand that received the fall of the cards when you shuffled.) You now have three piles of cards, face down before you. Make one stack of them by putting the three packets together on top of each other, in any order. You are now ready to deal off the top.

The central card gives the main answer to the present question; the one to the left represents past influences and factors; and the one to the right indicates future trends. We suggest you lay them out in order from left to right, saying mentally to yourself as you do so, 'That which was. That which is. That which is to come,' or any similar formula that appeals to you.

Our example presents a question asked by a lady who had just attended an interview for a temporary job for which she knows she has been successful. She is now wondering whether perhaps it might develop into a more permanent situation. The three cards that turned up were:

Past	Present	Future
Empress	Justice	Sun (reversed)

The Empress in the past gives a clear indication of the Querent's past circumstances in that she has been wholly involved for some years with bringing up children and work in the home. Justice in the present would seem to indicate that the time has now come for an expression of her talents and energies balanced between the home and outside work. The Sun in the future is a promising card to have, but its reversal seems to be a warning that all will not necessarily be as ideal as her current euphoria on getting the job would have her think. It would seem however that a step has been made in the right direction, and looking at prospects realistically, it is probable that the new job will be a satisfactory experience but no more than a temporary stepping-stone to something else.

The Querent, who in this case was also the Reader, remarked of this, 'Although the reading may seem a little inconslusive to an outsider, I believe that it is telling me that I shall learn from the job, and the experience and new knowledge will be useful to me later as life changes.' This certainly seems in keeping with the fall and general meaning of the cards, and the lady concerned has obviously used the Tarot in a self-supportive and self-educative way. It is important, however, particularly when dealing with small generalized spreads such as this, (that is, only three cards, and each position encapsulating a wide range of possible application – 'past, present, future'), that the meaning can be interpreted in a radically different way depending on the mind-set of the Reader. For instance, in this case had these cards fallen as they have and been interpreted by someone who, say, disapproved of women working outside the home, then an interpretation suggesting that the Querent was riding for a fall could have plausibly been made, that she was facing a situation of 'judgement' as to the rightness of what she was now doing, with the reversed Sun in the future suggesting that her current hopes would be rightfully dashed (that the Sun would in future cease to shine upon her).

We hasten to say that in the circumstances we would not agree with such an interpretation, and that the lady correctly read the cards for herself. But what we do want to stress is the wide range of subjective interpretation possible when only a very few cards are read in isolation, or with a very broad spread of possible application of their meaning. It is for this reason that a more complex spread is likely to be more accurate and informative, with say at least ten cards and the position of each card designated with a specific element in the situation. Such a spread is the so-called Celtic method. First published by A.E. Waite in his *Pictorial Key to the Tarot* in 1910 (republished by Rider, 1972), it has become very popular as a general-purpose spread. It has certainly stood the test of time and public exposure in the ensuing years, and we ourselves have found it to be capable of giving reliable results and impressing those for whom it has been used in a reading.

This spread uses ten cards. After the preliminary shuffling Card 1 is placed in the centre to represent the Querent or the subject of the question, Card 2 is placed over it to represent factors that are immediately affecting this; card 3 is placed above these two cards and represents the expected result, or goal that is wished for, Card 4 is placed below them and represents the root of the situation in the past; card 5 is placed to one side of them and represents events of the immediate past. Card 6 is placed to the other side and represents factors in the immediate future. (We should say that there are published variants to this procedure but we recommend the system originally presented by A.E. Waite, which was accompanied by a verbal formula that has a certain traditional simplicity and power [1] 'This covers him,' [2] 'This crosses him,' [3] 'This crowns him,' [4] 'This is beneath him,' [5] 'This is behind him,' [6] 'This is before him.')

The order of layout was also in the form of a cross, and A.E. Waite preferred to make his cross from top point to bottom point, and then from right to left. This gives the 'future' positions to cards 3 above and 6 to the left, and 'past' positions to cards 4 below and 5 to the right. However, if the first card (or the Significator if one was used – see below) had a figure that looked to the right, he would put card 5, representing the immediate past, to the left, 'behind' it, and card 6, representing the future, to the right, 'before' it. Actually this makes no difference to the signification of the cards as it is the order in which they are laid down that is paramount, according to the spoken formula.

Some later cartomancers have preferred to abandon the cross for a circular sequence, to begin at various points on the circle, and also to differ as to whether left or right of the centre represents past or future. It would be ludicrous to assert that any deviations from Waite's original will not work, when they have obviously served others very well. What does become plain is that it is the intention of the diviner that matters, and what seems right on the day. In fact virtually any order and method of selecting the cards can be effective, and in the course of time each cartomancer will evolve a personal method.

The remaining four cards are placed one above the other in a line to the right of the existing spread. Card 7 represents the Querent and his influence upon the issue, card 8 represents external circumstances that are affecting it, Card 9 represents the inner feelings, perhaps unconscious, of the Querent, that have a bearing on the matter; and Card 10 represents the final outcome that is likely. In the words of the A.E. Waite's verbal formula: [7] 'This is himself,' [8] 'This is his house,' [9] 'This is his hopes and fears,' [10] 'This is what will come.'

A practical example is probably the best way to demonstrate the spread. This reading was conducted for an attractive and intelligent young lady in her mid-twenties who wanted to know if she was likely to be married within the next three years. The cards fell thus (Figure 12).

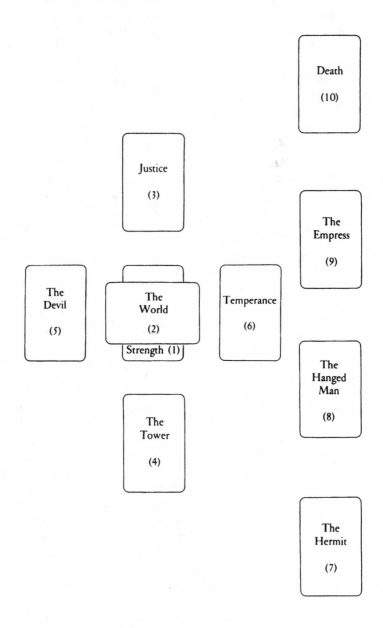

Death

(10)

Justice

(3)

The
Empress

(9)

The
Devil

(5)

The
World

(2)

Strength (1)

Temperance

(6)

The
Hanged
Man

(8)

The
Tower

(4)

The
Hermit

(7)

(1) **Strength** seemed to be a good image for the Querent, although it was not specifically selected to be such. (It can sometimes be useful to use a 'Significator', consciously and deliberately chosen from the pack, to represent the Querent or the question in hand. Such a card takes no further part in the reading but suffices to concentrate the mind, and to have a certain minor talismanic effect, physically 'earthing' or demonstrating the focus of the work.) The Querent agreed with the Reader's suggestion that this card also indicated that she expected support from any relationship.

(2) The second card in this spread specifically represents slightly opposing or challenging circumstances to the Querent or the matter in hand. **The World** in this position may thus represent the completion of a phase of life, giving a sense of impasse, or of disillusionment with present circumstances and past relationships. It also suggests that the Querent is concerned with her public image, which implies that in her mind it is about time someone of her age was getting married.

(3) The ultimate goal is here represented by **Justice**, and suggests a seeking of balanced expression in the Querent's life. She is certainly known to have a well-developed sense of fair play, which may have a bearing here. Also, of course, the legal aspect of this card can signify the formal marriage contract which is, after all, the subject of the Querent's question.

(4) **The Lightning Struck Tower** as past root of the matter may indicate a number of broken relationships in the past, although the Querent did not feel that any of them were traumatic or had led to new realizations. However, the cumulative effect must have had some influence upon her outlook insofar that she has come seeking advice on the matter. She is, after all, now seeking to know if she can build a solid edifice in the form of formal relationship that will stand.

(5) **The Devil** in the place of immediate past influence seems to confirm our inferences from the Tower: an unsuccessful relationship based on a mutual illusion. Here the Querent did admit that there had been 'a few disasters'.

(6) **Temperance** as the future influence looks hopeful and could mean a happy relationship in the near future, although in view of the later cards it would be as well to bear in mind the cautionary aspect of this card, which advises balance and the achievement of an inner harmony, if promising relationships are to be fulfilled.

(7) **The Hermit** as the Querent's present situation confirms that

she is currently alone and trying to assess her general position and direction. Seeking guidance in fact. The Querent agreed this. The time element in the old meaning of the card would also suggest that she is aware of time passing without her having found a partner.

(8) **The Hanged Man** as representative of outside influences confirms that she is feeling that her position is at odds with what seems expected of her. She preferred, however, to regard this as being a victim of circumstances.

(9) **The Empress** as representative of hopes and fears seemed appropriate to both. On the one hand the desire for a happy, mature and fruitful relationship, but on the other a rather sharply expressed dismay at the suggestion that this card might also signify the bearing of children. She feels, in short, both a desire for and a fear of commitment.

(10) **Death** as the final outcome suggests the end of an attitude or state of mind. She is undergoing a natural process of growth which requires the shedding of certain attitudes. This the Querent partially accepted but she remained somewhat apprehensive of the Death card being in this position.

To ease her mind a supplementary three-card spread was made, after reshuffling all the cards, with the query: 'Please clarify the meaning of Death in this spread.' This resulted in:

Past	Present	Future
Emperor	Death	High Priestess

The reappearance of Death in the present was most appropriate, and suggested that the image was meant symbolically to signify a transition from attitudes stressing control (remember her original Card 1 had been Strength), towards a more intuitive trust in herself and events. The Querent agreed to this assessment, and in lateral confirmation of this was the fact she had recently chosen to become vegetarian, and was clearly experiencing some sort of transition in her outer life in relation to inner values.

In conclusion we may note that there is no hard and fast 'Yes' or 'No' answer to the original question about getting married within a specific time, but rather a wise indication of the attitudes to be developed if the wished-for events were to come true. True Tarot work is more concerned with counselling than prediction. It might be added that the Querent had previously consulted a well-known psychic who had informed her she would change her job and marry within a certain period, both of which proved to be untrue. An example perhaps of the dangers of unsupported psychic impressions feeding back to a Querent what he or she would like to hear.

It may be noted that there are no reversed cards in the above spread. This is at least in part because this particular Reader prefers not to use them. The subject of reversed cards is a matter of some debate, and many beginners particularly are reluctant to use them. If one is approaching the subject in the usual superficial way then it does appear to demand twice as many 'meanings' to learn by heart. And the way that the controlled reversal of a number of cards is managed is seldom clearly explained, for normal shuffling does not cause cards to be reversed. However, if you have made personal contact with the complex of forces that naturally channel through each card, you should be able to comprehend what is intended when one of those cards is reversed. It implies a modification of the normal expression of those forces, but just what that modification is will depend upon the circumstances. That is, the nature of the question being asked, and the surrounding cards, together with any other intuitions that may come from the pattern of the designs or from talking to the Querent.

Please note that when reading the cards for another, talking fully with the querent is an important and valuable adjunct to the reading. We are not in the business of attempting to prove the validity of Tarot reading by predicting events from a blank wall of non-communication. We are trying to give advice to those who sincerely ask for it and who genuinely need it. Therefore full trust and faith should be a prerequisite of any consultation. One would not visit a doctor, solicitor or accountant and refuse to discuss any background circumstances on the grounds of 'scientific objectivity' or in order to make them prove their ability! Reading the cards for oneself is at least free of this problem but does present difficulties of its own. Certainly one is likely to have a comprehensive knowledge of background circumstances, but we all of us have blind spots that would more easily be avoided if another person was doing the reading. However, reading for oneself is an important part of training, and the Spirit of the Tarot is quite capable of getting the required message across even to those who resolutely refuse to see. As long as self-honesty and sincere intention are aspired to there is no reason why reading for oneself should be any less valuable than involving the assistance of a third party.

When you have finished a reading, gather up the cards and restore them all the correct way up. Return them to their box and restore the tablecloth and any other things you may use back to the way they were.

Working Plan

Diary Record

In connection with your preparation for your answer to Exercise 1 keep a record of your meditations upon each of the Trump images. You may use your work periods for actual readings or for pondering upon them, in which case make the appropriate note in the right-hand column.

Exercise 1

For all the Trumps list the way in which you might expect them to be interpreted if found 'reversed' in a Tarot reading.

Exercise 2

Conduct as many readings as you like, using your current knowledge. Keep a careful record of them, either on paper or audio tape. Coming back to them later will prove a valuable form of training, as you learn to assess your mistakes or inaccuracies.

Knowledge Notes

In this lesson we have been doing some actual divination, and although you should have already made your own acquaintance with the Trump images so that they 'speak' to you of their own accord, in the context of any layout, it may be helpful if we complete our list of brief suggested meanings, to give you something to fall back on if need be.

In the Knowledge Notes for Lesson 2 you already have suggestions for the main gatekeepers, that is the Fool, the Magician, Strength, Justice, Temperance, and The World. We will continue in the order of the Trump images in each of the halls that they keep, that is: Pope, Emperor, High Priestess, Empress; Devil, Death, Tower, Hanged Man; Hermit, Chariot, Wheel, Lovers; Angel, Sun, Star, Moon.

You will perhaps have noticed that some packs have the Trumps numbered differently from others. In fact there are various numbering systems in the traditional non-esoteric packs as well as in the esoteric ones. There is no need to bother too much about this. It has been dealt with at great length in Michael Dummett's and Sylvia Mann's monumental *The Game of Tarot* (Duckworth, 1980) and also in Stuart Kaplan's *Encyclopaedia of Tarot* (U.S. Games Systems, 1978). The earliest sets that we know of had no numbers, or even names, on them. The main discrepancy you may notice on modern esoteric packs is the counter-changing of the numbers of Strength and Justice. This is a result of the theories favoured by the Hermetic Order of the Golden Dawn in attributing the Trumps to various astrological signs in conjunction with the Qabalistic Tree of Life. It makes no difference to the significance of the cards as far as we are concerned, for we are dealing with the Tarot as a free-standing system in its own right, without trying to correlate it with other symbol systems. The only difference in practical terms will concern only those who choose to introduce numerological systems to their Tarot divination. However, we do not advocate this practice in our own methods – although we would not wish to decry the efforts of others in this direction. To those who do wish to experiment along these lines we would simply advise that they use the numbers printed on the particular set of cards they happen to use for divination.

The Pope is likely to indicate moral authority, conscience, the line of duty or accepted behaviour. Reversed or badly situated this could become hypocrisy, self-righteousness, 'busy-bodying', gossip, or interference in the affairs of others for moral reasons, or applying psychological pressure or disapproval.

The Emperor is an influence of general control, the ability to cope, perhaps influencing affairs from a distance, for instance, by line of authority. Badly placed or reversed it can be the autocratic abuse of power, a heavy-handed father approach, unnecessary rules and restrictions.

The High Priestess is an image of higher wisdom, not necessarily religious in nature, but encompassing the ability to take a dispassionate view of things and events. Reversed or badly aspected this can signify remoteness, or a cold-blooded attitude to affairs of the heart.

The Empress is a maternal influence in all senses of the word, supportive and giving. Reversed or badly placed it can signify the adverse aspects of motherhood, such as over-protectiveness and possessiveness; or it can signify the great demands of motherhood on a female querent.

The Devil signifies illusion or delusion, which usually results from pride of one kind or another. In a sense it could be regarded as similar to the reversed meanings of the Emperor or Pope. Reversed these adverse conditions may work in an unexpected way, perhaps bringing the realization of mistakes made, even if in a somewhat painful or embarrassing fashion.

Death is a card of change, of endings and beginnings. If reversed this perfectly natural process may be resisted and perhaps manifest in an unbalanced or unnecessarily painful way.

Tower, like the Death card, is likely to signify change, although in rather more rapid or violent fashion. This can be in the nature of a sudden revelation of what best to do next, or of where one might be going wrong. Reversed or badly placed it may emphasize the catastrophic element of the change, perhaps exacerbated by the querent's unwillingness to change or refusal to look changing circumstances in the face, until the situation just blows apart.

The Hanged Man may show the idealist or one who takes a different view of things from his associates. He may be right. If reversed or badly placed however the chances are that his attitude will be wrong, or expressed in a damaging or foolish way.

The Hermit indicates wisdom or guidance, sage advice or intuitive hunches. Reversed it can mean pettifogging advice, or any vices associated with age; it may also indicate delays or red tape.

The Chariot shows successful progress, things taking their course as hoped and planned. Reversed it may bring with it a certain riding roughshod over the interests and feelings of others, or bringing in its train a certain counter-reaction, a costly victory.

The Wheel of Fortune tends to indicate change in the sense of ups and downs, rather than the more final endings or eventful abruptness of Death or the Tower. This can be for better or worse, temporarily. Reversed, it is more likely to be for the worse, or perhaps coming at an inopportune time.

The Lovers is a card of making commitments; these commitments may be made with great love or mutual acceptance. Reversed, or badly aspected, such decisions are likely to be made with much reservation, difficulty or heart-searching.

The Angel or **Last Judgement** is another card of change, in the sense of waking up to new opportunities. Reversed or badly positioned, this may have its uncomfortable aspects, like any sudden awakening. The angel's horn might come like a bucket of cold water, and it may seem more comfortable to have things stay as they were.

The Sun is a warm, encouraging card to have, anywhere in a spread. Reversed it may be like the physical sun, shining rather too brightly in certain circumstances and having a parching effect, or may in its brightness reveal things one would rather have hidden.

The Star is a card of hope and fond aspirations. Reversed or badly placed these hopes may be simply illusory or pie-in-the-sky, or possibly not realized or realizable. Or the querent may lack the will to get down to more immediate practicalities.

The Moon is sometimes called The Twilight and indicates half-seen, half-hidden things. It carries considerable power, for the moon invisibly affects tides and the forces of growth. It can be regarded as an indication of strong hidden forces working within a situation, although not necessarily psychic ones. Reversed or badly aspected such forces may be working to the detriment of the situation and could thus appear in the form of false reports, bad opinions, hidden prejudices or similar conditions.

Having listed these general suggestions for meanings we would emphasize that there is really no substitute for getting to know the images for yourself so that they are capable of speaking to you, imaginatively or intuitively, when you are undertaking a reading. While one can arrive at a reasonable reading by following the general published 'meaning', divination that is really worthy of the name depends upon familiarity with the images through your own experience in meditation and divination. Like any art or skill, this comes with time and application in league with whatever natural talent you may be blessed with. Look upon this present emphasis on 'meanings' as a convenient half-way stage between having an intellectual knowledge of the Tarot and being able to regard it, through personal familiarity and experience, as a guide, philosopher and friend.

Questions and Answers

Q. I have not used reversed cards in any of my spreads, and I don't feel entirely happy with this concept.

A. I appreciate your reservations about use of reversed cards and initially I had very similar feelings myself. This is to be expected of anyone who has a broad philosophical approach to the subject, wherein it is felt that these ideal archetypes cannot possibly signify adverse factors. We do, however, live in an imperfect world, and when the Tarot images are being used to explain or represent events in that world then there must perforce be occasions when they must take on an adverse signification, otherwise they would have no bearing on life as it is actually lived.

The normal run of cartomancers and their clientele generally feel no concern with philosophical problems such as these, being quite content to take things, and the cards, as they find them. In the light of experience I have come to terms with the use of reversed cards and my readings have benefited considerably. You will obviously have to make up your own mind on this score but

I would recommend that you give it a try, as it would be a pity, I think, not to take advantage of this additional dimension to the interpretation of Tarot spreads.

Q. I was told early in my studies that you shouldn't read for yourself as no person is entitled to that much knowledge; also it's hard to be objective about your own situation.

A. I think the early advice you received about never reading for yourself is a bit on the harsh side, although it has a certain point. Reading for oneself certainly has its difficulties insofar that any blind spot one may have in dealing with life problems is likely to be matched by the same blind spot in reading the Tarot about them. However, having said this, at least one tends to know more of the intimate detail of any problem when reading for oneself, and it is possible over a period of time to build up a sequence of readings for oneself and learn from them by going back over to see what actually happened and maybe where one went wrong or failed to see the glaringly obvious. All this can be a very educative process.

Q. I've done some readings on family members and people I write to, but they're all at a distance. Do you think it makes a difference whether the person is present or not?

A. Reading for others at a distance is entirely feasible. It helps perhaps to have some kind of link with them, preferably a letter stating the query or problem, and failing that, anything personally connected with them. Even this is not essential, as it is spirtual intention and faith in your powers and those of the Tarot which are the key elements in the equation.

Q. I have been reading books on numerology in conjunction with the Minor Arcana. They seem to help - perhaps. At times I am not too sure. Any comments? There certainly seems to be a link, but each book seems to say something different.

A. I too have pondered long on this matter and found very little help in books on the subject, which for the most part are facile and contradictory. There seem to be at least two major schools of tradition, one Qabalistic and the other Pythagorean, and neither seems to tie up too well with the other. There is a fair quantity of catch-penny balderdash as well. I think one's only hope is to follow one's own lights from first principles - and to regard the number 1 as a whole and a unity, so that subsequent numbers are divisions of this Unity. This has quite an important effect on the role of zero. Is it a kind of half-way house between an infinite series of positive and negative integers stretching each way to infinity – or is it a profound No-thing from which the Unity miraculously appears? Or both? No wonder the Fool is identified with this profound enigma.

I have also found speculating on the relative frequencies of the tone scale to be of some help. And if you are interested in science there is quite a lot of mileage to be got from the numerical make-up of the electron shells and nuclei of the atoms of the various elements. Oddly enough I found these had correlations with the Tarot Trumps, although I hesitate to aver that the inventors of the Tarot were proto-atomic-physicists. But as a profound system of inner cosmic principles you never know where the Tarot is going to lead you!

Q. Although I have interpreted all the cards I find it hard to bring a reading all together to form a conclusion and actually answer the original question, which is what I'm supposed to do. Can you help please?

A. You raise a good point about the difficulty of getting a positive and definitive answer. Very often one will find, and particularly when reading the cards for oneself, that the reading tends to spell out the current situation very well but does not go on to spell out a definite prediction or come to any conclusion. There can be various reasons for this. One is that it is best that you continue to try to work out the answers for yourself. The other is that the final issue is as yet unresolved. As I indicated at the beginning of the course, the Tarot is like a wise adviser, and sometimes (or indeed it can be quite often), the wisest counsel to give anyone is either to turn back to his own resources or to honestly say that the outcome is still in the balance. There is also an ancient code of practice that says that even if one knows another's future one may not give information to him that might radically alter his destiny.

Q. I have noticed that if I do two or three readings for myself on the same day, the same cards tend to keep coming up in each spread and the same cards seem to get reversed, although I am not doing this on purpose. If I do a reading on the following day totally different cards may come up. Is this normal? Why does it happen?

A. One sometimes does find cards coming up several times in the course of practice readings. I was experiencing this myself very recently. This can mean that the Tarot wishes to get something across to you that you may not be asking about, and indeed is the first step towards the genuine and very valuable faculty of 'conversing' with the Tarot, so to speak, without asking formal questions in formal spreads. One can tune in to it just by playing around with the cards or shuffling idly through them. Again, this is a faculty that may come only after some practice and familiarity.

Q. The images have really come to life for me now. It's the interpretation that is not always easy for me at this stage.

A. It is good to hear that the images are strong for you. This is half the battle, and the technique of communication and interpretation, like using English grammatically, will come with practice.

Q. I would like advice on whether one has to put the cards back in order every time.

A. Although there are advocates of putting the cards back in order every time, in my experience it is quite unnecessary. However the Tarot works, it is quite capable of selecting the cards it wants, starting from any order. Therefore I think that putting them all in a set order after every reading is not only superfluous to requirements but a certain denigration of the Tarot itself, a kind of pseudo-scientific belief in statistical purity as opposed to the very human, irrational and yet very wise pragmatism of the Tarot in action. Personally I simply put any reversed cards the right way up, and then give a quick shuffle and triple cut after finishing a reading; with the intention expressed in my mind that this is a cleansing and sorting of the cards for the next time, and a formal cutting off of all connection with the reading just finished.

Q. I tried a 3-card, a 7-card and a Celtic Cross reading and asked the same question each time. The answer to the first was good, the same on the second, but when I asked the same question on the third reading it seemed that the question was ignored. I had the feeling I was being told that enough information had been given me. Is this feasible?

A. As I hinted in the text of Lesson One, the Spirit of the Tarot is quite capable of reacting to being 'pushed' or 'tested'. It is interesting to see that you got the appropriate message intuitively and were given the information the Tarot felt it was useful for you to know. This is a good sign and shows that you are making good contact with the inner forces, so that the Tarot becomes not so much a fortune-telling device but a language for expressing the intuition in regard to various aspects of life.

Q. I was doing a reading for a woman I had never seen before but knew to be married with children and materially well off. As I looked at her cards I had the strongest feeling that her husband was having or would have an affair. I didn't mention this for I thought I was most probably wrong and in any case there was no point in worrying her. I subsequently discovered my feelings were correct, and that in fact the woman was aware of what was going on. This pleased me in one sense (not that there was a broken home in the making, but that my deepest feelings were right) but made me wonder about saying 'extra' things which I do not pick up directly from the cards.

A. I agree that it can be difficult if you have a strong impression about a matter so personal, whether it is laid before you 'in the cards' or not. In a matter as sensitive as this it is no doubt best to err on the side of caution. This is where tact and counselling skills come in, and following your intuition you might have been able to draw her out in a manner that would have been a release for her and helpful in getting the most out of the reading. Of course the thing to avoid at all costs is sowing seeds of suspicion or doubt, well-founded or not, that may be harmful or destructive. This may be no easy matter, and emphasizes the great responsibility that one takes on in setting up to be a psychic or Tarot consultant.

Q. I found working on meanings of the reversed Trumps quite hard. I often feel I have a 'concept' of their meanings but cannot verbalize them. I also found it difficult to generalize a meaning out of the context of the other cards.

A. I agree that this exercise is not an easy one. For one thing it is something of a slippery task to concentrate on negative aspects consistently in this way. (In some ways it can be like mini-psychoanalysis for some people.) Moreover, as you say, the reversed meanings, perhaps more so than the interpretation of the cards when right way up, will vary quite considerably in a spread according to the context – not only of the question, but of the other cards around it – and its position in a particular layout.

Q. Could the reversed Devil be interpreted as freedom from ties and restrictions?

A. People often find difficulty in trying to understand what a malefic type of card is likely to signify when reversed – either the misfortune redoubled, or alternatively mitigated into less trouble than would be indicated by the card when upright. Freedom from ties and restrictions – which is the general opposite of the restrictions and obsessions associated with the Devil – might well be a valid interpretation of the Devil when reversed, but as it is a somewhat ill-fortuned card by nature I would expect the indicated freedom to manifest in an unfortunate manner, as lack of responsibility, or carelessness, recklessness, or the ignoring or contempt for established codes. This could include various forms of sexual deviance. It would certainly be the type of indication one might find in matters concerning divorce, particularly where there are children or other dependants involved, and also of course abortion.

Q. If the No 2 card crosses in a Celtic spread, which way is right way up and which way is reversed?

A. I always regard it as right way up if the top of the card is to the right, and reversed if the top of the card is to the left. However, A.E. Waite, who first published this method, always said that because this card is laid sideways on, it should always be read as if it were the right way up. However, as the meaning of the position of the second card relates to 'obstacles', then in a sense it has a certain amount of reversed meaning implied already when you come to interpret it. I suggest you think this over for a bit and then decide for yourself what seems right for you.

Q. One of the 3-card readings I did for myself went very wrong. I had taken three cards to see how a morning with a good friend would turn out. The three cards were the Knight of Cups, the Star, and the World. From these I understood that the meeting would be very promising. I saw the Knight of Cups as a deep companionship, the Star that all would be very hopeful, and the World that continuing on from the meeting I would be very pleased, and that what I wanted from it would be accomplished.

However, it was all very disappointing, for our meeting was cancelled. As a result I was very depressed.

A. Your problem here raises a number of interesting points. I am inclined to think that very often the Tarot is not predicting the future but reflecting the psychic or psychological factors in any given situation. If this is the case then the fall of the cards on this occasion could well have been an accurate assessment of the empathy that exists between you and your friend and your high expectations. It was not in the business this day of predicting cancellations or other accidental happenings. Were you in fact involuntarily setting up the Tarot as a mirror of your own emotions at the time? It's worth thinking about in relation to how you use the Tarot and for what purposes. Was this an important occasion? Or were you just plying the Tarot with trivia? Only you can answer these questions, and it is the way to hone a reliable means of working with the oracle.

Q. Recently whilst working with several of the images I have experienced vibratory sensations in my hands and body, culminating in a great 'fulness' of energy around my throat, such as I have occasionally experienced whilst meditating. These sensations are very good and give me a deep sense of relaxation and calm.

A. These sensations do indicate that some kind of growth is happening but you should avoid putting too much emphasis on them. They are side-effects and will probably pass away. Above all, avoid seeking to encourage them, as that is at best something of a time-wasting blind alley. The main result we are seeking is the quality of realization, and this will come about as your various inner centres come into use or increased activity. The sensations you feel are the astro-etheric effects of your deepening meditative work, and are just that – an effect rather than a cause. In a certain sense it is similar to a male adolescent experiencing a deepening of the voice, or suffering temporarily from acne. It is a side-effect of growth, not a cause of it.

LESSON FIVE

The Four Suits

We can now extend our research into the forces that are represented by the Suit cards. There are four suits, each with fourteen cards, numbering 56 altogether. Once again there is no great memory feat involved in learning meanings off by heart. The essence of these cards is met with in imaginative form, as were the Trumps. They in fact form four 'theatres' which we may visit in turn.

In occult interpretations the four suits are often equated with the four Elements of the ancient world – Fire, Air, Water and Earth – from which all things are made. And in a modern development from this, the psychological equivalents of these Elements are often cited – Intellect, Intuition, Feeling and Sensation. While these systems have their validity, and we can examine their merits in more theoretical studies, for all practical purposes the traditional Renaissance interpretation of the meaning of the suits, which has been handed down in cartomantic practice, will be of greater value to us. These Renaissance categories of human life are, for each suit: executive power, organization (Wands); opposition, external forces (Swords); love, social relationships (Cups); and wealth, gain, physical well-being (Coins).

A moment's reflection on the actual suit emblems reveals their intended meaning. We see the magician's wand, the field marshal's baton or king's sceptre; the soldier's or antagonist's sword; the loving cup or the social cups of celebration and good fellowship; and the coins, tokens of wealth. These four categories of human life have also been foreshadowed in the four Halls of the Tarot Trumps: Wands for the Hall of Strength, in which are to be found the Emperor, the Empress, the Pope and the High Priestess; Swords in the Hall of Justice, in which are to be found the Devil, Death, the Tower and the Hanged Man; Cups for the Hall of Temperance, in which are to be found the Hermit, the Lovers, the Chariot and the Wheel of Fortune; and Coins in the Hall of Worlds, in which are to be found the Last

Judgement, the Sun, the Moon and the Star. Beyond each of these Halls is an appropriate Theatre, of Wands, Swords, Cups or Coins. The way to each of these will now be shown, and once again it is a matter of making a journey in the imagination, starting with our friend the Fool, following him to the Hall of the Magician, and thence being invited into one of the appropriate Halls by one of the four Gate-keepers.

The Theatre of Wands

The first Hall we shall enter is that of Strength. See yourself invited by the figure of Strength into the circular room beyond her. Once there, we look toward the far wall and notice that there is a small door just to the right of the Pope. The figure of Strength is aware of our intention and we realize it is with her authority that the door opens to let in a shaft of bright light from beyond. And there, standing in the open doorway, is the figure of a Page. It is the Page of Wands, and impelled by a gentle gesture from the lion maiden, we walk over toward the open door.

When we visualize the figure of the Page he (or she) should be in the form shown on the Tarot pack that we normally use for divination. We have so far been dealing with deep archetypal forces and figures; when we move to the levels of the suited cards we come closer to the surface of everyday life. Therefore, when the Page ushers us through the door, out of the Hall of Strength with its mighty and impressive figures, we find that we are dealing with an ordinary human being. Although the Page, whilst in the Hall, had the formal appearance of the image that appears on the card, when we step into the brightly lit antechamber beyond, we find that the appearance of the Page changes to modern dress. We find that he (or she) is a smartly dressed messenger, as from a large and successful business organization, and we are being shown into what looks like the reception area of the head offices of such an organization. The Page is helpful and courteous, and tells us that we will be shown the innermost secrets of the organization. With that we are led down a maze of corridors until we come to a large open-plan office that is a hive of activity, with people bustling everywhere, and over all is an atmosphere of well run confident efficiency.

The Page leads us to a central desk. Upon it we see a framed picture of the traditional Tarot card, the Knight of Wands. However, seated at the desk there is a busy executive controlling much of what goes on in this office complex by means of a battery of telephones, video screens, push-buttons and other communication devices. He looks up and smiles, and indicates that everything around us is under his control. Still he has time and the willingness to show us further into the organization. He turns and indicates a balcony high at the far end of the office. The balcony is empty but at each end is a large painting; the painting on the right is of the traditional King of Wands, on the left, of the Queen.

The Knight indicates that he will take us to the balcony and we follow him smartly onward to the end of the office, where we find the shining chromium plated doors of a lift. Here he leaves us to return to his executive duties, but we are still accompanied by the Page, who presses a button in the lift wall. We are transported swiftly upwards. At the end of the lift's ascent the doors open and we step into a deeply carpeted area, where we find two figures approaching us. One is a man of middle years, smartly dressed in a business suit, approaching us from the right. And from the left a woman approaches, equally well dressed and apparently a senior executive or director of the company. They introduce themselves to us cordially. The man, who fulfils the role of the King of Wands, tells us that he is the overall head of all that goes on within the organization, responsible for its overall operation and success. The woman, who fulfils the role of the Queen of Wands, tell us that she is his co-director and mainly concerned with the people in the building and their well being, as well as with the fabric of the building and the details of the machinery of organization.

They say that they know we have come to view the secrets of the innermost workings of the corporation, and to this end they indicate at the far end of the room a wall that, like a theatre stage, is covered from ceiling to floor with heavy curtains. The King and the Queen move to stand right and left respectively of these curtains. We remain in the centre of the room with the Page. When we are ready, the room grows dark and the curtains slowly roll back to reveal, brightly lit before us and rising upwards to a point, what seems to be one side of a great pyramid.

The pyramid side has large rectangular panels upon it, and on each panel is emblazoned the emblem of one of the numbered cards in the suit of Wands. At the pyramid's apex is to be seen the great rugged club of the Ace of Wands, held by a hand, with rays of light sparkling from it. Below the Ace are two panels, the one on the right bearing the Two of Wands, and the one on the left, the Three. At the next level down are three panels. The central one bears the Six of Wands, the right-hand one the Four, and the left-hand one bears the Five. At the lowermost level are four panels. The Nine at the left-hand corner (near where the Queen is standing), the Seven next in line beside it.

At the right-hand corner (near the King), is to be found the Ten, with the Eight next in line beside it. Thus the overall pattern is like this:

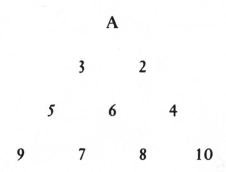

It can be seen that the Ace and the Six take up central positions, while the other cards are divided into odd numbers on the left and even numbers on the right. This general lay-out, known as the tetractys, is of extreme antiquity and was held in great veneration by early investigators of the mystical properties of numbers, such as Pythagoras. His name is still familiar through his famous theorem about the properties of a right-angled triangle. And the principles of proportion derived from certain right-angled triangles (known as the Golden Section) were used for many classical temples of antiquity and, rediscovered, were used in many of the great cathedrals of Europe.

These same principles were well known to the Renaissance adepts who framed the structure of the Tarot, which is why they are important to us here. Allied to these principles are those of the Jewish Qabalah, which was also much studied by men of the Renaissance, and which forms the basis of the divinatory meanings of the numbered cards. Before we proceed to examine the actual figures on the side of the pyramid we will spend a little time examining the general principles of this blend of Pythagorean and Qabalistic number theory, because it played an important part in the establishment of the Tarot.

One is the root, the upwelling centre of force of any particular kind, and so the *Ace of Wands* represents the fount of organizing energy or intelligent activity. **Two** shows the principle of duality or polarity, so the *Two of Wands* represents control of one thing, person or group by another. **Three** stands for the principle of establishment – a three-legged stool is a stable seat, whereas a two-legged stool is not! Similarly a triangle is the first plane figure that can be drawn with straight lines. The *Three of Wands* represents therefore established strength or power. **Four** represents the state of four-square manifestation, the form principle represented by the Three now more definitely established, an actuality rather than a plan or principle. The *Four of Wands* stands therefore for completion or achievement.

Five presents an unbalancing or 'sharp' principle at work, overbalancing the four-square situation. The *Five of Wands* thus represents competition or even conflict. **Six** is a most harmonious number. In the Bible God created the world in six days, and it was called a perfect number by the ancients. In the Tarot suits it shows the principle of each suit in successful fulfilment. So the *Six of Wands* is a token of success or victory in any enterprise. **Seven** represents an overbalancing of the state of achievement of the Six, and shows as courage, or the spirit of adventure or new enterprise, in the *Seven of Wands*. **Eight** is an application of the principle of each suit in the daily world, and so the *Eight of Wands* means activity, swiftness, being busy with things or hurrying with messages.

Nine, being a three-fold three, is a number representing great power residing in the background, as a conditioning influence upon events. It is no coincidence that in the lay-out of the pyramid it stands next to the Queen, for it has a strong ruling feminine ambience. The *Nine of Wands* is therefore a card of power and energy. **Ten** is similar to the nine but is more the outward show, the final outcome, and is appropriately adjacent to the King in the pyramidal lay-out before us. The *Ten of Wands* indeed indicates a certain surfeit of organizing energy and so represents a certain overbearing attitude, over-organization, supervision taken perhaps to oppressive lengths.

With these number principles in mind let us now look again at the panorama before us, the pyramid of panels rising to a point at the Ace, with the Six in the centre, and the King standing to one side at the lower right, overseeing the even numbers (2, 4, 8 and 10) and the Queen standing to one side at the lower left overseeing the odd numbers (3, 5, 7, and 9). We should first see the emblems of the cards emblazoned on the panels as they appear in any traditional Tarot pack. The precise details vary from one pack to another but the general principle is all that needs to be followed. We see the Ace as a hand holding up a large ragged club; the remainder of the cards consist of crossed wands, with a single wand upright through the middle for the odd numbers, a pair of upright wands for the ten.

As we focus our attention on each card panel we should see it light up under our gaze. As we look at it, we see its traditional pattern begin to fade, and it becomes more like a screen, with pictures appearing spontaneously on it. These pictures will illustrate the general meaning or complex of meanings that can be associated with each card. The pictures may well change, and will differ for different people observing them. However, the general meaning behind the pictures will be the same, for they will indicate the principles of the number and the suit combined and adapted to various circumstances.

An example of the kind of pictures that might occur is to be found in the set of lesser card designs in the Rider/Waite pack. This was perhaps the first to be published showing pictures on the numbered suit cards illustrating the divinatory meanings. The pictures are one indication of the type of images that may be seen, but one's own observations may well differ. A.E. Waite and his artist had a particular preference for seeing the pictures in a kind of medieval setting. If this stimulates the imagination, all well and good, but it is not a necessary mode of imagery. What *is* important is to use your own visionary imagination to see and maintain the picture for each card. They will then be easy to recall and adapt for later divination. This principle cannot be stressed too much. The secret of success in all this work is the building of pictures in the imagination. This was the basis of the art of memory practised by the ancient wisdom schools and later enshrined in Renaissance esoteric systems such as the Tarot. And the principles remain valid, if largely forgotten, to this day. If you have any trouble in recalling the meaning of Tarot cards it will be because you have tried to rely too much on intellectual analysis or theorizing. Simply build the pictures, and you will have an ever-ready magic mirror of true recollection which is not only effortless but thoroughly reliable.

Regarding the pyramid or receding triangle that ascends before us, we first gaze upon the Ace, near the apex. We know it to be a fount of organizing energy. See the Ace as it is traditionally depicted. Now its brightness gives way to other pictures that carry the same meaning. You may see a magic wand scintillating with light, you may see a transmitting radio aerial, you may see an orchestral conductor's baton, or a king's sceptre, a drill sergeant's pace stick, a flag pole – any emblem of energy or power.

Having observed this, drop your eyes to the central panel that depicts the Six of Wands, for this represents that basic principle we have just been observing, now in balanced action. Again, when you have observed the traditional design of six wands, crossed three by three, allow the pictures to rise depicting the balanced successful achievement of the principle of energy and intelligent activity that is

associated with the suit of Wands. A.E. Waite saw a figure with a
purple cloak, a victory garland on his head, riding a white horse richly
caparisoned, holding aloft a staff with a wreath of triumph upon it, in
procession before a crowd raising their staves on high. Your image
may well be different. It could be someone in modern dress in a
situation of victory or achievement or success, perhaps not on
horseback but riding in a luxury limousine! Or it could be a different
kind of picture altogether, an athlete winning a race for example.

The important thing is not to try to think up some picture that fits
by scratching your brain for ideas. Simply hold the two basic
principles in mind (you know what the number six tends to stand for,
and also what the suit of Wands stands for) and observe whatever
images arise spontaneously. If the images seem wildly inappropriate
then simply dismiss them and wait for other, more suitable ones to
arise. When you have become accustomed to this kind of mind-work
then wholly appropriate images should flow freely to you – and this
is what separates an experienced Tarot diviner from one who is
freshly starting out or who is trying to work off a superficial
understanding of the principles involved.

Now we can look at the other panels in turn. Concentrate upon the
Two next, and then the Three, which are to the right and left
immediately below the Ace. The Two should bring up images of
control; the Three should bring up images of established strength.
Following upon this, concentrate upon the Four and then the Five, to
the right and left of the central Six. Take your time over this, you are
establishing the foundation for a structure of ideas that will stand you
in good stead for a lifetime. It is quite a good idea to work with two
images at a time. The Ace and the Six first; the Two and the Three
next; then the Four and the Five; followed by the Seven and the
Eight; and finally the Nine and Ten. By the time you have finished
this, if you have built the pictures vividly, you will have no trouble in
calling to mind any card of the Wand suit and its likely significance
in any reading.

At the conclusion of each part of this meditative work, you should
withdraw by the way you have come. See the curtains close over the
panorama before you. Make your farewells to the King and Queen,
and accompanied by the Page, return down the lift and through the
busy scene below, giving due acknowledgement to the Knight. Pass
through the corridors and the reception area back into the Hall of
Strength. Here, being left by the Page, the figure of the maiden with
the lion will conduct you back into the Hall of the Magician, where
the Fool will take you back over the air bridge to the door in the rock
which leads to your normal physical surroundings. All this may be

effected quite quickly but should not be omitted. It may seem to be a complicated, formal convention, but it serves to establish a true pattern of inter-relationships with all the Tarot forms deeply within your consciousness. This is important; it establishes the Tarot system as an organic whole, a balanced system within which you can work and which can work within you.

Working Plan

Exercise 1
Describe the images that came up for you for each of the Wand cards, Ace to Ten.

Exercise 2
Write a paragraph of description of a typical person (or message or organization) that might be represented by each of the Wand court cards.

Knowledge Notes

While it is of greater benefit to allow your own images to represent the numbered suit cards, it can be useful to be aware of the results obtained by others who have previously worked at this task. We shall therefore take a look at some of the comments made by A.E. Waite and Aleister Crowley, both of whom spent some time working at their own designs. A.E. Waite's are in fact quite well known through the popularity of the cards he designed with Pamela Coleman-Smith, and since their publication in 1910 they have strongly influenced a number of others designs, such as the Royal Fez Moroccan, the Aquarian, the Morgan-Greer, and the Hanson-Roberts to name but four of the most popular modern packs. Aleister Crowley's ideas, which were put into effect by Lady Frieda Harris over the period 1938 to 1943, are perhaps too ornate and idiosyncratic in some respects for general popular use, but he used traditional ideas (based largely on the meanings formulated by the Hermetic Order of the Golden Dawn, of which A.E. Waite was also a member), and attempted to express them in the abstract design of the symbol layout. This is also a solution which I and Sander Littel attempted in the Gareth Knight Tarot, which we designed in 1962. The following notes are therefore designed to stimulate the imagination rather than to provide substitutes for your own creative faculties. Remember that the best possible designs, that will speak most to you and help you in your subsequent card readings, will be your own. The Tarot works best as a personal inter-relationship between you and the Tarot – and has no need of any 'expert' intermediary.

Ace of Wands. Traditionally called *Root of the Powers of Fire*, the fire that is meant is the creative fire of life. To Waite this was best expressed by a heavenly hand appearing from a cloud and holding a stout branch which is bursting forth with life in the form of buds and leaves. The later Aquarian and Hanson-Roberts cards show this perhaps even more dynamically, the rod being more a green stem from the centre of which burst flowers as well as buds from the sides. The Crowley image is more fiery still, all reds and golds and yellows, with a violently upthrusting rod bursting forth with flames. There is also a hidden meaning in that the flames are in the shape of the Hebrew letter *yod*, which signifies creative seeds. Crowley described it as 'a solar-phallic outburst of flame from which springs lightning in every direction'. The Gareth Knight image has a rod extending from heaven to earth, in the seven colours of the rainbow, in the midst of a lightning flash which extends from a 12-pointed white star at the top of the rod to a green and gold circled cross at the foot of the rod, from which red sparks fly as a kind of reaction to or reflection of the divine lightning flash.

Two of Wands. The traditional seed idea is *Dominion*. Waite described his image as a tall man looking from a battlemented roof over sea and shore, holding a terrestrial globe in his right hand and a staff in his left. Crowley showed two heavy-looking dorjes, crossed. A *dorje* is a Tibetan symbol for a thunderbolt. And in the Gareth Knight card we showed two crossed wands with creative fire at their centre, rather in the nature of a welding or fiery conjoining perhaps. The fire is also, of course, synonymous with the human will.

Three of Wands. The traditional seed idea of *Established Strength* is shown by Waite as a calm, stately figure with his back turned to us, looking from a cliff's edge at ships passing over the sea. Three wands planted firmly in the ground stand beside him. Crowley sees his three wands as lotuses in blossom because for him the meaning of the card is harmonious and associated with the beginning of Spring (that is, one might elaborate, the established strength of the winter roots that are about to send forth growth and renewed life). In the Gareth Knight image the established strength is shown by the central, upright wand being very sturdy and thick.

Four of Wands. *Perfected Work* is the traditional seed idea for this card, which Waite shows as four great staves planted in the ground with a large garland suspended between them. In the background is an old manorial house with various figures in apparent festive mood, two of them raising up bunches of flowers. The Crowley image shows the same idea in the form of four wands with their ends forming a circle about their fiery centre. Each wand has a ram's head at one end and a dove at the other to show their balanced polarity. In the Gareth Knight card the image is of four wands in a four-square lattice-work, with balanced four-square flames giving the impression of balanced work or design.

Five of Wands. The traditional seed idea is *Strife*, shown by Waite as a group of youths brandishing staves, although in his description in his book *The Key to the Tarot* (Rider, 1982) he suggests that they are indulging in sport or mimic fighting. Crowley's imagery is in the form of a massive, upright, authoritative winged wand establishing rule over two pairs of contrary powers, each topped with a phoenix head or a lotus (that is the implied contrasts between a bird of flame and a water-lily). In the Gareth Knight card we have much the same pattern although with plain rods; one sturdy and upright establishing its authority over the four lesser ones to the accompaniment of much angular flame and sparks of lightning.

Six of Wands. The seed idea is *Victory*, which is shown by Waite as a horseman wearing one victor's wreath and bearing another on a stave, accompanied by followers with staves. Crowley shows the three types of wand that appeared in the Five of Wands in a perfectly balanced and orderly array, with flames burning steadily as lamps at their intersection. Much the same idea is behind the Gareth Knight design.

Seven of Wands. The traditional seed idea is *Valour*, and Waite sees a young man on a hillock with a stave in hand defending himself against the six other staves raised from below. Crowley's representation shows the six ordered wands of his Six of Wands banished to the background behind a mis-shapen club. In his explanation in *The Book of Thoth* (Weiser, 1981) he amplifies his ideas by saying, 'The army has been thrown into disorder; if victory is to be won, it will be by dint of individual valour – a *soldiers' battle*. The pictorial representation shows the fixed and balanced wands of the last card relegated to the background, diminished and become commonplace. In front is a large, crude, uneven club, the first weapon to hand; evidently unsatisfactory in ordered combat. The flames are dispersed, and seem to attack in all directions without systematic purpose.' The Gareth Knight image is similar in outline but with plain rods, one of which dominates the rest, outlined in a red and yellow angular halo of flame.

Eight of Wands. The traditional signification is *Swiftness*, shown by Waite as a flight of eight wands through the air, propelled from some unknown source. Crowley picks up this idea by showing light wands turned into electrical rays, sustaining crystals by their vibratory action. In the Gareth Knight image eight wands rotate rapidly in a circle in the confines of four surrounding magnets, again picking up on the idea of the swiftness of electrical energy.

Nine of Wands. The traditional meaning of this card is *Great Strength*. Waite's image shows a man standing before a palisade, watchful and prepared to defend it. In Crowley's image the wands have become arrows, eight of them form a closely knit lattice-work and one, much larger, stands before them with a radiant sun at its upper end and a crescent moon at its lower. The Gareth Knight image is of a similar lattice-work, but the upright wand in the foreground is absolutely massive and adorned with a white rose, signifying ultimate spiritual authority.

Ten of Wands. The traditional meaning is *Oppression*, and this is shown by Waite in the figure of a man oppressed by the weight of ten staves which he is carrying. Crowley's geometric image is of two upright wands in the foreground before a background of eight interlaced wands. They are all of a metallic grey colour, suggestive of prison bars. In the Gareth Knight image the card is dominated by the two upright wands which are pressing closer together. Between them there is colour and light, but increasingly manifest as they squeeze together is a darkness that renders all into colourless patterns of black and white.

The Court Cards. None of the published sources is very helpful when it comes to the Court Cards, either in card design or in books. The traditional card designs show courtly figures, not too relevant to modern terms, or else, in an attempt to show archetypal psychological tendencies, they are more like angelic or elemental creatures than human beings. Similarly, the traditional fortune-teller's approach of equating cards with physical types (the 'dark lady' or 'red-headed man' and so on) is restricting and misleading in practice.

In an actual reading any of the court cards can stand for various people, irrespective of hair or skin colour, although the general type should hold good. Therefore the best advice we can give is that you make your own acquaintance with the court figures in the context of your work in going to and from the memory theatres of each suit. This will give you a basic type and function that will stand you in good stead when you come to actual readings, being firmly based on the basic function of the card concerned yet giving you the flexibility to interpret according to the needs of any given situation. For instance, sometimes the Pages are messages, or background gossip, rather than actual persons, and this must be left to your intuition and to the interpretative skills that you will develop with practice.

Questions and Answers

Q. The image of a building company came up immediately when I started working with the Suit of Wands and although I originally thought it a bit unsuitable I couldn't manage to get it out of my mind. I look forward to your comments.

A. Building has indeed a strong tradition in providing symbolism for esoteric work, not only in the sacred geometry of the ancient temples and pyramids and more recent Medieval and Renaissance cathedrals, but also in the lore of freemasonry, which is based upon the building trade. We do not have to get into these deep waters in the practical application of our Tarot work, but it is interesting to see how the traditions have their applications in many unexpected ways. So full marks for following your own intuition and pictorial imagination, and I trust that this exercise will have encouraged you to trust it. This will lead to accuracy and depth in reading the cards and possibly to a natural development and deepening of interest and ability in esoteric matters generally.

Q. I have noticed in various Tarot books that little, and sometimes nothing, is given on the reverse card images – I wonder why? As life is not all sweetness and light I would have thought the reversed image should rate the same importance as the upright images. They can certainly be more constructive. You have made certain recommendations as to how the cards should be shuffled which, in my view, do not seem to give enough opportunities for the reversed images to play their full part. In my practice readings I do, on occasion, swizzle the cards around face down on the table so that the reversed images are on an equal footing with the upright ones. I think the readings are better for it.

A. I think there is very sound sense in what you say, and a good case could be made for having at least half the cards in the pack reversed. However, there are many who feel distinctly uncomfortable about the use of reversed cards and I would not personally want to insist that they grasp the nettle, because I think that their disquiet is often the result, not so much of a squeamish attitude towards physical life as it is lived but more to an intuitive feeling that the images represent a vision of perfection that the world has fallen away from. The general compromising consensus is what I generally advocate, that is, the turning about of just a few cards. In practice I tend to fix on seven myself. Anyway, you go ahead and follow your nose in this and see how it works out for you.

Q. Why do you have the Page and other Court cards appear in modern dress and not Medieval clothes?

A. There is no reason why the Court figures have to be in modern dress. When writing this part of the instruction it seemed to me that most students would prefer it this way, but certainly I have found that there are others who like to have them in historical or traditional guise. If you feel happier with them that way, then by all means see them so.

Q. Is it right to think of the four Court cards of Wands as the 'Family of Wands' – with certain characteristics in common, for example their bold, fiery temperament? The King suggests to me that he is a more 'developed' version of the Page and Knight, and that all four Court cards are linked together in sequence. Is this right?

A. The Court cards can indeed be regarded as part of one family for each suit. The King and Queen can be regarded as more developed or experienced than the Knight, and the Knight in turn of the Page. Whether you find the King or Queen more mature depends on how much of a feminist you are!

Q. I didn't find this lesson at all easy. I think it was putting it into modern, everyday concepts that got me.

A. It can be a kind of culture shock I know, switching from the archetypal images of the Trumps to a modern ambience for the suit cards. It is possible of course to keep the imagery in 'old-tyme' guise but it seemed to me more appropriate to do it this way if one is concerned with eventually using the cards for interpreting spreads covering modern-life situations.

Q. I like your comment on my reading: 'the Tarot is rather fond of that', referring to the possibility of a hidden kick. It helps to personalize the Tarot for me, to make it feel like it's someone I can converse with and even expect a joke or a bit of sarcasm from.

A.   It is important to relate to the Tarot in a person-to-person way. It gets rid of any staleness of approach that can come upon us when we have been batting symbolism around in our heads for donkey's years, making pretty theoretical patterns, or even worse, seeing it as some kind of 'psychological mechanism'. Yet unless we get a certain sense of awe about approaching it as a pretty powerful kind of being, who chooses to communicate with us in this way, then Tarot divination is never going to get any further than subjective musing. It is, despite its familiarity, a magical process, with all that term implies. And the being behind it, whether showing himself to us as the Fool, or Magician, is Lord of the Dance, whether we choose to translate that title in terms of Christian, pagan or oriental mystical experience.

Q.   I can't seem to settle down to working with just one pack of cards. I hope you can deal with all my indecision here. I see my own images when I work with the cards anyway, whichever pack I am using.

A.   I think it is the personal element in the Tarot that causes us at one time to respond to one set of card designs and at other times to another. I have several sets that I use at different times and on different occasions and for different purposes. In one sense it is the Tarot in a different mood, wanting to play with us in a slightly different fashion. Incidentally, don't be afraid to be pretty wild in your experimentation. The Tarot can handle it if you can. If you want a really big spread, why not try mixing four packs together? That gives scope for some very subtle and detailed interchange. Of course it is best to use mini-size cards for this, unless you've got a very large table, and very long arms to go with it!

Q.   I have done a few more readings for friends as well as for someone I had never met before. Things come to mind during the readings which I am almost afraid to mention for fear of sounding foolish. There is the temptation to tell them 'safe' things rather than sticking my neck out. With friends I find that either I know what type of problem they have or which direction they are enquiring about, but the woman I had not met before told me she wanted to know 'anything'. In some ways this was better in that I was not preconditioned but on the other hand I thought I told her far too many trivial 'fortune-teller' things. I sensed though at a certain level it was this that she wanted to hear. I feel terribly nervous beforehand, then when I get started not so bad. Afterwards I think it wasn't too impressive. I find that some people are frightened of telling me too much, and also seem to expect me to know everything about their lives. All very daunting.

A. I note what you say about your experience of reading the cards for others. There is of course no better practice, although as you say, it can be a bit nerve-racking at first. But you will find that you will begin to take things more in your stride as you gain experience. Half the battle is getting tuned in to what the Querent is really wanting to know, or what expectations he or she might have, and maybe putting these right if they are unrealistic. Therefore it helps to get into conversation with the Querent as much as you can before and indeed during the reading. You should never allow him or her to dominate the proceedings, or get yourself manoeuvred into the kind of assumption that you are somehow on trial. Either Querents are seeking help and advice or they are not. And if they are not then there is not much in it for either of you. On the other hand, if they do genuinely seek help then it is in their interest to be as forthcoming and open with you as possible.

Q. Once each week I set out three cards for myself about some event, or rather, try to see what they are telling me, then afterwards I can see how well I had read them, without having to wait too long.

A. This practice of taking three cards to see their relevance to your own affairs is quite a good one, and some people make a life-long practice of it, sometimes every day, and report that they find it very helpful and illuminating.

Q. Is it all right just to meditate upon the meanings of the numbered cards rather than see pictures of them?

A. The intention of the exercises was certainly for you to meditate upon the meaning of the numbered cards but at the same time to have a visual image that demonstrates the meaning. I find that different students are helped in different ways and prefer to approach this stage of the course in different ways. Some, looking at the blank spaces that represent the cards, have images arise spontaneously that illustrate the relevant meaning. This means in effect that they are virtually designing their own pictorial Lesser Arcana. This is a very good way of forming a close association with the suit cards. The more imaginative students tend to turn up a whole mass of pictures or images illustrating the meanings of each card. The less imaginative tend to rely on some already familiar pictorial version of the card, usually the Waite design, and use this. You have gone straight to the meaning without recourse to a pictorial symbol or image; and if you find that this works for you, and that you can recall the meaning of a card whenever you think of its suit and number, then that's fine. However, in keeping with the methodology of the course, which stresses the importance of the image-making faculty of the human mind, I would suggest that visualizing pictures in association with each card has a lot to be said for it. It acts as a useful memory device on the one hand, and as a means of clothing psychic perceptions or higher intuitions on the other.

Q. I found the new experience with the Minor Arcanum in the Memory Theatre exciting and challenging. The images began to rise quite spontaneously after my second visit there. In order to memorize them I created a small story out of the sequence of each card representing the suit, and have included in the story the King, Queen, Knight and Page, without whom the story would not be complete.

A. The method you have adopted of a kind of story line is an excellent practice, and helps to key in the meanings of the cards in yet another dimension. Another student hitting upon this method in relation to the suit of Wands used a story of starting up and organizing a business.

This story-line method has been used in *Mythic Tarot* (Rider, 1986), in an approach conceived by Juliet Sharman-Burke and Liz Greene and illustrated by Tricia Newell. Stories from Greek mythology are used: the legend of Eros and Psyche for Cups, of Jason and the Argonauts for Wands, of Orestes and the curse of the House of Atreus for Swords, and of Daedalus the builder of the Cretan labyrinth of the minotaur for Coins. One could of course use any number of other stories taken from other bodies of myth or legend, or indeed made up by oneself. The art of story-telling is closely connected with the Tarot, and could well be used as a device for stimulating the imagination by would-be story-writers or novelists. However, our immediate purpose is not to set up a school of creative writing!

LESSON SIX

The Theatre of Cups

We suggest that we take the Cups suit next. The procedure is similar to that which we followed with the suit of Wands. We pass from the Hall of the Magician into the Hall of Temperance, and there too we find a hitherto-unnoticed small door open, in which stands the figure of the Page of Cups. We follow the Page through the doorway to find ourselves in a brightly-lit reception area. It does not have quite the same air of brisk business activity as did that for the Wands; here, although the general layout is similar, there is a more relaxed atmosphere. It is like a luxury hotel, or perhaps a stately home, with a general feeling of well-run ease. The Page again appears in modern dress and may be of either sex, in the function and perhaps the dress of a hotel page. We are ushered through a labyrinth of quiet corridors.

We come to a large area, which seems to be roofed and walled with glass. There are vistas of gardens on one side and of a sandy beach and blue sea on the other, where people are enjoying themselves. Around us are tables and easy chairs, where people are seated. Again it is rather like the lounge of a luxury hotel. In the centre is a desk, upon which is to be seen the framed picture of the Knight of Cups. The man behind the desk is seen to be acting in the capacity of genial host and organizer of all the activities about us. He welcomes us warmly and appears to know that we wish to see the innermost workings of this pleasure palace. He points towards the far end wall where there is a high balcony, at each end of which hangs a portrait – of the King of Cups to the right and the Queen of Cups to the left.

The Page ushers us towards the doors of a lift located beneath the balcony and we ascend. Once again we are greeted by a middle-aged man and woman who take the parts of the King and the Queen of Cups. They are genial hosts and welcome us cordially. They indicate the curtains at the end of the room and take up their positions at either side of them, the King to the right and the Queen to the left.

The curtains part slowly to reveal once again the sloping side of a pyramid, with panels upon which are emblazoned the ten numbered cards of the suit of Cups.

Once again we will find that pictures arise when we contemplate each one in turn, in accordance with its number and its suit. The *Ace* represents the very fount of ease and pleasure, an ever-flowing bowl or cup of love and plenty. The *Two*, the principle of polarity, shows love between two individuals or groups of people. The *Three*, the principle of establishment of the qualities of the suit, shows events or affairs giving great pleasure. The *Four*, the full expression of this quality, shows a certain over-plus of the pleasure principle, in luxury, surfeit, or a tendency to boredom or self-indulgence. Perhaps inherited ease or wealth, or success that has come too easily and may be taken for granted.

The *Five*, which is an unbalancing principle at work in the general ambience of pleasure, shows disappointment. The *Six*, which gives full balanced expression of the suit principle, shows enjoyment, the making of new friends and of discovering new pleasures. The *Seven*, which again is an overbalancing, sharp element in its number meaning, shows amid the pleasure principle of Cups, a certain reluctance to face hard reality, so it gives a situation of self-deception or illusion, of living in a fool's paradise. The *Eight*, which signifies application of the principle of the suit, again shows a little too much of a good thing, by way of a loss of interest, or indolence, and success or ease that has been abandoned. The *Nine*, which is the power closely behind physical appearances, is a signifier of wishes fulfilled, success and good luck. The *Ten*, the number of completion, the end of the number sequence, again shows conditions of great success that may well be long lasting and well founded.

We proceed on lines similar to those we followed with the Wands. Having observed the pictures that arise with each card, in the same suggested order of working, we take our leave of the King and Queen of Cups, and return the way we came, accompanied by the Page, past the Knight, and back through the Hall of Temperance.

The Theatre of Swords

We shall next make the acquaintance of the suit of Swords. For this we make our entry to the Hall of Justice and see the Page of Swords standing at the open door to guide us. When we pass through this door we find ourselves in a bare functional reception area that has few of the elements of gracious living. It is not a forbidding place but one

that has an impersonality, rather like a government office or large
waiting room, be it a doctor's, a solicitor's, or a room in which we
might await some kind of formal interview.

The Page, who again may be of either sex, is like a court usher, or
similar official, who conducts us through a complex of bare corridors
until we reach a large open area which is filled with desks and
benches. Here sit a wide range of people. Most are formally dressed
in some way, either with the wigs and gowns of the British legal
profession, or with the green gowns or white coats of surgeons or
doctors. Some are military personnel, in uniforms of different kinds,
including policemen, warders, and officers of private security forces.
There are scientists working at laboratory benches, hospital nurses,
civil servants, and officials auditing or inspecting ledgers and
documents.

We are led by the Page to a central desk upon which is a picture of
the Knight of Swords. The person behind it is somewhat stern-faced
and impersonal, but by no means unpleasant or hostile. By use of the
screens and phones and other gadgetry he monitors and controls all
that goes on within this hall. After formally greeting us he indicates
the far end of the hall where we see a balcony; to the right and left
there are portraits of the King and Queen of Swords. We are then
taken to the lift.

When we arrive at the higher level we are met by the King and
Queen. We are greeted courteously but with the kind of
impersonality that one might associate with an eminent surgeon,
lawyer or scientist. The general tenor is the same for both of them,
but with the King the masculine elements of detachment and control
are emphasized, and with the Queen the feminine attribute of
attention to the means whereby control is exercised. She might well
be the matron of a large hospital, and he its chief medical consultant.
However, we should not overemphasize the medical element. It
serves as a useful example but the suit of Swords is by no means to do
only with matters of physical health. It is concerned with any
impartial, testing, proving, correcting activity.

The King and Queen take up their stations. Once again the curtains
part and we find the familiar triangular pyramid side revealed, with
the ten cards of the suit of Swords emblazoned upon its panels. We
observe the pictures that arise with each one, as before.

The *Ace* shows a hand with a drawn sword, held point upward so
that it penetrates a golden crown. This is the root of all impartial,
testing, balancing forces, external to any system upon which they are
operating; also the root of growth. The *Two*, the principle of duality,
reveals pictures of forces, perhaps contending or conflicting, but in

balanced opposition. The *Three*, the principle of establishment of the quality of the suit, indicates events bringing sorrow or regret. The *Four*, the principle of four-square organization, has sufficient balancing power inherent within it to give images of truce, armistice or rest after conflict – perhaps convalescence after illness or injury.

The *Five*, whose 'sharpness' accentuates that same quality in the Swords, gives situations of defeat. The *Six*, which is a supremely balancing number, in the suit of Swords gives success after due effort or work, success that has to be well earned. The *Seven*, with its overbalancing characteristic, in Swords indicates situations of futile, unstable or unrealistic efforts. The *Eight*, which shows the principle of application of any quality of force, with Swords, perhaps because of fears of external opposition or hostility, gives situations marked by indecision, or pettyfogging bureaucracy and extreme caution. The *Nine*, giving a strong background atmosphere of the influence of the Swords, shows situations of loss, or of worry or depression. The *Ten*, the final outcome of the Sword principle, signifies the ruin and defeat of hopes and intentions.

Having worked through these images, we make our farewells and retrace our steps in the same way as we departed from the Theatres of Wands and of Cups, this time returning via the Hall of Justice.

Learning the Language of the Trumps

While we are learning the significance of the Lesser Arcanum, or the numbered suits, we must not neglect the Trumps. We can continue making spreads and interpreting them using the Trump images only. Indeed many cartomancers get by using only one Arcanum or the other (readers who use ordinary playing-card packs are in effect working without a Greater Arcanum).

If you are confining yourself to small spreads of no more than a dozen cards, then the twenty-two Trump cards may well be sufficient. It is also possible to use the suit cards only, particularly with fairly straightforward, mundane matters, as indeed, in effect, do all cartomancers who use the ordinary pack of playing cards.

It is a valuable exercise to try to put yourself into the position of the Tarot itself. The images of the pack comprise a symbolic language, and it is a language that you are trying to learn to read. Therefore, as a means of gaining fluency in this language you ought also to be able to express yourself in a message consisting of the Tarot symbols. After all, this is what you expect the Spirit of the Tarot to do! Let us take a well-known story as an example, the fairy story of Cinderella.

Suppose you, as Spirit of the Tarot, have been approached to answer a question from the querent Cinderella as to her prospects for the coming week. She wants badly to go to a ball but seems prevented by domestic circumstances. From your vantage point as Spirit of the Tarot you are able to foresee what is likely to occur. How would you express that message in the cards?

Let us use a fairly straightforward spread for this purpose - one recommended by Jan Woudhuysen in his book *Tarot Therapy* (Houghton Mifflin, 1979). This uses just seven cards laid out from left to right with the following meanings:

1. Character
2. Nearest and dearest
3. Hopes and fears
4. What is expected (but may not happen)
5. What is not expected (but might well happen)
6. Immediate future
7. Distant future

1. If we are restricted to Tarot Trumps, which one would we choose for the character of Cinderella? In her role of innocence she could be the Fool; or as one who lives entirely on hopes of a brighter future the Star might be appropriate. However, perhaps the Hanged Man might best portray her condition. Any one of these cards could be utilized, particularly if one or two of them are required elsewhere in the spread.

2. Her nearest and dearest being the frightful ugly sisters, wicked step-mother and negative and ineffectual father, it would seem that the Devil is the most suitable card here; although the Moon might possibly be used to represent the general state of deception or self-deception in the household.

3. Cinderella's hopes and fears centre about being invited to the ball, which in the circumstances seems highly unlikely. The Last Judgement might be most appropriate here - certainly an invitation for the mightily oppressed! A more general hope might be for Justice, or for a change of fortune, which would be represented by the Wheel. Or one might possibly also have the Star here, emblematic of her general hopes, which appear idealistic and remote.

4. That which is expected, but may not happen, is a continuation of the status quo. She will just continue to be a drudge. Thus the Moon might be the card here - or possibly Death, as the end of all hopes and aspirations.

5. That which is not expected, (but which from our inner vantage point we know is highly likely to happen), can be represented by a number of images. The Tower could represent a complete destruction of the current situation, the Chariot could represent her gaining control of the course of her life – with the added implied reference of her going off to the ball in a magic pumpkin coach – a marvellous chariot indeed! More general indicators could be the Wheel, showing change of fortune; the Sun, showing success; or the Lovers, showing the impending meeting with Prince Charming.

6. The immediate future we know is going to centre about the arrival of Cinderella's fairy godmother. She seems most appropriately represented by the Empress, as the bringer of good things; or by the Magician in view of her taking control of the situation by magical powers. A third possibility could be the High Priestess, in view of her wise-woman aspect.

7. The distant future is going to be one of great success. All dreams come true with marriage to the Prince. This could be shown forth by a number of cards – the Sun, the Lovers, or the World, signifying realization of all potential; or possibly Strength, in that she is now mistress of her destiny and the lower forces that formerly surrounded and controlled her.

From these general considerations it will be seen that some cards could appear on several positions. And indeed this is apparent from the signification of the stations of any particular spread. Hopes and fears may well foreshadow either the expected or the unexpected, and these in turn could be an aspect of either the immediate or the distant future. The exercise of using the images to spell out messages, using any story line, is an excellent way of gaining facility with interpretation of the cards in a spread, and developing a deeper understanding of the inner dynamics and modus operandi of the oracular Tarot as a whole. We recommend you make up your own exercises along these lines, as well as take every opportunity to practise actual reading of Tarot spreads.

Working Plan

Exercise 1

Describe the images that came up for you for each of the Cup cards, Ace to Ten. Also, write a paragraph of description of a typical person, message or organization for each of the Cup court cards.

Exercise 2
Do the same for the Sword cards.

Exercise 3
Write out a brief story line, from any source, and then express it in images of the Tarot Trumps, as in the example of Cinderella given in the lesson.

Knowledge Notes

We will continue in these notes to describe some of the images that have been associated with the numbered suit cards, looking first at Swords and then at Cups.

Suit of Swords

Ace of Swords. The image for this card is very much the same in the Waite, Crowley and Gareth Knight designs; that is, a sword held point upward, the point of which passes through a crown. In the Knight and Waite versions the crown is festooned with garlands, Crowley's is more a crown of light. As *Root of the Powers of Air* (its traditional title) it represents the mind, penetrating mental analysis or the intuitional piercing of obscuring emotions, fixed ideas or preconceptions. There is also an element of 'the spirit, which bloweth whithersoever it listeth'.

Two of Swords. The seed idea for this card is *Peace Restored*, and Waite sees this as a blindfolded female figure, with crossed arms, holding swords upon her shoulders. He describes this image as representing, in his mind, 'conformity and the equipoise which it suggests; courage, friendship, concord in a state of arms, affection, intimacy.' Crowley's image just shows the two swords crossed, but united where they cross in a blue rose that emits white rays. The Knight image has two curved swords or scimitars, hilt upward, and within the space between the blades a heart sending forth white rays.

Three of Swords. Waite sees a heart pierced by three swords, with clouds and rain behind, representing the key idea of this card, which is *Sorrow*. Much the same image is found on the Knight card, though without the storm clouds. Crowley, however, has menacing dark clouds as a background to his image of three swords cutting a white rose to pieces.

Four of Swords. The seed idea here is traditionally *Rest from Strife*, or as Crowley prefers to call it, *Truce*. The Knight image is similar to that for the *Two*, only with four swords, within the space between them is a red heart radiating white rays. In Crowley's image the four swords are in the form of a St Andrew's cross, with their points touching the centre of a large white rose. Waite however sees the effigy of a knight lying on a bier in an attitude of prayer, which he says represents vigilance, retreat, solitude, hermit's repose, exile, and the ultimate 'resting in peace' associated with the tomb.

Five of Swords. The traditional idea behind this card is *Defeat*, shown by Waite in the scene of a disdainful man picking up discarded swords and looking at two dejected and retreating figures, whom he has just defeated. Crowley's more abstract image shows five swords in the shape of an inverted pentagram, that is, point downwards, which has always had sinister connotations. The swords droop and the rose of the previous card has disintegrated completely – its dispersed petals outline the inverted pentagram. The reason the pentagram or five-pointed star has these unfortunate connections is that it is, point upwards, a symbol for the unity of the spirit that controls the four elements. In the reversed position it indicates duality, or contending forces having the upper hand over the threefold worlds of the spirit. The Gareth Knight image is similar to that for the 3 of Swords, but with five swords transfixing the heart.

Six of Swords. The key idea here is *Earned Success*. The Knight image is of six swords locked into the pattern of a hexagram, or six-pointed star, with a red heart in the centre with white rays. Crowley prefers to call the card *Science*, and shows six straight swords in balanced array as radii of a circle, their points meeting at the centre of a red rose on a golden cross. He describes it as 'the perfect balance of all mental and moral faculties, hardly won, and almost impossible to hold in an ever-changing world.' Waite's image is of a ferryman carrying passengers to a far shore. A deeper symbolic meaning for this scene, taken from ancient mythology, is possibly the earned success of souls of the departed being taken to their heavenly reward by the ferryman over the River Styx. Thus a meaning in ordinary life could well be of achievement through long effort, or the making of a fresh start based on past earnings.

Seven of Swords. The traditional title of this card is *Unstable Effort*. Waite's image is not easy to connect with this at first sight, as he shows a man in the act of carrying away some swords from a camp by stealth. The man carries five but has left two behind. The Knight image is of seven swords in something of a higgledy-piggledy formation, some curved and some straight, the one in the centre quite serpentine, with its blade of various colours. Crowley calls the card *Futility*, and sees six downward-pointing swords in a crescent formation contending against a much larger upthrusting sword, as if there were a contest between the many feeble and the one strong, with neither side getting the upper hand. Thus a lack of decisive action, and general hindrance, on all sides.

Eight of Swords. The traditional title here is *Shortened Force*, which is certainly portrayed and no mistake in the Waite scene of a woman blindfolded and bound in a desolate landscape. The Knight image is of eight curved swords, which although arrayed in neat formation just do not connect with each other, leaving a gap down the middle so that any defence they might attempt seems likely to prove ineffectual, through lack of organizing ability or will to fight or succeed. Crowley calls the card *Interference*, which also highlights a common meaning of the card in divination, particularly of bureaucratic interference or petty officialdom and similar restrictions on individual or creative growth or action. He shows this as two long swords, their points downward, hindered or crossed by six small swords of various odd shapes.

Nine of Swords. This card is traditionally called *Despair and Cruelty*. Waite depicts this as a figure lamenting on a couch against a background of swords. The Knight image is simply of nine swords forming a sinister, close array, with all their points upward. The Crowley image is of nine jagged and rusty swords pointing downward and dripping with blood and poison. It should be said that all these images are rather more sinister than the actual interpretation might be when the card occurs in a spread concerning affairs of daily life. Certainly it is not a welcome card but must be read in the context of the rest of the spread. Generally it will mean disappointment or unhappiness about something in life, and the advice for dealing with it is likely to be patience, resignation, or acceptance of the inevitable or unavoidable, perhaps by passive resistance.

Ten of Swords. Similarly, this card has a traditionally malefic meaning, namely *Ruin*. This could hardly be more total in Waite's image, which is of a prostrate figure, pierced by all ten swords. The Knight image is a close network of blades, suggesting a complete barrier against passage. Crowley shows the ten swords in the basic pattern of the Tree of Life, which signifies a ground-plan of the soul of man and of the universe in Qabalistic philosophy, but here the crucial central blade is shattered. The remarks we have made about the 9 of Swords also pertain to this card when it turns up in a reading.

Suit of Cups

Ace of Cups. The Ace of Cups is traditionally known as *Root of the*

Powers of Water, by which is meant the emotions and particularly the emotions of love and affection. In its full sense this also comprises divine love as well as love between people, which accounts for the dove that appears in the Waite, Crowley, and Knight images, descending from on high and plunging downward towards the cup. The Waite cup is also a fountain, the streams of which ultimately fall into a pool of water-lilies below. There are also waters below the Knight cup, which has signs of the zodiac about its rim. Waite's dove bears a sacred host, marked with a cross, this image also appears in the form of a circled cross behind the dove on the Knight picture, against a background of divine rays. In the Crowley image a shaft of light descends from above into the cup, which stands in the centre of a white rose and overflows with water turning into wine. In an actual reading these sacred connotations do not necessarily imply a religious element in the circumstances being reviewed, but rather the principle of love, that may be expressed in many ways according to the surrounding cards in the spread.

Two of Cups. Traditionally called *Love*, Waite shows this as a loving couple pledging one another, with a healing rod of entwined serpents rising above their cups, surmounted by a winged lion's head. Knight and Crowley have similar images, a white lily or lotus overflowing via two conduits in the form of fish into two cups. Crowley has a second lotus floating on the sea, between the fish and the cups, and the flowing liquid is translucent water. The Knight image has no background and the liquid is red wine, not water, with one fish being silver and the other gold.

Three of Cups. This card is traditionally called *Abundance*, and Waite shows three maidens in a garden pledging each other with cups. Crowley sees three cups in the form of pomegranates (ancient symbols of fertility) being filled to overflowing with water from a lotus plant. The Knight image is similar but the cups are not in the form of pomegranates and the liquid is wine rather than water.

Four of Cups. Although this card is traditionally entitled *Blended Pleasure*, Crowley prefers to call it *Luxury*. The Waite picture shows a young man seated under a tree looking at three cups on the ground before him, with a fourth cup being offered to him by a hand issuing from a cloud. His expression is none the less one of discontent. Waite explains his idea of the card to mean 'weariness, disgust, aversion, imaginary vexations, as if the wine of the world had caused satiety only; another wine, as if a fairy gift, is now offered him, but he sees not consolation therein.' This element of satiety or world-weariness accords quite well with Crowley's title for the card. Both the Crowley and Knight images show cups being overfilled. As Crowley comments, 'this implies a certain weakness, an abandonment to desire. This tends to introduce the seeds of decay into the fruit of pleasure.'

Five of Cups. The traditional meaning of this card is *Loss in Pleasure* or, as Crowley has it, *Disappointment*. Waite shows a man, cloaked in black, looking disconsolately at three spilled cups, with two other cups apparently empty behind him. The Knight picture is of five cups, each one below a stunted lotus bud with no flow between them. This is also Crowley's theme, but here the lotuses are also being torn by stormy winds, and the five cups are over an arid, stagnant sea.

Six of Cups. This card carries the seed idea of *Pleasure* and in Waite shows two children in an old garden, their cups filled with flowers. The Knight picture is of six cups being generously filled with wine from a lotus, whilst with Crowley the lotus stems filling the cups with water are grouped in an elaborate dancing movement, and the cups are not yet filled to overflowing.

Seven of Cups. This card is known as *Illusory Success* and Waite shows a man standing in wonder before seven chalices in a cloud, each with a strange vision appearing over it. The Knight image is simply of seven empty cups with a lotus plant that is completely devoid of any bud or blossom. In Crowley's picture, the lotuses have become like poisonous-looking tiger-lilies – they ooze with slime rather than water, and the sea below is a malarious morass. The cups are iridescent in a poisonous-looking kind of way. Somewhat in keeping with his imagery of corruption Crowley calls this card *Debauch*; one is reminded of the line from Shakespeare's Sonnet 94, 'Lilies that fester smell far worse than weeds'.

Eight of Cups. Traditionally entitled *Abandoned Success*, Waite shows a dejected man deserting a pile of eight cups on a lonely shore under a waning moon. The Knight picture is of eight cups, each with a lotus blossom, all of which however are in tight bud; no wine or water flows. The Crowley image shows cups that are shallow, old and broken, some of them empty, and only a meagre trickle of water for the others. The lotuses droop for lack of sun and rain, the sea has dried up into separated pools of dark, brackish water under lowering, leaden clouds. His name for this card is *Indolence*.

Nine of Cups. Traditionally the card of *Material Happiness*, Waite shows this as a goodly personage feasting to his heart's content. Both the Knight and Cowley images are of nine cups being amply filled by lotuses.

Ten of Cups. Traditionally called *Perfected* or *Perpetual Success*, Waite shows a loving couple, attended by two dancing children, standing beneath a rainbow. The Knight and Crowley images are similar to one another, showing cups in the formation of the Tree of Life being amply filled by wine or water. It is just possible that this card is too much of a good thing; Crowley expresses this by having some of the cups tilted.

Questions and Answers

Q. I found with both the suit of Cups and of Swords that the cards themselves gave such a specific picture that it was difficult to visualize an alternative. However, when they have appeared as part of a practical reading they have sometimes told me something more. For example, I read the 10 of Swords as relevant to a barren garden. Is this way off the track? It seemed appropriate and sensible at the time, but looking back I'm not so sure.

A. Yes, do feel free to interpret the cards in quite an open fashion during an actual reading. They may well want to supplement their meaning to you in various ways, which will usually come to you as an intuitive hunch, or else as a particular visual image, or maybe a particular configuration on the design of the cards that you happen to be using. I would have said that the barren garden is by no means way off the track for a 10 of Swords interpretation, suggesting as it does a particular application or interpretation of the general influence that this card represents.

Neither would I be too worried about having had second thoughts or later doubts. This is indeed quite a healthy sign, because card-reading is not an exact science, and anybody taking a serious and responsible attitude towards it will inevitably have doubts about the various complex matters that come under review. However, I should say that as a general rule first impressions of an intuitive or psychic nature do tend to be more accurate than the later intellectual doubts or speculations that one may have. It is what one felt when 'tuned in' to the cards and to the querent at the time which has the greatest likelihood of being the truth.

Q. There are times when I find I am at variance with what other people have written and that can undermine my confidence.

A. I know it can be difficult but you should try to avoid having your confidence sapped by published interpretations at variance with your own. There is a strange glamour about the printed page in that it seems to lend a certain authority to whatever appears on it. Yet something is by no means more accurate or wise simply because it has been put through a printing press. In the occult field particularly, comparative reference between texts shows considerable differences of opinion. Hence my efforts to get students to come up with their own images and ideas in a direct personal relationship with the cards themselves. Never mind the pundits.

Q. When I do my practice readings I am constantly having to refer to my notebook to get the 'one-word' interpretation.

A. Having to look up meanings suggests that you are not treating the exercises in a visual enough way. If you can concentrate on a picture image rather than a conceptualization you will find this problem will disappear. (Harry Lorayne in his *Develop a Super Power Memory* (Thorsons, 1986), which is pure magic, demonstrates this point very forcefully. Using pictorial visualization, quite incredible feats of memory are possible. As soon as you start to conceptualize, it falls apart.)

What I suggest you do is to try either drawing or painting your own set of cards, which is admittedly the long way of going about it. More immediately, you could try riding on A.E. Waite's bandwagon and take the time to lay out all the cards and visualize the pictures. This is the reason why many people prefer to use a fully pictorial pack for all their readings, and it works well enough, although it is something of a compromise from my purist advice to use an old-type Marseilles pack and let your own images arise.

Q. Should I commune with the people on the suit cards as I did with the twenty-two Trump cards?

A. It was not part of my intention to encourage a personal approach to the minor cards as was done for the Trumps. There is a difference between the two sets of cards, the minor cards standing for events or actions rather than principles, for the most part. So I do not think it is necessary to take the same approach as you would for the Trumps, although if you feel that you would like to do so I would not wish to stop you. It would certainly deepen your awareness of their potential but would extend the course more than is generally necessary for the average student. Let us put it in the category of more advanced personal research.

The Court cards, however, are a kind of halfway house, and it would be useful for you to make their acquaintance. Then see how you feel about going on to formulate a kind of tutelary genius associated with each of the numbered cards.

Q. I hope you don't mind but I've added sketches to my record. I found it easier to do that way. Pretty primitive artwork but the basis is there.

A. It is an excellent exercise to actually draw the images, and were it not for the fact that many people get into a bit of a stew over what they regard as a lack of artistic talent, I would ask all students to draw pictures of their realizations. Indeed the logical conclusion is to go on and make your own complete set of Tarot cards – which is a very rewarding exercise indeed. You might want to try it some time.

Q. During my work on Cups I had to make a long journey, and passed through Euston Station in London. There I had the extraordinary experience of observing people knitted into a pattern of relationships, the origin of which lay outside them at a periphery but which worked through their intentions and actions. I have since on reflection become equally aware of the operation of Swords among people. Neither Wands nor Coins have yet revealed themselves in this way as yet, though perhaps this is yet to come. Are these real forces in life? How do you work with them? Are there spiritual beings at work within or behind them?

A. The forces represented by the Tarot suits are indeed those which stand behind all life, although of course there are various ways of interpreting this in detail. The Tarot is but one of many systems that can give some systematic indication of them. However, as regards the Tarot itself in this context, the feelings you got on Euston Station and elsewhere reminded me of some of the similar impressions conveyed by Charles Williams in his novel about the Tarot called *The Greater Trumps* (Eerdmans Publishing Co, 1976) which you might find an interesting read some time.

Q. I find that occasionally three men in white garments appear. They say little, though I often find that they stand about me in a triangular formation. The experience is not threatening or menacing – they seem to just wait patiently. On some occasions they have led me further up the steps beyond the Tarot Hall to a white temple. There the cards are projected onto the walls, held sometimes by three pillars, sometimes seven. The Minor Arcana are projected from the roof to the floor. The Major form a large crystal at the centre of the hall when sunlight descends from a central dome. I am always free to refuse this journey if I wish. I am not sure what to make of this. Should I just wait and see?

A. The three men in white garments would seem to me to be helpful figures, although they may choose to play their cards close to their chests, so to speak. I fancy they have something to do with you spiritually, probably in connection with your other esoteric interests. They may or may not appear again, or make their intentions known. However, they would seem to be interested in stimulating your curiosity toward higher aspects of the Tarot, so it might be useful for you to follow their lead and actively contemplate the scenario that they seemed to present to you.

   This place could be identified with the castle high up the mountain which seems to be the habitation of the Fool, and which a number of students have picked up on. I have not encouraged any systematic investigation of this; there will be time enough when the elementary course is done.

Q. A question I have which has not resolved itself is whether the Tarot is an independent path of spiritual development needing nothing beyond itself to bring the meditant forward.

A. I first learned about the Tarot in conjunction with other paths, notably the Tree of Life of the Qabalistic system. However, as I grow in experience (and hopefully in wisdom) I realize that the Tarot is perfectly capable of being a path in its own right, without need of support from any other system, although for those who are sufficiently interested it is possible to make cross-connections with other systems. This is because they all, if they are valid, describe the same internal verities.

Q. The picture I got of the 6 of Swords (*Earned Success*) was a figure drawing a sword out of a cube of stone. I am not sure of this one. Have I made it too much of a success?

A. One way of looking at it is as a matter of destiny, almost a gift of the gods, and therefore hardly 'earned' so much as given. However, the poor young Arthur certainly has to earn it later, what with establishing his right to rule the realm against the prejudices of the old kings, and then all the problems of running the Fellowship of the Table Round, up to the final scene at the lake. So it depends whether you feel that something to be earned in time future is as relevant as it being earned in time past. Of course, if it is the sword-drawer's destiny then presumably he earned his present right and position by work in past lives or other conditions of being. In the last analysis it is how you feel about it that is important. And if the sword in the stone is a good hook for you to hang your ideas upon then by all means use it. This debate about it will certainly have fixed it in your memory I should think.

LESSON SEVEN

The Theatre of Coins

We start our work upon this suit by entering the Hall of the Worlds and there, through the small hidden door, we are met by the Page of Coins. We are shown into a reception area that, in stark contrast to that of Swords, is opulent, although with a sense of solidity which differs quite perceptibly from the equivalent areas of Wands or Cups. The Wand reception area showed a modern business gleaming with functional efficiency; that of Cups was altogether more luxurious and devoted to pleasurable pursuits; it had a soft, comfortable, leisurely feel. This place has the feel of a bank or financial institution, of well-polished mahogany and brasswork, an ambience that suggests traditional values, conservatism and financial probity. The Page who shows us through the corridors might well be a bank clerk or teller, or a stockbroker's messenger.

The large area into which we are shown might well be a large bank, for it is full of desks devoted to the business of making, exchanging or accounting for money. The figure at the desk, upon which is a picture of the Knight of Coins, works at the nerve-centre of all this financial activity. We see beyond the desks, outside the windows in what are obviously security areas, well-guarded vans collecting and delivering bullion in the form of ingots and coins, and indeed even documents and objects of value that one might expect to be stored in deposit boxes.

The figure at the desk has the demeanour of a bank official, although with a considerable vitality as is to be found, for instance, in those who have to have the quick wits and detailed knowledge to operate the money markets and fluctuations in stocks and shares, exchange rates, options and commodity prices. At the balcony at the end there are the usual pictures of the King and Queen. We are ushered through to the lift and up to the floor above where we are met by the King of Coins, who is very much a patrician stockbroker figure, a man of substance, used to dealing in money – which is in a sense concentrated energy, the fruit of people's labours. The Queen is also a lady who is well used to money and the power and influence that go with it. In a sense she exudes the ambience one might expect from, say, a dowager duchess, used to running a stately home.

The King and Queen take up their stations to right and left of the rich curtains, which part to reveal the pyramid's side with its panels on which are the ten numbered cards of the suit of Coins.

The great golden disc of the *Ace* is the fount of wealth and material success, and the picture or pictures that shine within its panel indicate this. The *Two*, the principle of duality, in the suit of Coins shows a change of state or location, in harmonious and controlled circumstances. The *Three*, the principle of establishment, shows a business enterprise. The *Four*, the fulfilment of an established principle, shows power and influence.

The *Five*, with its sharp aspect, indicates worry or concern about possible financial loss. The *Six*, with its harmonious fulfilling principle, indicates conditions bringing success, money, and/or gifts. The *Seven*, with its overbalancing aspect, indicates affairs or enterprises not coming to fruition, at any rate not yet. The *Eight*, with its principle of application, in Coins shows conditions of skill, ability, and acumen. The *Nine*, with its powerful background influence over outer events, shows material gain. The *Ten*, the full material expression of the principle of Coins, shows money or wealth. (Of course in any divination there will be an element of appropriate proportion in all of this. Remembering the parable of the widow's mite we should bear in mind that to many people, quite a modest sum may well represent considerable wealth, and that the appearance of this card in a spread does not necessarily mean gaining a vast fortune.)

When we have finished contemplating the pictures of the Theatre of Coins we are shown back, as is the custom, through the way that we came, retracing our steps to the Hall of the Worlds.

Basic Principles of a Tarot Spread

Although there is a great variety of possible spreads, most of them are based on certain general principles. The popular 'Celtic' spread, first published by A.E. Waite and which we have already described, embodies these principles very well. If you are aware of the principles you will be better able to construct and modify your own spreads and so improve and develop your own individual technique of Tarot reading. There are three basic steps to making a spread: a) the selection of the cards; b) their arrangement in a significant pattern; and c) the use of extra cards to amplify or resolve difficult points.

In selecting the cards (a), there is also an underlying principle. If the intention is right and sincere, then the selection of the cards will be right, no matter how this is effected – whether by a complex and predetermined ceremonious procedure or in the most casual and seemingly haphazard way. Over-riding all, and this only comes with experience, is the 'feeling' for what is right for any particular occasion.

The standard general procedure, (if indeed anything can be called standard in the fluid and intuitive world of Tarot reading), is a well-tried and simple one to follow, until individual custom and practice are established. This procedure is as follows:

1. Querent and Reader discuss the problem, in a relaxed way, and define it in terms of a precise verbal question. This should be mutually agreed and fully understood by both parties before passing on to the next stage. Writing it down may be of help, or formally reciting it aloud.

2. The cards are shuffled. We have already described our recommended method and we suggest you use it, at any rate for a start. There are, however, many variations of procedure. Some cartomancers do the shuffling themselves before passing the pack to the Querent to be cut. Others, and probably the majority, have the Querent do it all. The actual shuffling can be either a normal hand shuffle as in preparation for an ordinary card game, or by swirling the cards face down on the table (provided the surface is suitable), after the manner of shuffling Scrabble or Domino tiles. This method makes automatic provision for reversed cards, as opposed to the more self-conscious provision for them in ordinary shuffling whereby a few cards have to be deliberately turned. Some cartomancers like to have the pack arranged in formal order before each reading. Others, and again probably most, do not bother with this formal nicety, feeling that this is somewhat pseudo-scientific and that the cards will be truly selected no matter what their original statistical order. However, if the normal shuffling method is used, all cards should initially be placed the same way up, unless one is content eventually to have the situation whereby about half the cards in the pack have become reversed. Some recommend that the mind be made a blank while shuffling. This is easier said than done, particularly for anyone who is not well practised in meditation. It seems far easier, and indeed more appropriate, to concentrate the mind on the already defined question (but not on a pre-conceived answer!), to which the mind has been attuned by the preliminary discussion.

3. Cutting the cards. This is fairly standard practice and signifies the end of the shuffling process. It is usually given to the Querent to do, but sometimes the Cartomancer prefers to do it. Traditionally it is done with the left hand into three piles. Variations upon this theme are a matter of personal choice and general feeling.

With the arrangement of the selected cards (b), there are again certain simple principles. These are not rigid laws but they do have resonances deep within the human consciousness, and so are worth working with rather than against. In general terms we could say that, when we consider the bare table upon which the cards are to be set, the area *up* the table, or away from the reader, tends to represent the future, and the area *down* the table, towards the reader, tends to represent the past. Also, the *left* of the table tends to represent restriction and confinement, and the *right* easier conditions and relationships. By this same token the left/right axis can also represent the past-to-future continuum, as to many people the past tends to feel restricted, and certainly fixed, and the future more fluid and mobile, an area of hope. (Also, if one should proceed to deeper symbolic considerations, and use a spread based on, say, the Qabalistic Tree of Life, then the left- and right-hand sides of the table will correspond to the Dark and Bright pillars respectively.)

Up the table can also represent more spiritual or idealized factors in a reading, whilst down the table is more material and down-to-earth. In all of this the *centre* will tend to represent, if not the present situation, then the focus of the question under review. All this gives us a basic field of influence, with the past, restriction, and mundane matters towards the bottom left of the table; and the future, freedom, and more spiritual matters tending towards the upper right. (The right- and left-hand dynamics could be considered reversed for a left-handed person.)

It can be seen that the first part of the Celtic spread fits readily into this field. After the Cards 1 and 2 are laid, which represent the focus of the problem, Card 3, which represents future goals, falls naturally at the centre top; Card 4, representing the general, background past falls naturally at the centre bottom. Card 5, which represents the immediate past, would fall to the left hand; and Card 6, which represents the immediate future, would fall to the right hand. In general terms, cards 3 and 6 representing future, fall to the right and above an imaginary diagonal line across the table from top left to bottom right, and cards 4 and 5, representing the past, fall to the left and below it. The Celtic method is thus basically a six-card spread: two in the centre, representing the present, two cards representing the past, and two the future.

The four further cards to the right, sometimes known as the 'staff', are, in a sense, a formalization of the traditional principle (c) that allows a further four cards to be selected in addition to any spread, and to be consulted or not as desired for possible amplification or clarification of any particular question arising from the cards of the spread. In the Celtic spread these have been placed to one side, but again show the general principle of the dynamics of the 'field of reading' in that they proceed generally from past/present to future as one goes up the table – 7 representing the Querent, 8 the environment, 9 hopes and fears, and 10 the outcome. In fact, the Celtic spread has the additional feature that further consultation can be undertaken by placing the 10th card, 'The Outcome', in the centre, as a Significator, and constructing a whole new reading based on this.

This is an appropriate place to consider the use of a Significator, which is a card pre-selected and placed on the table to represent the Querent or the problem, and which otherwise takes no active part in the reading. Some cartomancers prefer not to bother with a Significator. However, in appropriate circumstances it can serve to concentrate the mind on the issues involved and may also be a useful preliminary for dealing with certain types of querent, who need calming or steadying with some preliminary discussion. This may more than compensate for the slight disadvantage of taking what might prove to be a very useful card out of circulation for the subsequent reading.

It is also possible to build a spread by increasing the number of cards located in any particular station. Three is perhaps the optimum number for this, thus a ten-card spread can become, by extension, a thirty-card spread. However, paradoxically, a certain lack of definition can result from having too many cards on the table, and certainly in the earlier stages of practical work it is more instructive to use a limited number of cards. This should enhance the intuitive powers and bring a great deal of knowledge about the cards that *are* used. However, the greater subtleties of more advanced techniques of reading are the result of the ability to interpret cards in combination, whether in pairs, threes or greater numbers. This can only come with practice. For the earlier stages, if you should decide to use more than one card for any particular spread position, it is probably best to take them in threes, and regard one as having the prime meaning and the other two as modifiers. To this end you should decide beforehand which card is to be the one with the prime meaning, the first, second or third laid. From working with threes in this way you can then extend to working with fives or sevens, if this form of expanding a reading appeals to you.

The Court Cards

In the traditional packs the various distinguishing marks, attitudes or emblems of the Court Cards are often overlooked. And whereas in the later esoteric packs the Court Cards vary significantly from one pack to another, there is quite a remarkable consistency in the various traditional Marseilles designs. It can therefore be a useful exercise to take a close look at the actual images of each of the Court Cards of the pack you usually use to see what characteristics may be suggested to you by the portrait and configuration of the card itself. The aim of this exercise is that by examining the cards in this way it may be brought home to you that with the Court Cards we should be dealing with specific characters and not just stereotypes. In a Tarot reading the Court Cards may well represent people, and by becoming familiar with the sixteen characters of the Court Cards we will be in a better position to align them with actual people in the world through their character traits. This is a better method than the cut-and-dried categories of some card reading instruction books that talk in terms of 'a dark man' or 'an older woman'.

In general terms the Court Cards are not necessarily to be interpreted strictly according to sex. A Page may well represent children or young people of either sex, or simply the bearer of a message, be it the postman, a casual acquaintance or a close confidant. Similarly, a Knight can represent someone of either sex in an active, bustling, managerial capacity; one who leads or inspires others by example. The Queens and Kings may represent older people according to sex but this is by no means universal. Certainly they represent people in established positions of authority, but this may well be in the totally domestic context of father or mother – or indeed something or someone that takes the place of father or mother. It could be a company, committee, social worker or peer group. Organizations may be represented by Kings or Queens according to whether they are active and authoritative or caring and cooperative. Thus a firm of solicitors or a factory's management might be represented by a King, a hospital or social service establishment by a Queen. Organizations have personalities just as do people, and this should be borne in mind when we are considering Court Cards that appear in Tarot divination. The watch word is to make personal close acquaintance with each Court Card through imaginative discourse with them, the required meanings will then be apparent in any later context.

If we go back to our Cinderella story, it is a useful exercise to nominate which Court Cards might represent the various characters.

For Cinderella herself: the Page of Cups? For her confidante Buttons: the Knight of Cups or Page of Wands? Her Fairy Godmother: the Queen of Coins? The Ugly Sisters: Queen of Swords? Her Father: King of Wands or Swords? Prince Charming: King or Knight of Cups? The Court Official with the Glass Slipper: Knight of Wands? Think about it, and apply the same exercise to characters from fiction or real life.

Working Plan

Exercise 1
Describe the images that came up for you for each of the Coin cards, Ace to Ten. Write a paragraph describing a person, message or organization each Court Card represents for you.

Exercise 2
List out the sixteen court cards and against each one name a famous character from fact or fiction who you think would be well represented by the card, or else a two or three-line description of the kind of person that might be so represented.

Knowledge Notes

We continue with a review of the traditional images for the suit of Coins (also known as Pentacles or Disks).

Ace of Coins. This card traditionally represents the *Root of the Powers of Earth*, which is to say that it is the principle of physical actuality, of getting things 'down to earth'. Thus Aleister Crowley chose to have his personal seal as the centrepiece of his vision for this card, containing much of his philosophical ideas. Much the same principle is to be found in the Gareth Knight version but with a more universal pattern of symbolism, that is the seven colours of the rainbow surrounding the disk, which is quartered in the traditional colours of Earth – citrine, olive, russett and black – and in the centre of which is a red rose on an equal-armed gold cross. Waite's picture is of a hand, issuing as usual from a cloud, holding a disc upon which is engraved a five-pointed star.

Two of Coins. This card, of which the seed idea is *Harmonious Change*, is depicted by Waite as a young man dancing and juggling with two disks which are conjoined by a ribbon in the shape of a figure eight. This pattern is rendered more abstractly in the Knight version, which shows the two disks in the form of Chinese *tai ge'tu* signs (symbols of counter-changing polarity) conjoined by a serpent in the shape of a figure eight, with its tail in its mouth. This device is the same as that conceived of by Crowley, who remarks that it represents the harmonious interplay of the elements in constant movement. These rather general interpretations of the principle of harmonious change may well, it should be said, within the context of an actual Tarot reading be rightfully interpreted as nothing more cosmic than a pleasant holiday. As in all practical Tarot work, the cards have to be interpreted according to their general context.

Three of Coins. This card is traditionally assigned the concept of *Material Works*, and Waite shows the picture of a sculptor at work in a monastery. The Knight design is of three disks forming a formal triangle, decorated with roses. Crowley shows three wheels at the base of a triangular-based pyramid.

Four of Coins. Traditionally designated *Earthly Power*, this card as seen by Waite is of a crowned king, hugging a golden disk possessively, with another under each of his feet, and one on his crown. The Gareth Knight picture is of four disks in a four-square pattern firmly interlocked with a central rose, whilst Crowley sees the four disks as the corner towers in a plan view of a square fortress.

Five of Coins. The traditional meaning of this card is *Material Trouble*, which Waite sees as a pair of beggars passing in the snow before a lighted window. The Knight arrangement is five disks in the form of a pentagram or five-pointed star, in the centre of which is a reversed pentagram, a sign of evil omen. Crowley has his five disks in a reversed pentagram formation, with a background that implies stability under intense strain. His title for the card is *Worry*.

Six of Coins. This card is by tradition designated *Material Success*, and Waite shows a merchant with a pair of scales weighing out money to the needy. The Knight layout is of six disks in a circle, forming a six-pointed star about a red rose on a golden, equal-armed cross that radiates light. This is on much the same symmetrical layout as the Crowley design.

Seven of Coins. This is called traditionally *Success Unfulfilled*, which for Waite is depicted by a young man leaning on a staff gazing somewhat disconsolately at a bush growing pentacles, presumably in insufficient quantity. The Knight picture is of seven disks trailing roses that are not, however, in full flower, and in such a way as to leave a gap at the bottom, suggestive of an upturned and empty bowl. Crowley, who calls the card *Failure*, shows leaden disks, suggestive of counterfeit money, against a background of blighted vegetation.

Eight of Coins. Regarded traditionally as the card of *Prudence*,

Waite sees this as a stonemason busily working, presumably depicting the prudence of one who has provided himself with a trade and skill. The Knight picture is simply of eight disks arranged neatly either side of an upright sprig of rosebuds. Crowley shows the disks as the flowers or fruit of a great tree, presumably planted by people of prudent foresight. He describes the ambience of the card as being 'intelligence lovingly applied to material matters, especially those of the agriculturalist, the artificer and the engineer', which accords with Waite's picture.

Nine of Coins. This card traditionally signifies *Material Gain*, and Waite shows this as a woman with a bird upon her wrist, standing before a prolific grapevine. The Knight image is of nine disks in close-knit formation, decorated with roses in full bloom. Crowley sees the arrangement of the nine disks as a central trio surrounded by the other six in a hexagonal formation, the idea being that multiplication of the original three has taken place by virtue of good luck and good management.

Ten of Coins. The traditional meaning of this card is *Wealth*; both the Crowley and Knight images are of the ten coins arranged in the formation of the Tree of Life, that is, three triangles culminating in a tenth circle at the bottom which represents the full, successful material expression of the spiritual, mental and emotional conceptions represented by the three triangles. Waite sees a man and woman standing contentedly beneath an archway that leads to a great house and domain. They are accompanied by a child, and a seated, grey-bearded patriarch with two dogs looks benignly upon them.

The Three-dimensional Structure of the Tarot Halls

That which follows is not directly related to the use of the Tarot cards in divination but may be of interest to more philosophically-minded students as an example of the way that the Tarot can structure itself, if left, in good faith, to its own devices.

The way that this course was written was largely after the fashion in which it has been taught. First the Fool was met, which led to the Magician, and thence to the four circular halls – of Strength, Justice, Temperance and the Worlds. Having established these four circular halls leading off from the central circular Hall of the Magician, the doors then opened to let in the respective Pages of Wands, Swords, Cups and Coins. Each of these led in turn through their respective foyer and labyrinth of passages to a great hall supervised by the Knight. From thence our attention was drawn to a balcony behind which was an upper room to which we ascended by a lift or spiral stairway. Here we found the King and Queen and the relevant Memory Theatre which consisted of a pyramidal wall of illuminated panels behind a concealing curtain.

It may not have been realized but when we were led by the Page through the groundfloor passages we were being taken to the far end of each hall, so that when we entered each one we were facing toward the central Hall of the Magician. When we ascended to the Memory Theatres we were in fact proceeding to a level above that of the circular halls of the Trumps. The four pyramidal walls behind the curtains were therefore part of a single hollow pyramid that formed a square dome over the Magician's table. Thus the four Aces are directly above the centre of that table of power, and the forces of the four suits descend to that table to be redistributed by the Magician as he deems fit.

When I realized this fact I found it helpful to build a cardboard construct of the building, complete with little figures from a mini-size Tarot pack. I am not suggesting that there is any need for you to go to this length unless the idea really catches your imagination. It can, however, be quite illuminating to bring symbolic conceptualizations to life at the material level. The interesting thing to me was the way this quite complex structure was formulated independently of any conscious thought or planning on my part. Does it in fact have an objective existence on what is sometimes called the astral plane? I leave this to your conjecture. It is notable that some students also find things there that I have not mentioned in the lesson material. Let me quote from one example: 'The Hall of the Magician was certainly a power house. It seemed to have unseen humming machinery and a powerful light source coming from above. I visited each card in turn and the Magician often came round with us. Sometimes the cards rose from the table and spiralled round our heads. There was not much conversation. Sometimes we were wrapped in the aura of each. Once the four came to the centre and we were all bathed in rainbow light from the roof.'

If you are interested in the deeper powers behind the Tarot images, and in the ways in which they may lead you, then I would suggest you look at my book *Tarot Magic* (Destiny Books, 1990), which recounts some of these experiences. We will also go on to describe other advanced paths of the Tarot in the latter part of this book.

Questions and Answers

Q. I'm a bit puzzled by the 6 of Pentacles. Six is supposed to represent balance and harmony, yet the Hanson-Roberts card shows an older man giving pentacles to children, and the Rider-Waite card depicts a well-off man giving coins to kneeling beggars. This wouldn't seem to be a balanced situation; it seems that the giver is in a position of superiority, and usually someone on a higher level doesn't give out of the purest motives but rather does so in order to feel superior or to make the other person beholden to him. I guess I'm just uneasy with the picture.

A. My own view of the 6 of Pentacles is that it represents exchange in the broadest sense, an exchange between polar opposites if you like, and what is important is to home in on this concept of inter-flow. In the card – never mind any negative feelings you might have about the concept of charity – the interchange is of money on the one hand and gratitude on the other. This latter concept is most important – the 'giving of thanks' – in almost all areas of human relationship. It means a lot more than common courtesy, and in its deeper levels it reflects upon the importance of prayers of thanksgiving – which outside of any ecclesiastical ambience mean being grateful for being alive, accepting the universe for what it is and what it can be, and loving all creatures great and small.

All of this is contained in the card, which should not be interpreted in any narrow fashion of charity or patronization – although if reversed or ill-aspected it could well refer to this in any reading. If you look upon the picture not as depicting a hand-out to beggars but, say, the paying of salaries for good work done, or an appreciative gift for services rendered, and the gift being duly appreciated, I think you will come to a closer awareness of the potential of this quite profound card. Like all the sixes it is a very good one to have turn up in a reading.

Q. I find the 6 of Pentacles particularly complex. The card tells me a different story every time I meet it, and has to me been the one card most influenced by others surrounding it and giving the most conflicting interpretations.

A. I agree with your notes on the complexity of the 6 of Coins. It seems to me that this card can mean a lot of things, and in some respects it has a lot to do with 'polarity' in the broadest sense, and with the inter-relationships between human beings, individually and collectively. It is this broadness and depth in many of the Tarot cards (in fact, probably all of them in the last analysis) that makes it such a valuable system, seemingly capable of infinite extension as one's understanding grows. It is starting people off on this road of expanding realizations that is my main motivation in producing this course.

Q. When I greet the Fool in my meditation period it is with a handshake which has become Masonic in its nature, that is, pressure is exerted with thumb and little finger. Any comments?

A. I regret I have no explanation for the Fool greeting you with a Masonic handshake. I trust he has not taken to having one trouser leg rolled up? However, there is a great deal of common ground between esoteric symbolism in the Western Tradition in its many aspects, and Masonic custom, symbolism and practice – even if most Freemasons these days seem to be astonishingly ignorant about the rich esoteric heritage that is contained within their rituals and regalia. I do not know how familiar you may be with such, but you might find it an interesting exercise to take a look through the Rider-Waite pack particularly to see how many bits of Masonic symbolism you can spot.

Q. Would you please tell me if it is better to think of the last suit as Coins, Pentacles or Disks? I have seen it referred to as all of these. Doesn't it matter which you use?

A. It makes very little difference. Use whichever seems most appropriate to you or which appeals to your imagination. My own choice is Coins, as I am pretty well convinced that this is how the Italian Renaissance originators of the Tarot saw them. Pentacles was really an introduction by 19th-century esoteric students who wanted to make the Tarot seem more 'magical'. It really does not need this kind of artificial aid, it is quite magical enough as it is.

When I gave a weekend workshop on the Tarot earlier this year I emphasized this point by having a sword, a wand and a cup to represent the other three suits, laid out on a table and for people to handle. For the fourth suit I had a metal plate piled high with £1 coins – about sixty or seventy pounds worth. The significance became immediately obvious. They had a certain power about them – the immediate symptom of which was whether one should take security precautions during the coffee and lunch breaks! So this suit represents material power, by and large, and I feel that Coins is really the most appropriate term and symbol. Coins, or money in any form, are crystallized energy. They represent people's work, people slave for them, steal them, fight for them, live by exchange of them, and so on.

Q. I am far more interested in the deeper powers behind the Tarot images, and find the Lesser Arcana irksome and difficult to remember. They seem to be unconnected and unnecessary to the work of the Spirit of the Tarot, almost like two separate systems.

A. I sympathize with your feelings about the Greater and Lesser Arcana being different systems, or at any rate working on different levels, with perhaps the Aces being intermediary junction points, as the powers of the Magician which can be unfolded on another level of manifestation. I think the Lesser Arcanum does have an important role in divination, however, because great as the Trumps themselves are, to have a spread consisting entirely of Trumps, if not entirely limiting, is rather like dining entirely off lobster thermidor – one needs a bit of bread and scrape to help digest it. So the suit cards serve I think very well as indicators of the general circumstances of life, with the Trumps being interspersed as the important operative elements. When it comes to systems of spiritual development I agree that the Trumps are in a class of their own. However, even here there is a basic structure or ground-plan that is well delineated by the fourfold nature of the suits – the cardinal points of the temple, as it were.

Q. I had slightly negative feelings towards Pentacles before studying them, due to their mundane, materialistic quality. I rather liked Rachel Pollack's extended vision of them as symbolizing 'magic' in ordinary creation, beauty in nature. How do you feel about this?

A. Glad to hear that you have come to be on better terms with the suit of Pentacles. It is indeed quite an important suit because where would we be without the good old earthy physical world? One of the main troubles that one finds with many esoteric students is that they want to run away from the earthy, which is the last thing we should do, because the very reason we are here in incarnation upon this Earth is to learn the lessons of working in and with its dense, physical substance. I did once rather shock a group of students by saying that no occultist had any excuse for being poor. Some took it to mean that one ought to be doing rituals to make money. The point however was that if the study of the spiritual side of life does not make us more able, rather than more ineffectual, there is something wrong somewhere.

Pentacles are also known as Coins, and money is said to be the root of all evil. I don't think so myself. It is just difficult to handle because it is raw power. It is crystallized energy, human energy, spiritual energy, in the most concrete form. Like most things it is generally only a problem if we haven't got it, or feel we haven't our fair share of it; although there can of course be problems for some in having too much. As in all things, it is treading the middle way that seems the secret of success and a happy life.

LESSON EIGHT

Divination Using the Suit Cards

We are now in a position to use the whole Tarot pack in our readings. It will be no bad idea, however, to consolidate our appreciation of the conditions represented by the suit cards.

Take each suit in turn from the pack and lay it out, then take each card of the suit in turn and practise seeing or feeling the related images that you have come to associate with it. This will at first be more easily done by taking one suit at a time. When this has been practised a few times, then take the whole pack and pick out cards at random. These are the 'five-finger exercises' of creating and maintaining a rapport with the whole conceptual range of the symbolic language we have created in order to communicate with the Spirit of the Tarot.

In an actual reading the significance of the cards may well be modified by their position and also their relation to the circumstances of the querent and the nature of the question being considered. We should also take into account the possible significance of cards being reversed. It is quite possible, given the use of the full pack of 78 cards, that using the principle of reversed cards is unnecessary. This is indeed a valid view and there are some readers who get quite adequate results without them. However, the process of divination is one of using a symbolic language, and the more subtleties and nuances a language has, then the better is it able to be used as a means of communication. With the method of gaining familiarity with the cards that we have used there should be no difficulty in coping with this larger range.

With Court Cards found in reverse, it can be taken that there is some difficulty in the relationship, whether the card represents a person or a group. There is a minor practical difficulty with some of the numbered cards in that some designs look the same whether they are reversed or not. However, depending on the pack you are using, certain subtle differences will be found on some of the cards, and these you should become familiar with. For instance, on the odd-numbered Sword cards the single sword will be blade uppermost when the card is the right way up. With other cards, however, there may be only minor differences in the floral design; and in others no difference whatever. You should decide which way up you feel is correct and mark the card accordingly. In a number of packs this has already been done for you, often with a small roman numeral lightly printed at the top or bottom of the card. This will not be the case however if you are using a pack that has been manufactured and sold principally for gaming rather than for cartomantic use, and you will have to perform this small task yourself.

Reversed cards imply a modification or muting of the energy or medium that the card represents. It can be a useful exercise to go through each card in the pack contemplating what its reversed significance might tend to be. In practical terms, however, this will depend very much on its position in the spread and the general tenor of the question in hand. For this there is no substitute for practice in actual divinatory reading.

Sample Readings Using the Full Pack

We have already demonstrated the use of the 10-card Celtic spread in Lesson 4. At that point, however, we were using Trump cards only, and without reversed images. We will therefore now run through a Celtic spread using the full pack and also the possibility of reversals. It may also prove useful to demonstrate the possibility of getting things wrong, particularly if one is reading the cards for oneself in a somewhat stressful condition or circumstances.* What follows then is a spread laid by a lady who had just put in for early retirement and was perhaps feeling (consciously or unconsciously) uneasy about the fact. This led her to read some of the cards in an overly negative

---

*Note: In this reading and the one that follows we are particularly indebted to the two students who have given permission for their work to be published, which we are doing anonymously because of the critical nature of some of our comments. Let it be said that both students completed their studies successfully and are, in our estimation, highly competent readers. The point is that if you do not have a personal teacher or candid and competent friend to do so, looking at your own work with a constructively critical eye is the most effective way to improve your reading skills. This is what we have tried to convey in this section of the work. Naturally some interpretations are open to discussion or disagreement and it would be a foolish commentator who felt his or her own views to be the only valid ones. Let the reader exercise personal judgement in assessing the pros and cons of all the comments and interpretations in this lesson and indeed the following one. This will form the basis for the correct attitude of sincerity and faith in one's contacts when actually doing a reading combined with cool, unbiased intellectual analysis at a later stage.

fashion. The spread is as follows, with the lady's comments, and my own (in *italics*), as to each card.

(1) **Queen of Swords**. The subject-matter or the instigator of the question. Probably me, Quick, decisive, wanting to get on with something new. A feeling of separation. (*Agreed.*)

(2) **Ace of Swords**. Covered by a sense of freedom, cutting loose, growth. (*Agreed.*)

(3) **The World**. A successful completion. The goal is expected to be happy and fulfilled. (*Agreed. This card seems particularly apt in summing up the end of a career.*)

(4) **10 of Swords**. The root of the matter. Ruin. Sorrow and defeat of hopes. Could be sorrow on behalf of a loved one. (*Why? This seems to be some other previously unstated concern breaking in. And this fourth position relates to the past, not to the future. It seems to me a direct confirmation of the reasons for wanting to retire. Things have just become too much of a hassle at work.*)

(5) **Temperance**. The immediate past was well balanced. I began to feel I should have left things alone. (*I can't see the reason for this anxiety. You have just been in the process of considering the pros and cons of changing the pattern of your life, which is aptly represented by this card.*)

(6) **7 of Wands**. Courage will be needed to deal with future trends. Obstacles overcome. (*Sure! Retirement, and a new lifestyle is bound to be a challenge.*)

(7) **5 of Wands**. My position during the time asked about will be one of strife and conflict. Things seem to be going from bad to worse. I have obviously made an erroneous decision. (*This ominous view is not justified at all, and comes partly from taking 'potted meanings' or 'key-words' for the cards too much at face value. This simply confirms what was indicated by the 7 of Wands in Position 6. The 5 of Wands usually means some kind of challenge or testing phase. Waite refers to the young men on his card as taking part in a 'mock' battle. It thus frequently means some kind of initiation to new circumstances and the adjustments called upon to meet them. It can indeed be a joyful and fruitful experience, and certainly by no means implies that you are bound on a course of disaster.*)

(8) **The Devil**. Environment factors hold more obstacles and material difficulties. Could lead to despondency and disillusionment. (*I do not see it in quite such negative terms. Having got rid of past problems with an ideal goal [The World] in mind, what is the future situation going to be? The 7 and the 5 of Wands showed that giving up a lifetime's work is in itself something of a challenge.*)

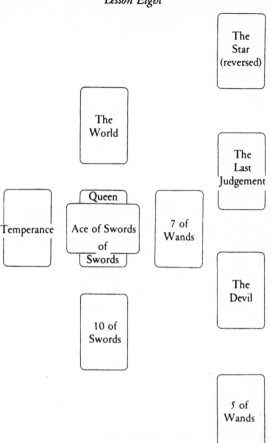

When it comes upon you you will probably find yourself looking back
on the old working days as something that took you out of yourself and
the home and was, in its way, a more balanced existence, at least in
principle. With this gone you are likely to find it something of a
challenge to find a new meaning and direction to the rest of your life.
It is then that I think you are likely to find the environment 'the very
devil', but you have to remember that the Devil signifies illusion, and
very much your own illusion. You can transform it.)

(9) **The Last Judgement.** My inner emotions hope for a new cycle.
   Renewed interest and new life. The rest of the spread indicates
   this may be premature and could be an unhappy awakening.
   (*This card in this position suggests that you are looking for a great
   transformation, and everything in the garden from henceforth to be
   paradisal and lovely, but the other cards indicate a need for a more
   realistic approach.*)

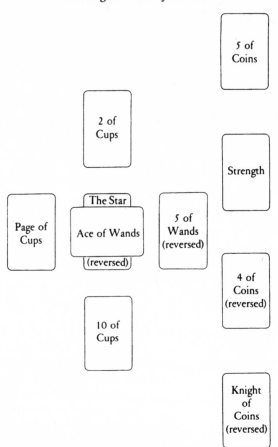

(10) **The Star** (*Reversed*). At last a good card and hope for the ultimate
outcome, but unfortunately it is reversed! So probably hopes
will be dashed. A feeling of living in 'cloud-cuckoo land'. I was
now feeling completely chastened and felt I had done quite the
wrong thing. (*I really do not think you need think so. The reversed
Star is simply confirming what is indicated by the previous card. That
is, that you should not expect too much. That however stressful the
situation you have emerged from you are likely to find a certain
amount of difficulty in adapting to being without it.*)

The Querent then went on to do another spread based upon the
reversed Star, but got into something of a downward spiral of
depression and began reading all kinds of ominous portents into the
cards (none of which has since transpired).

(1) **The Star** (*Reversed*). Placed here as Significator, with the question being why would my hopes be unfulfilled? (*This of course is making the assumption that your hopes will in fact be unfulfilled. You are putting the Tarot into rather a difficult position it seems to me, in asking it to justify an answer that it never really gave!*)

(2) **Ace of Wands**. New beginnings, energy. Could be a birth. As both our daughters are pregnant I felt this had some significance. The babies would be born in the middle of the period asked about. (*I would see the signification as having a more general application. The challenge is going to be new beginnings when you retire. Of course if you are an expectant grandmother this will have an important bearing on your future, whether or not you retire.*)

(3) **2 of Cups**. The goal seems to be the renewal of friendships, or new friendships, cooperation and love. Each 'goal' card is a good one, as I supposed it would be if it represents a hoped-for outcome. (*In the light of the question you have asked the Tarot I would think it is saying that this is the kind of goal you need to have in mind if your hopes are to be fulfilled. New friends and wider circle of acquaintances.*)

(4) **10 of Cups**. The root of the matter is the success of pretty well everything in my life so far, and the supposition that it would continue. But the rest of the cards seem to be saying 'Ever been had?' (*Again, referring to the exact question in hand, it seems to me that with this card in this position the Tarot is bending over backwards trying to reassure you that all is not as dismal as you have surmised.*)

(5) **Page of Cups**. The immediate past seems to be the children I am leaving by giving up my job. Another mistake? Could represent the trustworthy worker I felt I had been. (*Indeed it seems very likely that as a teacher of obvious dedication you are going to miss the kids that have always surrounded you.*)

(6) **5 of Wands** (*Reversed*). More strife in the near future! Indecision. Trickery. (*The Tarot is only saying what it said before. Retirement is going to be a bit of a challenge. Don't take your problems the wrong way, Again you are getting hyped-up in a rather negative fashion by putting too much ominous weight onto this really quite innocuous card, which simply means a challenge, which all our daily lives are full of in one way or another.*)

(7) **Knight of Coins** (*Reversed*). The Querent's position. Could it be one of stagnation and idleness? Lack of material progress. Inertia. (*Yes, I agree that this probably does refer to you; Knight because you are a very active person, and Coins I would think because with retirement you are certainly going to have rather less money coming in*

than you are used to. Hence the reversal. The Tarot is indicating that
you should think of this in the light of your question about being
disappointed in hopes. And of course you may well have an inactivity
problem at first. It stands to reason that everyone in this situation does.)

(8)　**4 of Coins** (*Reversed*). The environment suggests setbacks in
material gain. Obvious if I have given up work but I had intended
to do some supply work or some other type of work completely.
Perhaps a fairly successful change of occupation. Not propitious
again. (*I think you are reading too much negative significance into
this. It is simply reiterating what was implied in the previous card, and
it is indeed obvious. We should not expect startling revelations, or great
promises on the one hand, or doom and gloom on the other, from every
card. The Tarot is simply replying to your question as to future
circumstances in a perfectly rational way, as any other adviser would.*)

(9)　**Strength**. I feel I have enough strength to deal with what comes.
Good job by the look of it. (*I'm sure you have. The Tarot is again
being very supportive and encouraging, in the face of your apparent
determination to see the worst side of every possible portent. It is also
implying that you are likely to find greater fulfilment through pursuit
of higher or less material things in life.*)

(10)　**5 of Coins**. Just about the last straw! The outcome will be
material trouble. (*You should remember at this point the negative
tone of the question you asked. 'Why won't my hopes be fulfilled?' The
answer can hardly be 'Because everything in the garden is lovely!' The
three Coins cards in the Staff are suggesting that you may find things
a bit more restrictive than your optimistic dreams thought because there
will not be quite so much money around, but the presence and position
of Strength suggests that you will be able to ride well over this.*)

The Querent now felt overwhelmed, however, and began to see all
sorts of horrors. The Ace of Wands signifying birth underlain with
the 10 of Swords seemed to portend tragedy – mental or physical
handicap, stillbirth or worse. She took the 5 of Coins as the
Significator for a further spread to ask how long this seeming round
of despair, needing so much strength and courage to get through,
would last.

(1)　**5 of Coins**. The Significator, the question being more detail
about this material trouble and how long it would last. (*Again we
are putting a very loaded question to the Tarot based upon a
misinterpretation of what it has already replied. And putting a time
factor in, in this fashion, is really unanswerable in the mode of
divination that we are using. How can it possibly reply adequately?*)

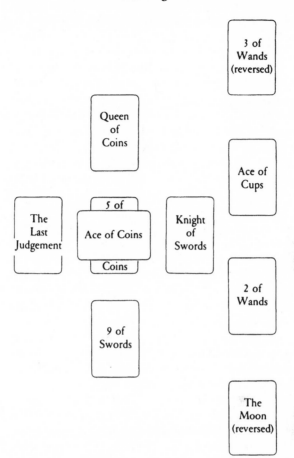

(2) **Ace of Coins.** What covers it is good, and indicates material and spiritual prosperity. (*This interpretation is really slightly irrelevant and suggests the Querent is here whistling in the dark, desperately trying to look on the brighter side. In our view, coming at the position of opposition, the Ace of Coins is simply repeating what it said in the Staff of the last spread. Less money about, that's all.*)

(3) **Queen of Coins.** The ultimate goal is again a good card showing a generous and charitable person who can afford to be so. A worthy goal for someone without a job! (*This would seem to indicate the Querent and also the matter of finance, but does not imply anything really drastic. It is simply reiterating what has gone before. Note we have had three more Coins cards already in this spread; the intended meaning could hardly be more obvious.*)

(4) **9 of Swords.** The root of the matter. A card difficult to tie in with the above. Maybe the goal will be so difficult, if not, impossible to obtain, despair will take over. One meaning could be miscarriage, or worry. (*Rather than being difficult to tie in it is a card dead in line with the nature of the question and the assumptions being made about what the Tarot has already said. One has to remember that this fourth position indicates a past state, or present root assumption. The Querent is here projecting some kind of disaster into the future out of her own worries.*)

(5) **The Last Judgement.** The recent past. A change, a new cycle of experience. Again an obvious card in the circumstances. (*Yes, and here once again pointing to an unexpected degree of change in the circumstances. In that this is in the position of the immediate past it would seem to be representing your recent action of resignation.*)

(6) **Knight of Swords.** Another card indicating courage and activity. Could be impetuous. (*Yes, I think it sums you up quite well, and is showing need for other activities.*)

(7) **The Moon** (*Reversed*). The Querent's position. Another change? Perhaps being reversed mitigates it somewhat? Could be deception or something to do with health, both physical and mental. (*I think, before we get too involved with speculations about physical or mental breakdown or other deteriorating changes, that we consider the rather more obvious hint from the Tarot that the Querent is perhaps just getting things a bit wrong?*)

(8) **2 of Wands.** The environment suggests dominion. A dominant person. Could be the Querent is beginning to take charge of things? (*Maybe the Querent will need to, but I would suggest that what is being indicated here is that the environment and general circumstances of life in retirement will play a dominant role, and challenges will have to be met.*)

(9) **Ace of Cups.** Inner emotions are of love, joy, happiness. A favourable outlook. Abundance. Another turn for the better. (*Well, in terms of the question asked, you are certainly being advised to cheer up and look on the bright side!*)

(10) **3 of Wands** (*Reversed*). The completion should be established strength but as the card is reversed this is mitigated somewhat. Diminishing adversity is perhaps the only optimistic slant one can hope for. (*Once again I do not think this interpretation quite hits the mark. Partly because the Querent is thinking in terms of stereotyped key-words, and partly because she is getting into a state of anxiety. The nature of her problems, which is the question asked of this spread, is simply that her established position, assumptions and income will, after retirement, be not quite so established as once they were.*)

The Querent confessed to finding all these spreads rather shattering. However, on the contrary, all that was being revealed by the spread was simply sound common-sense to someone in the Querent's position. If much of it seemed to be obvious that is simply because life, for the most part, is like that. We cannot expect the Tarot to predict major adventures where none exist, although in this case it was more in the nature of imagined disasters, and above all demonstrates the difficulty of reading the cards for onself, particularly in a situation where one is heavily emotionally involved, consciously or unconsciously. It should be said that none of the disasters came to pass.

In our next example we may see how reading for oneself in a somewhat fraught situation can have the opposite effect, and lead to an over-optimistic interpretation of the cards.

This spread concerns a gentleman who had set up in business on his own but who found to his dismay that as a result of an oversight on either his part or his accountants, he was liable for a crippling demand from the tax authorities. This threatened the very existence of his venture, and he turned to the Tarot for guidance.

(1) **King of Cups**. Deliberately chosen as Significator to represent the Querent, because 'it represents the happiness and contentment that I want.' (*In light of the nature of the enquiry the King or Knight of Wands or Coins might have been more appropriate, concerned as they are with business organizations and finance. Choice of the King of Cups does suggest a certain inaccuracy of motive for a businessman.*)

(2) **Wheel of Fortune**. Like it or not, changes are in the offing and it is no longer possible to maintain the status quo. (*Agreed. And this being in an opposing position in the spread, these changes may be enforced and not too well-liked.*)

(3) **5 of Cups**. Whilst I have the basis of a happy and secure lifestyle I can anticipate being under a strain until the problem is resolved. (*Yes, we have the seeming anomaly of a rather disappointing card in the position of 'goal', however, the question in hand relates to how best to deal with a disappointing set of events.*)

(4) **The Emperor**. The root of the matter is that I am solely responsible for, and in charge of, this situation, and it is up to me to sort it out; to assert myself to get things done to my advantage and to use my authority and inner resources to the best advantage. (*Agreed.*)

(5) **6 of Swords** (*Reversed*). Originally the tax bill was much larger.

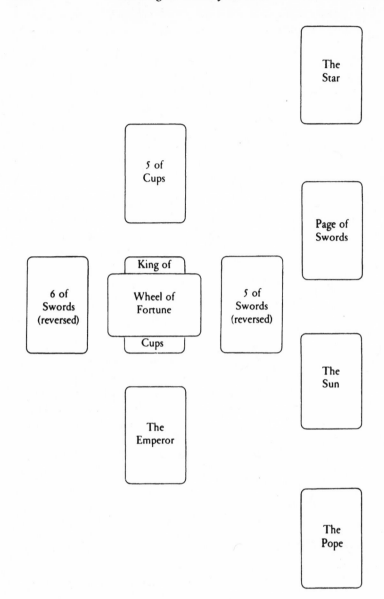

The Star

5 of
Cups

Page of
Swords

King of

6 of
Swords
(reversed)

Wheel of
Fortune

5 of
Swords
(reversed)

Cups

The
Sun

The
Emperor

The
Pope

This was contested and a lesser amount agreed. This to me is a compromise as I did not consider anything was due at all. (*This does seem to refer to the tax demand: a card that usually refers to work or earned success being reversed so that what was earned has been largely taken away!*)

(6) **5 of Swords** (Reversed). I will be able to meet the demand of the authorities, although it will be a struggle. (*There seems to be an unsupported element of optimism inserted here, perhaps understandable enough. No one is likely to relish having the card representing defeat in the immediate future. It depends perhaps on whether one regards the reversal of a 'bad' card to be a mitigation of its unfortunate aspect, or whether reversal means that things will be even worse. One needs perhaps the guidance of other cards in the spread to indicate which way the cookie will crumble. And in light of subsequent events it should be said that the Querent did struggle through, so his interpretation seems borne out by the acid test of what in the end actually happened!*)

(7) **The Pope**. This represents myself and the need for me to have confidence and faith in my own inner resources. The need to feel sure I have made the right decision and will succeed. (*A Trump in this position suggests that this is an important part of the message the Tarot is trying to get across – that much depends on the Querent. There is a certain aloofness or impracticability that might be inferred from the Pope image, but as it is not reversed we may assume that this is not the main tenor of the message. Is there something to be learned from transition of the Querent from Emperor in the past to Pope in the present? And is this a good transition, or a bad one in the circumstances? Does it mean a falling away of outer dynamism and control? Or an increase in inner wisdom and discretion? Again other cards in the spread should help to elucidate this; with the help, if one were reading the cards for another, of discussion and exchange of ideas on the matter.*)

(8) **The Sun**. The very few people I have spoken to on this matter have given me confidence by their understanding. This has revitalized me to greater efforts. (*It certainly helps to have a supportive environment in adversity, as this card suggests in this position. Again, being a Trump, this could have quite a strong bearing on the situation. Outer support being given, even if only moral or psychological.*)

(9) **Page of Swords**. It is my wish that I will soon hear of an end to this problem. That I will soon be able to resume my modest lifestyle without the authorities breathing down my neck. As the Page seems to be sheathing his sword on the card, perhaps I will hear news to this effect. (*Yes, but remember this card represents only*

hopes and fears, not what will necessarily happen. One is obviously expecting some kind of official or legal communication, that may or may not let you off the hook.)

(10) **The Star**. The outcome of this problem will be to my satisfaction and I will be able to relax and pursue a lifestyle free of a heavy financial burden. (*Certainly the Star signifies hope, but for the successful resolution of the situation in quite such fulsome terms as is suggested in the interpretation, I would have preferred to see a more concrete card, concerning success or material works. My own general interpretation would be that much depends on the Querent, in terms of inner resolve and moral resources, to pull through. However, there are promising signs of support from the Querent's immediate circle, as indicated by the Sun in position 8.*)

As so often happens we see the Tarot more or less restating the problem, a point that no doubt led the Querent to lay a further spread, with the Star as Significator. Although as we found in the previous set of readings, there is, at least to my mind, a considerable amount of 'question-begging' or unwarranted assumptions shown in the way the follow-up enquiry is framed.

(1) **The Star**. The hopes and wishes that I have will be realized. How will this come about? (*This seems to me to put the Tarot in a difficult position, for it never did say that the hopes and wishes would be realized! How then can the uncertain, or even unlikely, come about? And how can such a misunderstanding be sorted out in a message limited to being framed in a mere ten pictographic images? We often ask a great deal of the intelligence behind the Tarot.*)

(2) **3 of Swords**. My differences with the tax authorities have been settled and I have to go along with the decision. (*In other words, saying pretty plainly that all hopes and wishes are* not *going to be realized, and that a considerable amount of heartburning is going to come the way of the hopeful Star.*)

(3) **Page of Wands**. I can soon expect to hear of changes that I can make to my business to improve its viability. (*Well, the goals do seem to concern messages or advice about business organization. So agreed.*)

(4) **The Last Judgement**. The root of the matter is that not only do I have to make changes but that now is the right time to do so. (*The root of the matter has been the rude awakening, which has already occurred in the past, and which is what we asked about in the beginning. But certainly radical changes might be called for now, although the card in this position usually refers to the past.*)

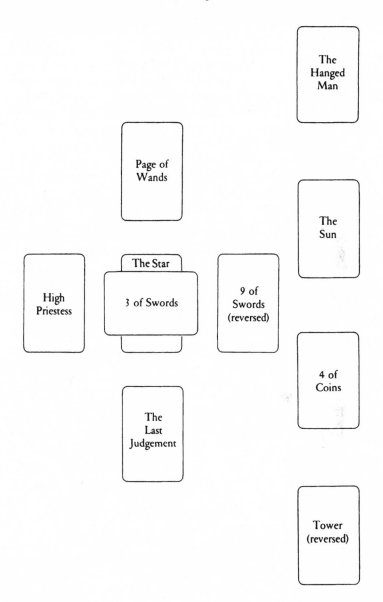

The Hanged Man

Page of Wands

The Sun

The Star

High Priestess

3 of Swords

9 of Swords (reversed)

4 of Coins

The Last Judgement

Tower (reversed)

(5) **High Priestess**. Advice I have received recently from a highly intuitive person of great spiritual insight and awareness. (*Possibly so. As we do not know of this person or the nature of the advice this is not something upon which we can usefully comment. Again, in the event of doing a reading for somebody else, this would serve as a basis for discussion and further elucidation of the factors involved.*)

(6) **9 of Swords** (*Reversed*). My responsibilities will soon come to an end. (*Once again in the immediate future a pretty dreadful card in reversed position. The Querent's statement is somewhat ambivalent as to whether he sees this as a good or a bad thing. End of responsibilities could be interpreted as bankruptcy or selling up – which hardly accords with the opening statement vis à vis the Star.*)

(7) **Lightning Struck Tower** (*Reversed*). I usually have to be forced by circumstances into making major changes and this is no exception. A time of forced change. (*Probably right, and the admission is perhaps worth bearing in mind in relation to the Pope, who occupied this position in the first spread – a figure very much representing retention of the status quo.*)

(8) **4 of Coins**. External factors or influences will ensure that I will get my business on a sound financial footing. (*The card indicating material work is certainly relevant to the problem, in this environmental position, although it does not necessarily imply the optimistic conclusion. However, as indicated before with the Sun, help seems to be available in one way or another.*)

(9) **The Sun**. Having done this, energies will be released which will enable me to act with the confidence necessary to use my initiative to the best advantage. (*Certainly there seems no shortage of optimism, in this position of Querent's hopes and fears.*)

(10) **The Hanged Man**. The outcome will be that I will have to proceed with caution and, if necessary, make sacrifices to maintain my new-found sense of security. (*We would agree with the general inference made, although once again it is being assumed, without very much justification, that all will turn out for the best. Very much the kind of attitude one might expect from the King of Cups character, the original Significator. However, although the Querent seems to be reading rather too much assurance of a happy ending into the reading, the Tarot seems to be pressing home the general message that a change of attitude, and seeking outside help and support from friends, is the best chance of pulling the chestnuts from the fire.*)

The Querent now undertook a third reading, having got the message that external help was likely to be important. The eighth card of the last spread, the 4 of Coins, was used as a new Significator, since he had taken it to mean assurance of a sound financial footing.

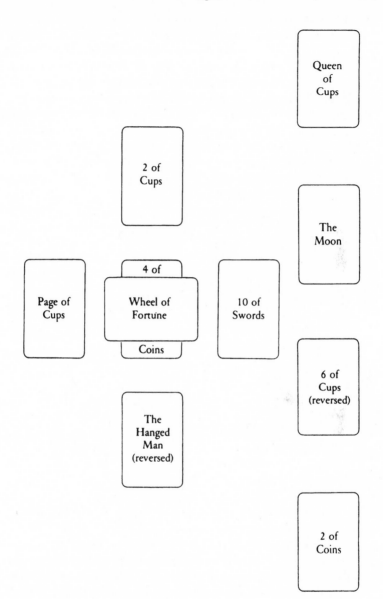

(1) **4 of Coins**. How may I expect and how attain this financial stability? (*Again, a somewhat unsupported assumption. Nothing quite so concrete and assured seems to have been promised.*)

(2) **Wheel of Fortune**. Indicates that changes are taking place now which will affect the situation. (*A repetition of what was indicated in the first spread. A statement of the obvious perhaps rather than any startling new revelation.*)

(3) **2 of Cups**. The goal I am seeking is to be found in the realm of new ideas, diversifying my activities. Perhaps a partnership. (*New ideas and diversification are not normally the significance of this card. However, we have to make allowance for what may be genuine intuitive insights on the part of the Querent as he applies his faculties to the problem through the cards. My own view would have been that this card signifies the kind of external aid already mentioned, not necessarily financial but morally supportive.*)

(4) **The Hanged Man** (*Reversed*). The root of the matter is poor judgement, carelessness and lack of caution in the past. (*Words of wisdom, dearly purchased!*)

(5) **Page of Cups**. I have already had notification of these changes and benefits to be derived from them, from a medium friend. (*An interesting parallel to the High Priestess in the last spread. Again we cannot sensibly comment as we do not know the facts, but it is interesting how the Tarot will often repeat [or hammer home!] points that have already been made.*)

(6) **10 of Swords**. The prospects are that I will satisfactorily end my dealings with the authorities. (*I regret that I cannot see how so optimistic an interpretation of such a negative card can be justified, particularly in light of the previous cards that have fallen in this position. Whatever the eventual outcome, it would seem that the immediate prospect is a pretty thumping bill from the Inland Revenue.*)

(7) **2 of Coins**. My present position, of trying to make £1 do the work of two. Constantly juggling to make ends meet. (*The Mr Micawber-ish observation may be accurate, although my usual interpretation of this card is Change, often harmonious. Change has been showing up quite a lot throughout these spreads and one hopes that it will be met with harmoniously by the Querent in the form of successfully learning lessons in the school of experience.*)

(8) **6 of Cups** (*Reversed*). Shows that external social factors are, if anything, adding to my tension and not helping my peace of mind at all. (*Odd that we should have this slightly negative showing in a position that has indicated a very supportive environment before. The 6 of Cups does of course represent happiness but generally in a kind*

of childlike, irresponsible fashion. Its being reversed here may well emphasize this dependence element. In the context of the question asked, it would tend to suggest that there is a bit too much of the happy-go-lucky attitude, as originally suggested in the choice of King of Cups as personal Significator.)

(9) **The Moon.** My inner emotions are very strong and only add to my determination to find a satisfactory way out of my predicament. *(Full marks for general attitude but this is not what my interpretation of the Moon in this position would be. To me it suggests a certain amount of negativity and even self-deception. However, at least it is not reversed. But I feel it confirms a certain lack of decisiveness and outward drive. The Querent comes across as a fundamentally nice person, but one who in his situation needs more of the aggressive attitude of a busy supermarket manager if his small business is to succeed.)*

(10) **Queen of Cups.** The solution of the matter lies in a partner. This will be a person whose outlook is complementary to my own – the Significator of the first spread having been the King of Cups. *(One interpretation of the card if one is looking for a rosy future. However, although a complementary partner might be an advantage, it seems to me that the Queen of Cups here is simply the original King of Cups in more passive mode. This means that the resolution of the situation depends much on the character and attitude of the Querent.)*

So ended the reading, and it was not one that rendered any great revelations or startling future prognostications. But this, it will be found, the Tarot or any valid divinatory system seldom does. What is provided is an outline of the general situation, inner and outer, for inner consideration and outward discussion. For this reason reading for another, or having another read the cards for one, has its advantages over reading for oneself. Not that working with the cards on one's own is ever without instruction and good use, provided one cultivates the right attitude of mind and approach.

The subsequent circumstances of the Querent of the above spread are that he is battling on, has not gone under, but as he more or less predicted himself, he has met the demands made upon him and is continuing on his way, though not without a struggle. The purpose of his undertaking the spread, in the first instance, had something in the nature of seeking reassurance rather than an unqualified desire to predict the future, warts and all. Not many of us, in fact, really want to know that. The alleged ability to predict the future can indeed be a dangerous assumption, particularly when reading the cards for another. Take the case of a married woman who has for some years been beset by the problem of infertility, and is now seeking some kind of assurance through a Tarot consultation. Here is a sample spread, and in this instance using Trump cards only, unreversed.

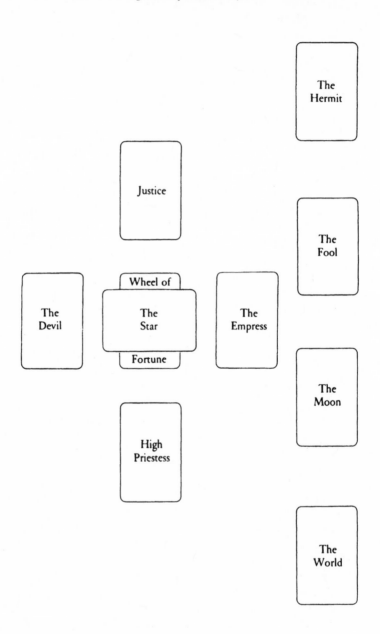

(1) **Wheel of Fortune**. Represents her present position, seeking a change of fortune.

(2) **The Star**. The Star crosses her, and this indicates the hope that has become harder to hold onto with each passing year.

(3) **Justice**. In the crown position of the Celtic spread this suggests that she needs to face the situation squarely, accepting the possibility of childlessness, and judging whether even if she were to be childless whether this would be the worst thing that could befall her; that she should count what blessings in life she has, as a counter-measure.

(4) **High Priestess**. Would seem to indicate that she has the hidden reserve to face the situation dispassionately; and these two virginal figures top and bottom of the spread indicate that she may well have to, that it is a particular burden she has to bear.

(5) **The Devil**. In the immediate past position this indicates that for some time her thoughts have become almost obsessive on this matter; that desires and attempts to start a family have dominated her life.

(6) **The Empress**. Placed as it is, in the immediate future, this would seem to be a hopeful sign; although with the other cards taken into account it would seem unwise to predict an immediate pregnancy. Rather it could alternatively mean a coming to terms with her situation and finding ways to a fulfilled life without children.

(7) **The World**. At the base of the Staff, this balanced card would seem to represent a coming to terms with things, whatever the eventual situation.

(8) **The Moon**. In the position of surrounding circumstances this would seem a clear indication of the recurrence of the monthly menstruation cycle, connected as it is with the Moon cycle.

(9) **The Fool**. As a representative of hopes and fears this suggests that present hopes may be far-fetched. These hopes and fears certainly relate to the birth of a child, for in certain packs the Fool is depicted as a baby.

(10) **The Hermit**. This card as final outcome is a lone figure on a mountaintop, which suggests that the whole struggle will not have been in vain, and that the Querent may have grown spiritually as a consequence. The Hermit in this position does suggest a negative outcome to a question concerning fertility. For a more positive response one might have expected to find here the fruitful Empress, or the World (with its womb-opening connotations that can be interpreted from the design), or other of the more hopeful cards such as the Star, or even the Chariot.

Had the reader used reversed cards the Tarot would have had scope to be rather more specific, but here again, before taking on even by implication the role of prophet of future happenings, the aspiring Tarot reader needs to be very sure about the kind of position in which he or she is volunteering to be placed. Counselling skills are indeed at least as important as any clairvoyant or intuitive ability, although ideally the two go together. A large element of common sense also is a requisite, preferably based upon life experience.

Working Plan

Exercise 1
Lay out the two spreads (Figures 13 and 16) that have been critically annotated in this lesson. It is quite important to do this physically in order to impress the images and their positions upon your mind. Follow through all the comments made and note whether you agree with them or not.

Exercise 2
Lay out the third spread described (Figure 19). Imagine you have been approached by this Querent and write out your reading for her a) in the form of a postal reading; b) in the form of a face-to-face reading, with a note of supplementary questions you might ask her; and c) private notes that you would make, not necessarily to be revealed to or discussed with the Querent.

Exercise 3
Get in as much practice as you can performing readings for yourself or for others using the whole pack.

Knowledge Notes

The Celtic Spread

As we have remarked, there are almost as many ways of laying out the cross of the Celtic spread as there are books on the subject. We have indicated our preferred method, but it is up to each student to adopt whichever method most appeals in the light of experience and personal preference.

We are indebted to Miss Dawn Wilson-Singer, however, for what may be an early version of the system, dating from before even A.E.

Waite published this method. This is a fifteen-card system that was used by her grandmother, to whom it was given by an old lady who used to do her cards in France. Hence the original formula was in French, and as follows:

(1) *à toi* (to you). Things personal to you, happening in the 'now'.
(2) *à la tête* (at your head). Your thoughts, dreams, hopes, reflections.
(3) *à la pied* (at your feet). Things you least care about; you know they are there, but they are not a problem. Things past or already dealt with, or things you can afford to ignore.
(4) *à coté* (by your side). Your support, or opposition, depending on the cards.
(5) *ta surprise* (your surprise). Things you least expect to happen.

The method is as follows:

1. The cards are shuffled by the Querent, cut, and handed back to the Reader.
2. The Reader spreads the cards out and tells the Querent to concentrate on the question (if there is one), or just to keep his or her mind blank and focused on the cards, then to pick cards out and put them face down one at a time where the Reader points, in the order shown in Figure 20.
3. There should be three cards on each of the five points.
4. The cards are then turned over and read in order. Extra cards may be added if the Querent wishes to know more about a particular aspect.
5. If reading the cards for yourself then lay them out from the Querent's position.

It is possible that something after the nature of this spread, with a four-card 'staff' added to indicate personal factors, was the beginnings of the Waite 'Celtic' spread. Adding this to the above, with three cards at each position, could give an interesting 27-card spread, based on a practical old tradition. You may care to experiment along these lines.

The Attitude of the Querent

When you have gained some confidence in reading the cards for yourself you will probably wish to read them for other people. This means that you will have to take into account, to some degree, the attitude of mind of the Querent. Is he or she coming to you with a

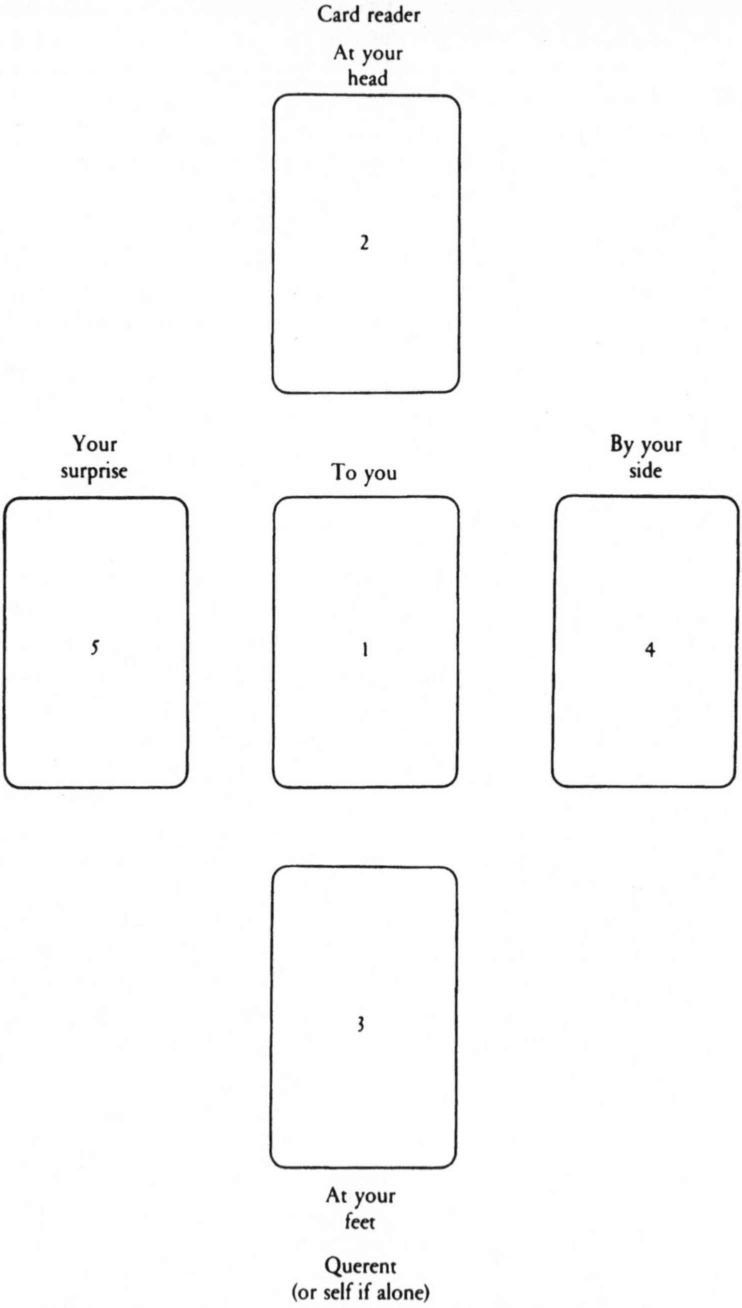

Card reader

At your
head

2

Your
surprise

To you

By your
side

5

1

4

3

At your
feet

Querent
(or self if alone)

genuine enquiry, seeking advice in good faith on some concern that he or she may have? You should not be too willing to do a reading for anyone who is simply doing it for idle curiosity. Nor should you let yourself be put into the position of being 'tested' by a sceptical enquirer. However good you may be, the attitude of mind of the Querent is an intrinsic part of any reading. It is all part of a three-way flow, between yourselves and the Spirit of the Tarot.

Should the Querent come to a reading with a frivolous attitude then more than likely he or she will receive a frivolous answer, whilst those who seek to prove it all wrong may well find that the Tarot lives up to their expectations. None of this will be very helpful to you, to the Tarot, or to them. However, if anyone comes with an open mind, even if not necessarily a believer in it, the Tarot can work very well indeed, often to the Querent's considerable amazement.

On the other hand you should beware of anyone who is too superstitiously dependent upon whatever you might say. It is a very grave matter for anyone to become so passive to outside advice, particularly of a psychic nature, that he or she is unable to take any independent decisions. The Tarot, being a wise oracular device, is not likely to be too helpful and may even give misleading advice in order to bring this type of Querent up short and jerk him or her into being more self-reliant. This again is not likely to be an easy situation for you to handle, and you would do well therefore to be a little selective in your choice of clients. Do not be afraid to talk matters through with the Querent before the reading, or as an immediate preliminary to shuffling the cards. You are engaged in a team effort to throw some light on to some problem area in the Querent's life. You are not on trial, nor is the Tarot, and the more the Querent gets involved in the three-way process the better are you likely to be of help.

An important point at this stage lies in getting the Querent to define a specific question. This is another reason why prior discussion can be helpful. Have a pad and pen handy so that the agreed question can be written down – this will serve to concentrate the mind no end. Ideally the question should need no more than about a dozen words. If you do not go to the extent of writing it down, at least make sure that it is plainly and clearly verbalized. Get the Querent to state it just before you start the reading, perhaps as you hand the cards across to be shuffled.

You will find that a number of Querents will not have sorted out in their minds exactly what their problem is. Either they are so confused that they do not know what to ask, or more often they have two, three or even more questions and possible solutions all jumbled up together in their heads. It is your first job to help them sort this out into a clear basic question. As with computers, so with Tarot: 'garbage in – garbage out'. If neither of you is sure what the question is, it is unlikely that you are going to get very clear guidance from the Tarot, for although the Tarot is capable of heroic efforts in circumventing the incompetence of Querent or Reader, there comes a limit to the efforts of even the most dedicated caster of pearls before swine.

Most multiple questions will boil down to one central issue. If not, another session can always be fixed, either after an interval or as a direct run-on, but in any case the ground will have been cleared of too much woolly thinking.

Another problem can be the loaded question, when the Querent is just not coming clean with you. A simple enough sounding enquiry put in terms of 'moving house' might really be concerned with walking out on home and family. Here again, some preliminary discussion should help to define what the question really is. Although the Tarot is very adept at detecting the real root of any problem, the trick will be whether you are sufficiently adept at picking up what the Tarot is trying to convey. This may involve circumstances at variance with what the Querent has led you to believe. It is possible of course that the Querent is genuinely mistaken about certain circumstances described to you; remember that in the Querent's account you are only hearing one side of the story. People are very good at kidding themselves, which is one reason why the Tarot can be a useful tool when properly used. Such proper use depends of course on the skill of the Reader, and that is up to you, and will only come with practice.

Yet even practice can bear little fruit if you do not approach it in the right way. Therefore, to get the most out of your Tarot reading experience, endeavour to take and keep notes, and go back to them at a later date to see if you still interpret things the same way, or if circumstances, if they are known to you, have been borne out by your reading or not. This is particularly applicable in the case of readings you have done for yourself, and can be especially useful in aiding self-knowledge as it becomes apparent how you kidded yourself into reading what you wanted to read in some situation in the past. On the other hand you may well see how, in light of events, the Tarot was trying to say something that was a bit too subtle for you to comprehend or read in the right way at the time. When reading for others, note-taking can be somewhat off-putting for the Querent, as can the running of a tape-recorder – and secret taping is ethically dubious, for however altruistic a motive. It is best to retain the cards in order after the spread, so that you can lay it out again easily and make notes from it after the Querent has departed. Again, avoid kidding yourself or the Querent that you can prophecy the future with amazing accuracy. If this were so, then Tarot consultants would make a good living off the stock exchange or turf accountants, without going through the hassle of doing personal divinations.

Cultivate a feeling of responsibility for any advice for action that you may give. A shrinking violet may well feel disenchanted with current opportunities, but take care before encouraging a paperclip stores clerk to throw up his job and set up selling double-glazing on commission only. If the cards seem to indicate that the Querent needs to come out in life a bit more, it is up to you to see that this is done in a sensible and circumspect manner – one little step at a time. Try to ascertain whether Querents are seeking information or simple encouragement, or someone to tell them something they know very well already (usually a moral problem their conscience is nagging them about). Any of these are legitimate aims for the Querent, apart perhaps for seeking justification for wrong-doing. In this regard, involving yourself in domestic problems, particularly those threatening marital breakdown, is an area where even angels would show some reluctance to tread. Ask yourself very clearly if you are genuinely in that category before doing likewise. Apart from any moral quagmire your advice may get you into, you don't want an irate spouse breaking your windows.

All of this probably suggests to you that those who set up as professional Tarot consultants probably deserve more money than they get. It is quite a responsible and demanding job – if done properly.

Statistical Probabilities

It is always worth taking a look at the number of cards of each type that happen to turn up in a spread. A comparative shortage of Wands would, for instance, suggest a lack of initiative or organizing ability; a shortage of Cups indicates a starved emotional life, of Court cards a lonely, unsocial ambience. A greater-than-average number of Swords or reversed cards would indicate a generally difficult patch. More than the expected number of Aces speaks of a lot of new beginnings. And so on.

It is possible to work out the average number of each type of card that one might expect in any spread by a little simple arithmetic. There are 78 cards in the pack, 14 of each suit and 22 Trumps. It follows that, however many cards you laid out in a spread, 22 out of 78 (or 28 per cent of the total) would be Trumps. And that 14 out of 78 (18 per cent of the total) would be comprised of each Suit. And 16 out of 78 (just over 20 per cent) should be Court Cards. And of the Aces, or any other number or Court Card type in the Lesser Arcanum, 4 out of 78 (5 per cent of the total) would be expected to show.

To make things easier, in a 21-card spread one would expect the following numbers on average. (Halve the number approximately for a 10-card spread.) Trumps: 6; Court Cards: 4; of each Suit: 4; any numbered Suit card: 1. So if you get significantly more or less than these averages then you might find it helpful to take account of the fact in your interpretation.

When it comes to reversed cards it depends of course on how many you reversed in the first place. If you reversed half the pack then 50 per cent of your spread should show reversed cards. If you reversed only six or seven then the expected percentage would be no more than one or two reversed cards (one and a half to be exact, but this is of course a physical impossibility).

Some cartomancy books give lists of meanings for finding specific numbers of different suit cards. Two sixes would mean one thing, three sixes something else, and four sixes something yet again. And so on through all the suit cards. We do not find this a particularly helpful approach, although obviously it has a certain logic. Those interested may like to speculate or experiment: it might be expected that a number of Aces, as we have said, would indicate a general atmosphere of new beginnings or creativity; sixes would imply a generally beneficent atmosphere, as these are mostly 'good' cards, whilst fives would imply a less cheerful scenario. However, this would show in your general reading of the individual cards anyway, so there seems no great point in specially allocated meanings for duplicated, triplicated or quadruplicated cards. What is more at question is how these cards collectively affect the general tone of the spread.

Questions and Answers

Q. In the case of one reading I felt that it did not refer to a present life but pointed further back. Also it pointed quite far forward. Is this sort of thing really possible? Is it permissible to do it?

A. Permissibility depends entirely upon your own motivation and spiritual intention. If done merely to satisfy an intellectual curiosity it is probably not a good thing to do, although I feel that the Tarot is quite capable of looking after the interests and spiritual privacy of others if need be. However, if it is done from a genuine desire to help, and not a personally-motivated moral meddling in the lives of others, then I would consider it not only acceptable but also even a duty to do so. After a time one develops a feel for these things, and one can find the Tarot itself giving you a nudge to consult it upon some particular issue.

Q. I learned one thing on this reading – how difficult it is to interpret a spread when there is no one there to give you some response. You can't help feeling that everything you are saying is wrong, even though the meanings given can apply to the cards shown. I certainly wouldn't take up doing postal readings!

A. You are of course right in your comment about how difficult it can be to do full justice to a Tarot reading without personal face-to-face involvement. In this regard postal reading is a poor substitute, although by no means without worth, and may be the best alternative in certain circumstances. Moreover, as I am sure you will have gathered, the greater part of Tarot counselling is as much in one's own feeling for people and their problems and one's experience of life as in any clairvoyant gifts. A good intuition, and practice in interpreting the cards, are of course important factors, but of little practical good without the other human skills.

Q. How can you tell if the Court Cards in a spread are true to their physical colouring or whether it is the personality of the card that matters most? How can you tell whether the Page represents a young boy or a young girl, or a baby? Also, how can you tell if the Pages are real people or just messages?

A. I regret that there is no easy answer to your question. Interpretation of the Court Cards is very much a matter of experience and your own intuition. There is no set formula whereby a particular suit represents hair-colour and such like, although if you are selecting a Court Card to be Significator for somebody then you can if you wish use colour of complexion as a guide to your choice. The basis on which you do this is up to you.

When it comes to the Court Cards turning up in the body of a spread then very often the function of the person represented will follow the suit. Thus a rather amiable young man, perhaps the Querent's boyfriend, might come up as the Knight of Cups, because Cups tend to represent friendship, love and so on. If it were a business relationship (one's male employer at work, for instance, or a partner in some activity), the suits might be Wands. Or, if the relationship were based upon finance, then Coins. And if a quarrel were involved, or a misunderstanding, then Swords.

Knights may represent male or female people who are active in any situation. Kings and Queens however tend to be male or female respectively, and often figures of authority, having an influence on the matters in hand although perhaps not as actively involved as are the Knights. It can happen that the same person is represented by two or three Queens, Knights, or Kings appearing in different parts of the spread, if it is a large one.

When it comes to Pages, they can represent children, although in my experience not very often, unless children have a major influence on the question in hand. More often they stand for messages of some kind, usually according to suit: Wands about organizational matters or some kind of activity, Cups love letters or messages from an old friend, Coins money, even something minor such as a postal order or cheque, and Swords legal documents or notices. Sometimes however it is not an actual message or letter but strong thoughts that are affecting things, or talk with or by other people. Thus the Page of Swords might signify malicious gossip, or the Page of Wands a discussion about work.

LESSON NINE

The Gareth Knight Spiral Spread

In this course we have concentrated on the simpler types of spread, using no more than ten cards at any one time. I have, however, evolved a spread of my own which uses 21 cards and which I have found to be accurate and very useful. It is based upon the principle that the table on which the spread is laid represents the past towards the bottom left-hand corner and the future towards the upper right-hand corner. The 21 cards are dealt out, starting from the centre, in a spiral fashion. Please refer to Figure 21 for the order and position in which the cards are set out. Although it may at first look complicated it is based on very simple and ancient principles of the spiral of manifestation, combined with the plane of past, present and future that runs diagonally across the table.

In effect one then finds one can read in easily assimilated patterns. The four cards at the bottom left give together a picture of the past. The four cards at the top right give together a picture of the future. Eight cards cover the present in two sets of four. The four at the top left give things in the present that are tending to be ignored, disregarded or otherwise concealed from obvious perception. The four at the bottom right give things in the present that are closer to conscious observation and things known about. The line of five cards down the centre of the spread give the psychological condition of the Querent, from the higher levels of spiritual will and intuitional awareness at the top to emotional 'gut reactions' and physical conditions, subjective or objective, at the bottom. The central card of all, which is the first card lain, represents the conscious mind of the Querent and also the question that is being asked.

Let us go through each card one by one to consolidate the pattern.

(1) The Significator. The Querent's conscious mind now. The problem now.

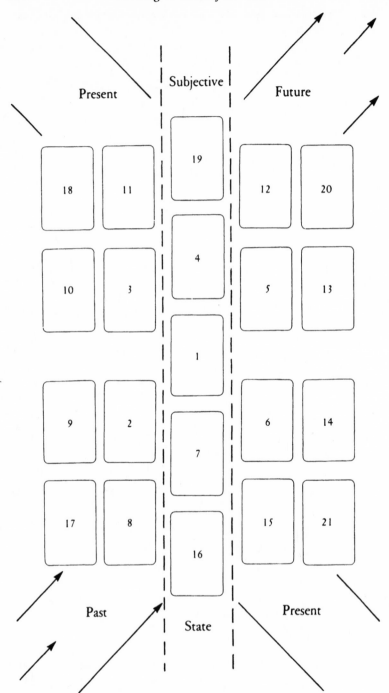

(2) The immediate past. Subjective prelude to the present problem. What was it recently that has led to the current situation?

(3) An important factor in the present that may not be obvious, or that could be being taken for granted or ignored.

(4) The intuitive content of the Querent's mind. It is possible that this may differ from the conscious preoccupation that led to the question. This level can represent the Querent's better judgement or personal wisdom, even conscience.

(5) The most likely eventuality in the immediate future, as things stand at present.

(6) An important factor in the present that is uppermost in the Querent's mind or that seems obvious to all.

(7) The Querent's gut feelings about the matter. Again this can differ from his or her conscious mental attitudes or the intuition.

Note: It is possible to conclude the layout at this point, for a short 7-card reading. However it is recommended that you continue with the rest of the layout, which contains important modifying factors to the basic situation here laid out.

(8 & 9)   Influences from the past, objective or subjective, that have a bearing on the matter, and which may well modify or perhaps have brought about the factors represented by card 2.

(10 & 11) Current influences on the matter, not immediately obvious, that have a modifying influence or other action upon the factor represented by card 3.

(12 & 13) Likely future influences that have a bearing on the situation, particularly as related to the factor represented by card 5.

(14 & 15) Current influences on the matter that are fairly obvious to those concerned, and that have a bearing upon and may well modify the factor represented by card 6.

Note: The above cards are largely Modifiers in their influence or action. The following six cards are important, but slightly more remote from the immediate problem or action. They form keystones, or cornerstones (so to speak) for the problem as a whole.

(16) Physical situation of the Querent. This can refer to bodily health and well-being, or to the Querent's physical circumstances of life.

(17) The root or seed of the matter in the past. This could relate to something that happened some time ago but which was nevertheless important in relation to the present problem.

(18)   A current matter taken for granted as yet unknown that bears
       on the problem. This is likely to be more objective than the
       factor represented by card 3, and could be somewhat more
       remote – such as the influences behind some immediate facet of
       the problem. It may represent unquestioned assumptions in the
       back of the Querent's mind that have a bearing on the problem.
(19)   The spiritual will of the Querent. This is almost certain to be
       unconscious. It is a compelling drive that may make its effect
       felt either in the general direction of the Querent's life or in
       patterns of circumstance that happen to him or her. It can be
       regarded as the force of destiny or, in eastern terms, of
       unresolved karma.
(20)   The likely future goal, event, or marker relating to the
       problem. It is towards this that events are inclining.
(21)   What the Querent needs to think about now or to meditate
       upon in order to achieve a solution to the problem or a safer or
       easier passage.

The factor raised by the last card is quite an important element to bear
in mind when performing a reading, particularly if the reading seems
to be somewhat adverse in its prognostications. If things do not seem
likely to turn out too well, or if the Querent seems likely to act in an
unwise fashion, the layout can be used as a basis for remedial action.
That is, you may find that you can select one or two key points where
things seem likely to go awry and suggest that the Querent meditates
upon them. In a simple case this can just be card 21, but there is no
need to be limited by this. If certain crucial cards in the spread were
reversed, it may be worth while to suggest that the Querent meditate
upon them as if they were right way up, with the consequent
improvement in the situation that this could entail. One could even
go so far as to try rearranging cards in the spread, or substituting
fortunate cards for unfortunate ones. This is not necessarily an
exercise in vain hoping or self-deception, but is a positive response
that can do no harm and may very well do much good, particularly
if it gets the Querent into a more advantageous frame of mind. For
those so inclined, a little formal ceremony could be suggested – even
just lighting a candle and placing the relevant card or cards beside it
for meditation or affirmation of purpose – which the Querent could
perform alone or under your supervision. From your own experience
of working with the Tarot images you will have realized that the
Tarot can be asked for direction and advice without recourse to the
fall of the cards in a spread, and there is no reason why you should not

pass on this benefit and information to your querent, if circumstances are appropriate.

In any spread it is worth while taking up all the cards from the spread and laying them out in a series of lines, with all the numbered Wands together, all the numbered Swords, all the numbered Cups, all the numbered Coins, all the Court Cards, and all the Trumps. This can often help you make an overall assessment of the general situation, which can bring good advice to mind.

Work out how many of each kind you would statistically expect to find. There are 10 numbered cards of each suit (approximately one eighth of the pack), 16 Court Cards (approximately one fifth of the pack), and 22 Trumps (between a quarter and a third of the pack). In a 21-card spread you would therefore statistically expect to find three numbered cards of each suit, four Court Cards, and about six Trumps. If you find significantly more or less of any of these, then ask yourself why. (For a ten-card spread simply halve these approximate numbers.) A shortage of Wands may indicate a lack of organizing ability or will to act. More Wands than expected may mean too much activity or organization around the problem. Too few Cups? There may be a lack of love in the situation. Too many? Then maybe people in the situation are too much in each other's pockets or are being over-possessive.

If there are too few Coins then there is either a shortage of resources or things are not being brought down to physical reality enough. If more Coins than might be expected turn up, then maybe things are being bogged down in financial considerations or perhaps there is too much concern with the physical. Alternatively there might be the not usually unhappy situation of there just being a lot of money about, comparatively speaking. A large proportion of Swords suggests more than a fair share of grief or aggravation. Few Swords suggests that things may be running along very easily, all things considered.

A shortage of Court Cards suggests that the querent is perhaps not making sufficient contact with other people. More than the statistical average of Court Cards might suggest that there are too many people around, or that the problems are very largely personal ones, if you bear in mind that it is possible for a Court Card to refer to the same person in different parts of the spread. I have known one person to be represented four times by the four Pages in different locations in one spread. A dual use of Kings, Queens or Knights in this way is not uncommon, and even three turning up is not all that rare. A large number of Trumps suggest weighty matters that run very deep with the Querent or the problem. On the other hand, few Trumps may suggest that things are on rather a superficial plane, for better or worse.

Finally, a thought about the number of reversed cards. It is difficult to arrive at a statistical average for these on rigid arithmetic grounds, but if more than a quarter of the cards are reversed then the indications are that the Querent is in a somewhat confused or disturbed state. If most of the cards are reversed it is probably best to assume that the pack has been turned up the wrong way at some stage in the proceedings and to regard the majority of cards to be the right way up and the minority in the reversed position. If in serious doubt in a situation like this, do not be afraid to suggest a reshuffle, or to fix another date for a reading. You cannot expect one hundred per cent performance from yourself or the cards all the time. You are going to let yourself down, as well as the Tarot and the Querent; so only work when you feel intuitively that things are right.

It is also quite possible to do a Tarot reading at a distance, telling the Querent to shuffle the cards on his or her own, whilst thinking about the problem, and then letting you know the first 10 or 21 cards (depending on which spread you intend to use) dealt off the pack. It is no bad thing to allow yourself 24 hours between laying out the cards and interpreting them. This 'sleeping on it' gives the Spirit of the Tarot a chance to work upon your subconscious.

Let us now turn to some actual examples of using the Gareth Knight 21-Card Spiral Spread to see it in action – an ounce of practice being worth a pound of theory, as they say.

Our first example concerns a lady in her early thirties, single and unattached. She wants to know if her love-life will improve, and in particular if a platonic friendship with a former flatmate might develop into a romantic attachment. The 21-card spread turned out as seen in Figure 22.

We can see right away from Card 1, *The Last Judgement*, that the question involves seeking radical change in life or an awakening to new possibilities. The vertical column that represents the Querent's current subjective state confirms the general problem at all levels. At the level of action in the world concerning the problem we have the *7 of Swords*, representing futile or unstable effort; and the reversed *3 of Cups* at the level of the emotions indicates the frustration she feels at her current lack of fulfilment in any meaningful relationship. She has at least realized the nature of the problem consciously, as is indicated by Card 1, which represents both her conscious mind in the present and the question at hand. At a spiritual level *Justice* indicates that she has reached a stage in her life when her innermost self and root of her being is requiring her to balance up the pattern of her life. She has asked a specific question about a former flatmate, but the

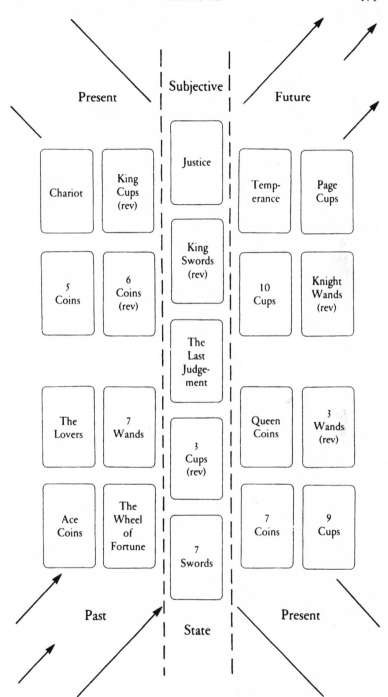

Present · Subjective · Future

Chariot · King Cups (rev) · Justice · Temperance · Page Cups

5 Coins · 6 Coins (rev) · King Swords (rev) · 10 Cups · Knight Wands (rev)

The Lovers · 7 Wands · The Last Judgement · Queen Coins · 3 Wands (rev)

Ace Coins · The Wheel of Fortune · 3 Cups (rev) · 7 Coins · 9 Cups

7 Swords

Past · State · Present

reversed *King of Swords* at the intuitive level suggests that she knows within that this is not quite the right course – otherwise why would she have come for a reading on the matter?

Turning to the four cards that represent factors from the past that bear upon the question, the two Trumps (the *Lovers* and the *Wheel of Fortune*) indicate a life of ups and downs in terms of affectionate relationships, and the fact that we have Trumps here, as well as in the places representing the current question and the spiritual condition of the Querent, indicates that these are important matters in her life. We do not have the situation here of someone asking idle questions about emotional trivia; the Querent has plainly come to an important watershed in her life, when a right decision is going to be crucial to her future self-expression in the circumstances of life. The Lovers and the Wheel impinge upon or modify the *7 of Wands*, which signifies that this situation is what she needed courageously to face up to (half the battle in life is in learning to ask the appropriate questions about ourselves, after which the answers tend to become obvious!) *The Ace of Coins* in the root principle position suggests that these romantic ups and downs, which although common to most young people's experience seem to be going on just a bit too long in the Querent's case, and the problem may centre somehow on her attitude to money, career, or security. In conjunction with the 7 of Wands it could indicate a career-orientated attitude which has prevented any emotional commitment. This is where discussion with the Querent can be helpful to establish if this is the case – and if not, whether the Ace of Coins perhaps represents some other persistent assumption or attitude concerning finances or material conditions that might have blocked the Querent's forming any romantic attachments. In this, encourage the Querent to seek an underlying pattern in the history of past relationships and their break-up. This is likely to be far more helpful than trying to make quasi-authoritative psychic prophecies about what the future holds. The present and the future have their roots in the past.

Let us now look to the present position, which is represented by two groups of four cards each. The top left-hand group tends (though not always) to represent issues that are less consciously obvious, the lower right-hand group those that seem more apparent to the Querent. In light of what we have been saying about the Ace of Coins indicating some problematic attitude towards finances or material conditions, it is interesting to see that four of the eight cards representing the present are of the Coins suit. In a face-to-face reading the Querent might well be asked at this point what these cards might signify to him or her. If we are engaged in reading at a distance, however, then we have to rely upon our own intuitive resources.

Taking these cards at their face value we see the Querent herself represented by the *Queen of Coins* – in fact, if one is using the Waite designs, she clearly appears to be nursing her problem on her lap in the form of the huge pentacle or coin. She is accompanied by the reversed *3 of Wands*, which represents things not being fully in control, although perhaps as a result of her trying to be too much of a controller. Does she tend to be a bit too manipulative in her relationships? Or is it again career ambitions tending to get in the way? The other accompanying card that modifies the Queen is the *7 of Coins*, representing a lack of fulfilment. However, the card in 21st position, which plays a dual function in this layout in that it often indicates a matter the Querent should meditate upon, is a very 'good' card, namely the *9 of Cups*. Its counterpart in the ordinary playing-card pack is the 9 of Hearts, usually called the Wish card, and indicates fulfilment of wishes. Here we would say that it indeed means this, but also that the fulfilment of wishes depends upon the Querent putting more emphasis on her own feelings and those of her partners, and that if she does this all will blossom for her romantically.

Turning to the other four cards, however, we see what seems to be a warning about the idea of teaming up with the former flatmate. He would it seems be a likely candidate for the position of the reversed *King of Cups* and together with the unpropitious *5 of Coins* has an ill-aspected influence on the reversed *6 of Coins*. The *Chariot* at the root of things suggests that the idea of this relationship is one that typifies the Querent's tendency to get things wrong in this area; it is set up intellectually and almost manipulatively as a rational possibility. It is another form of the 7 of Wands, often depicted as a young man defending himself fiercely with a club. A more relaxed attitude seems to be called for than that of valorous young man or charioteer. The 6 of Coins often puzzles people and has much wider meaning than merely charity; it signifies right relationships and the flow of good will, both emotionally and materially. In this context and in reversed mode it indicates plainly that the proposed relationship is not likely to prosper along the terms outlined.

Turning to the future then, represented by the four cards to the upper right, we see promise of great emotional and physical fulfilment in the *10 of Cups*, but this is contingent upon the modifying cards *Temperance* and the reversed *Knight of Wands*. Temperance, being a Trump card, indicates that its message is important, and that the Querent needs to moderate or temper her past and current attitudes when it comes to romantic relationships. The reversed Knight of Wands may well indicate the Querent herself and the manipulative tendency already shown in the 7 of Wands and the Chariot. This rather over-active determined young knight needs to be tipped off his horse. When this is done, then the future will open up, with the *Page of Cups* most appropriately representing new opportunities in matters of the heart.

Our next example is of a woman in her early twenties. She is having an affair with a married man who appears reluctant to leave his wife. She is also in something of a financial pickle and rather unhappy about the flat in which she is now living; she would like to live in a house. She wants to know what her prospects are in this situation.

This is the kind of question and situation that place something of a burden upon any system of divination and the person who is operating it. Should the cards fall a certain way, is one in the business of encouraging the break-up of marriages? Before setting up as a Tarot reader, one does well to come to terms with the implications arising from such matters. Are you prepared for the risk of facing an onslaught from an irate, deserted spouse, possibly with children and rendered destitute, blaming you for being an accessory before the fact? Apart from such extreme consequences, supposing one operates safely from behind a box number or at a distance, what are the moral implications? And are you prepared to live with them? Tarot reading, like any form of counselling, is no soft option in terms of responsibility to all parties concerned.

Bearing in mind that our counselling skills and experience of life are as important in Tarot reading as any ability in interpreting the fall of the cards, we can only do the best we can, being true to the cards and to the Querent, not distorting or suppressing anything out of our own preconceptions but seeking a harmonious way through the labyrinth of any personal problem. It is the figure of Temperance that comes to mind, the archetype that rules over the suit of Cups, governing the emotions and close relationships. One will find in all of this that the Tarot has a wisdom of its own that resolves, in its practical application, most difficulties of this nature that may occur, as long as you are adept at reading the cards. Let us turn to the actual spread that was laid as a result of this particular young woman's question (Figure 23).

The root of the problem, indicated by the *Ace of Coins*, would seem to rest on money and material circumstances rather than on any depth of feeling for another person. This is implied by the actual question, with its emphasis on money and the Querent's type of living accommodation.

Looking at the vertical line representing the Querent's present inner state, we find at the physical event level the *Last Judgement*, which

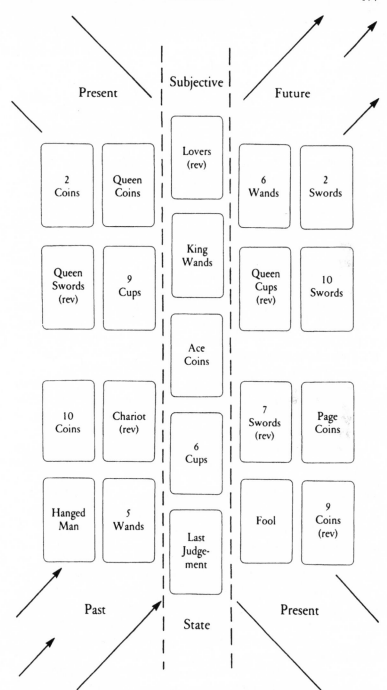

indicates that things are due for a radical change, even if it be a rude awakening whether for herself or another. The *6 of Cups*, at the emotional level, although generally speaking a beneficial card, carries with it what might be called perhaps too much of a good thing, which means very often a childish kind of contentment, or in this position an emotional immaturity. By her own intuition the Querent obviously perceives a stable provider as something to be desired, seen here in the form of the *King of Wands*. This is very likely exactly what she does need, although whether it is to be realized in the gentleman with whom she is currently involved is another matter, and the subject of this reading. The Trump at the top (the *Lovers*), representing her true spiritual will, would suggest that he is not; and reversed in this position indicates that she is currently getting things somewhat wrong in her outer life.

Turning to the four cards that represent the past, we find this confusion confirmed by the *Chariot* reversed, driving headlong in the wrong way in her quest for the fruits of a mature relationship and no financial worries (*10 of Coins*), despite whatever strife may be met with as a consequence (*5 of Wands*). The *Hanged Man* at the root of the matter indicates a sacrifice to be made by somebody in all of this, whether herself or others, and not too much concern over accepted social or moral conventions.

Turning to the present and the set of four cards at the lower right we see futile effort (*7 of Swords*), accentuated by being in reversed mode, with its modifiers the *Page of Coins*, or primary concern with money and material benefits, and the *Fool* as an inexperienced and inherently foolhardy way of going about things. The root of the problem is indicated by the *9 of Coins* reversed. Again the suit of Coins shows that the main concern is material and financial rather than loving. This card generally stands for wealth or benefits that are not earned; a prize in a lottery, or a legacy or some unexpected gift would normally be its signification. Here these expectations are reversed, showing, it would seem to me, the lesson that in this life one does not get anything for nothing, dream as one may.

The four cards on the upper left, indicating more concealed or less obvious present factors, show two Queens, which may be held to represent the Querent and her lover's wife. An interpretation could work either way. The Querent could be the *Queen of Coins*, as she hopes she soon will be, overturning the wife (the reversed *Queen of Swords*) in the man's material commitment. The root of the matter is harmonious change (at any rate for the Queen of Coins), indicated by the *2 of Coins*. Alternatively the Queen of Coins may represent the wife, who is currently in the dominant position, with the Querent as the ousted Queen of Swords; the harmonious change for the wife being the exit of the Querent from her husband's life. This seems, whichever way one looks at it, an apt summary of the situation, and whichever way it goes is going to prove a major emotional triumph for the victor, as indicated by the *9 of Cups*. For its resolution we must needs look to the cards that represent the future.

These turn out to be the *Queen of Cups* reversed, flanked by two seemingly contradictory cards, the *6 of Wands*, which is usually held to represent victory, and the *10 of Swords*, which generally stands for disaster. One person's disaster is of course another person's victory, and in the confrontational situation that is brewing we have to decide from other factors pertaining which is which. My own interpretation is that the reversed Queen of Cups is in fact the Querent, rather than the wife, whose situation as well as the matter's conclusion seems indicated by the final card, the *2 of Swords*, that is the condition of 'peace restored'. Thus the disaster of the 10 of Swords applies to the Querent, particularly if she tries to force things to a conclusion with a man who is, I feel intuitively, closely related to the 6 of Wands card, particularly bearing in mind the illustration in Waite's pack of a man on horseback riding off triumphantly (and out, I think, of the Querent's life!). The five wands depicted surrounding the figure on this card have resonance possibly with the *5* of Wands that figures in the past situation.

The counselling task that results from this spread therefore is to indicate gently to the Querent that things are unlikely to turn out as she hopes with this particular man, and that she would do best to disengage herself from the situation and look for love and money elsewhere. A meditation upon turning the reversed 9 of Coins the right way up might prove beneficial to her in the coming weeks, if she is open to this kind of inner self-help.

Finally we turn to a more mature woman, who had been married for some twenty years and had brought up a family. A few years ago, however, following a health problem and series of operations, her marriage came to an end as a result of her husband's adultery. She has since remarried, and with her new husband plans to sell the house in which they live and move to a seaside resort to start a small business. However, her husband has very recently begun to express doubts about the wisdom of this move. She is anxious therefore to know what her future prospects are, and she is also beginning to worry about whether her new husband may be 'cooling off', and whether her health may start to deteriorate again. The cards laid were as shown in Figure 24.

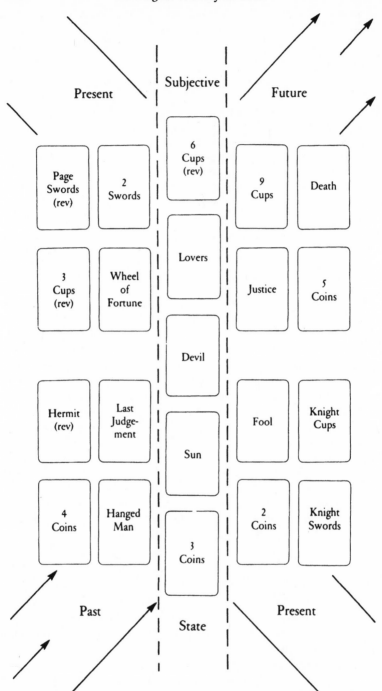

Present

Subjective

Future

| Page Swords (rev) | 2 Swords |
| 6 Cups (rev) |
| 9 Cups | Death |

| 3 Cups (rev) | Wheel of Fortune |
| Lovers |
| Justice | 5 Coins |

| Devil |

| Hermit (rev) | Last Judge- ment |
| Sun |
| Fool | Knight Cups |

| 4 Coins | Hanged Man |
| 3 Coins |
| 2 Coins | Knight Swords |

Past

State

Present

A notable feature of this spread is the large number of Trumps that appear, indicating that there are crucial and far-reaching issues at stake as far as the Querent is concerned. We see that the upheavals in the past have a strong bearing on the matter at hand. Their basis is the very material fabric of life, indicated in the past by the *4 of Coins*, which may signify here not only domestic conditions but those of the body also – in other words the past health problems. All has seen radical change and a new start, as signified by the *Last Judgement*, before which she found herself partly in the role of victim (The *Hanged Man*), and with all her previous wisdom and values turned topsy-turvy (the reversed *Hermit*).

I have mentioned the past first because it would seem that it is showing signs of poisoning the present and the future. The *Devil* in the centre shows a state of considerable anxiety, which is probably based upon illusion, although no less unpleasant to experience in spite of that. Otherwise within herself she seems to be all right. The *3 of Coins* indicates that her circumstances are currently stable; the *Sun* in the place of the emotions shows a fulfilled relationship; as may also be indicated by the *Lovers* at the intuitive level, although this card can also represent a decision or a choice of ways to go, and this is obviously exercising her mind. At the spiritual level we have the *6 of Cups*, which is (generally speaking) a happy card, although often indicating happiness expressed in a somewhat childlike fashion. Here it is reversed, which accentuates this. In some sense this would appear to indicate that deep within her self this Querent feels somehow guilty about her present happily married state, and at the same time haunted by how things went unexpectedly and radically wrong in the past. This results in her present conscious mental anxiety despite the otherwise even tenor of her life and circumstances. It is perhaps also these spiritual and intuitive factors that are or were at the back of her wanting to up-stakes and move elsewhere to start a completely new kind of life; almost a kind of insurance against the old pattern recurring. Now that her husband, perhaps rightly, is questioning the wisdom of this change, it stirs up unconscious worries fuelled from the past. Let us look at what the cards for the present portray.

On the one hand we have the *Fool*, set upon wandering off into pastures new, abetted by the *2 of Coins* signifying harmonious change, and the *Knight of Cups*, who signifies much the same kind of thing but in search of or in affirmation of love and partnership. To this beneficent trio we have added the very active and somewhat disruptive *Knight of Swords*. Is he perhaps indicating that there is a danger of forcing the issue, of over-hasty action?

The less obvious, almost unconscious motivations seem to be

indicated in the four cards at the top left. Here we see the *Wheel of Fortune* indicating change, or desire for it, but rather equivocally aspected by the *2 of Swords* and the *3 of Cups* (this last reversed). This indicates a desire for a restoration of some previous harmony allied to a wealth or abundance that, being reversed, is not giving the satisfaction that it might. At the root of all this is the reversed *Page of Swords*, which simply means anxiety, although there could also be an element of gossip, or malicious neighbours talking about what's gone on in the past. Is this perhaps a contributing factor to her wanting to sell up and start a completely new life elsewhere? This is a question that would have to be elucidated by discreet questioning of the Querent. Without that opportunity we have to rely on our own unaided intuitive perceptions.

Turning to the future we find not so much a prediction as a line of advice, represented by the Trump figure of *Justice*, who is set between two complementary cards, the *9 of Cups* and the *5 of Coins*, indicating that the future is in the hands of the Querent to mould by her own choice. The figure of *Death* should mark an end to her worries, guilts and old anxieties. In other words, the task for the Reader in this spread is one of reassurance to the Querent, laid on confidently; tell her that what is past is past, and that while it is perfectly natural to feel worried because of past misfortunes they must not be allowed to spoil the present or the future. She should also be told that the present and the future rests with herself and her new husband, and that she should take things as they come as part of a new partnership, to be assessed in terms of present happiness and fulfilment without allowing anxieties from the past to intrude nor seeking something completely new, rich and strange as a way of escaping them. Whether or not she and her husband move or stay is a matter that will develop from their own mature desires as their relationship develops.

The image of the Knight of Swords may serve as one to think upon, indicative as it is of the need to take the initiative and not be passive to external gossip, real or imagined, or worries from the past. Indeed the knight can cut up all these negative emotions and thoughts.

Sample Readings

Tarot readings will obviously be a very personal matter, and the approach of one reader will differ from that of another, not only in style but in nuances of interpretation. Also there will be differences in tone between a face-to-face reading and a postal one.

The spread that we have just analysed (Figure 24) is here given two further readings by different individuals. The first, by Libby Valdez, as if done face-to-face; the second done as a postal reading by Rosemary Simmonds.

The Face-to-face Reading

The thing that strikes me most about this spread is the apparent discrepancy between what looks like your own unconscious or intuitive assessment of the situation and the problem as your conscious, thinking mind sees it. Intuition and our gut feelings about a thing are often better at getting to the truth than our 'thinking' minds, which tend to get pretty cluttered up with extraneous ideas and fears.

Intuitively your unconscious perception of things looks very good to me: we have the card for the *Lovers*, which is *the* card for love and romantic fulfilment, dominating everything here. Your gut estimation of where things are at is the *Sun* – possibly the nicest card in the pack as an indicator of general well-being and good fortune. I think when two people are married it's very hard if something is seriously wrong in a relationship for the partners not to pick up on this fact, at least on an unconscious level. The fact that these two cards are so positive suggests to me that as far as the romantic, sexual or emotional side of the relationship goes there is nothing at all to worry about. If these cards were reversed or less auspicious in themselves I might have doubts, but I feel very reassured by their placing here. So what is the *Devil* doing glaring out in the middle?

In this position he represents your overall attitude to the problem now, your conscious mind. The Devil can stand for any aspect of our lower natures, from our shadow side, to sex, to illusion and projected emotion, to our capacity for evil. Don't worry – I don't think what we are seeing here is an eruption of primal evil. He has for me a certain over-the-top quality that partly suggests a lot of passion and anxiety. Whatever has triggered your worry at present has caused the release of anxiety, which seems to me to be washing about and likely to attach itself to anything you can think of as an explanation for your unease. I think the real source of most of your anxiety is the past; but obviously there are also problems in the present contributing to it, and these two sources of anxiety seem to be fusing into one big wave, making it harder for you to see the heart of things.

If I look to the cards representing the past root of the problem, we have the *Last Judgement*, which is to do with an awakening: perhaps this refers to your husband rather suddenly and unexpectedly voicing his misgivings about the move and the new business, since I feel this came as a bit of a surprise for you. The *4 of Coins* seems the ultimate cause of his doubts – and this implies a preoccupation with material provision and security (financial or otherwise). The figure in the card seems to me to be wrapping itself round its coins in a protective way – that is, holding on to what he's got for fear of losing it. This is combined with two cards (*Hermit* and *Hanged Man*) that seem to me to have a hidden, retreating quality, so it may well be that your husband kept quiet for a while before voicing his doubts, brooding on them within himself. It's almost as if he has been slowly waking up (Judgement) to the fact that he didn't want to jeopardize his material security, and feels rather apprehensive about the future and about getting older generally (Hermit, Reversed). In this bottom left-hand corner I believe also lies the root of some of the anxiety represented by the Devil. I think this sudden awareness of not being of one mind with your husband has created a sense of distance and maybe triggered associations with the break-up of your first marriage, associations which are now overflowing in an irrational way into the present situation.

Let's now look at the top left-hand four cards, which represent factors not sufficiently taken into account. The key card here is the *Wheel of Fortune*. I get a tremendous sense of an airy, floating quality in the wheel, as if it is spinning through space in an unpredictable manner. I feel this represents both your husband's emerging feelings and an objective comment on the flaws in your plans. I get the feeling that the man hanging on to his security in 4 of Coins feels on some level that if he uproots himself from house and job he will be taking quite a gamble on his material future, literally putting his goods on a roulette wheel. The *Page of Swords* (Reversed) hovering rather menacingly in the background to me represents the potentially, negative consequences (both perceived and real) of making 'a bad move'. It represents the spectre at the back of your minds of 'change for the worse'. The Page seems to stand for other things too: your husband's fear that if the move went badly it might affect his relationship with you, and a residual fear on his part that all the upheaval might strain your health. His initial reluctance to voice his doubts – that I see in the Hermit and Hanged Man – may stem from this fear of bringing discord into the relationship. I believe the balancing between *3 of Cups* (Reversed) and *2 of Swords* on either side of the symbol for change stands for the slight cloud over your relationship caused by this unresolved difference between you. In the 2 of Swords I sense a tacit agreement not to discuss the matter, and this uneasy stasis is creating a low-key tension in the relationship. I think any kind of tension causes a slight withdrawal of one partner from the other, and if this rather unconscious withdrawal manifests itself on a sexual level, it's easy to misinterpret. You think your husband is drawing away because he no longer finds you attractive, when really it is due to the vague tensions that are undermining his sense of closeness in the marriage. I think the fact that the move is important to both of you means that while the issue is unresolved it is acting as a slight check on the flow of the relationship: that is why 3 of Cups is reversed – this tension. The 2 of Swords suggests to me a sense of quiet deadlock or unspoken opposition and disagreement. Some of the Devil's energy also comes from your combined negative tension here. To clear it all up I think you need to discuss it in an open way.

If we look to the lower right-hand corner we find the factors which you are both more conscious of: it tells us how you are dealing with the problem at the surface level. The key card here is the *Fool*. To me this card is mainly giving off a lot of optimism and happiness, greatly reinforced (in this central circle of Trumps) by the positiveness of the Lovers and the Sun. In a way the central pattern of Trumps looks to me as if the Devil is a powerhouse of passion and anxiety, and its axis spins the other Trumps round. The Lovers, Sun and Fool are the positive, joyful expression of the Devil's energy, while the three darker cards are there to stop the whole thing spinning away into a euphoric oblivion, and to give a bit of shape, discipline and order to all that energy, bringing it down to the ground. All these Trumps show just how much you care about all this.

Now as far as the cards for the conscious present go: the Fool seems to me to be fairly unearthed. I think this may be to do with your general enthusiasm for the move, the way the plans were at first discussed – maybe in a whole-new-life, sky's-the-limit sort of mood? Also I sense the general happiness of being married. I also feel it may symbolize the attitude that you felt was the best way to react to your husband's doubts till now: stay cheerful and optimistic, keep off the subject and hope his worries will go away. I feel it is relevant that the Fool and the *Knight of Cups* – with whom I identify your husband – are both looking in opposite directions, back to back, as if deliberately not connecting with one another's point of view. Although you as the Fool seem fairly in tandem with the Lord of Harmonious Change (the 2 of Coins), the Knight of Cups has his back to him also and appears quite oblivious to his presence. I feel it's indicative of your husband's lack of interest in getting down to the whole business of moving. From a certain tension which I feel between the dreaminess of the Knight of Cups and the struggles of the juggler in the *2 of Coins* I think your husband may feel rather inadequate to the joint challenge, and not confident that he is the right sort of person for it. It may be he needs to call on professional advice to give him more confidence and a sense of direction in this. He doesn't seem to me to be in the mood for big changes; he is rather hoping things will sort themselves out and trusting it will all come right in the end.

At this point I think it is worth asking – where are all the Wands in this spread? If you are going to move house and set up a new business Wands are pretty vital, since they represent executive power, organizing activity and the will to act. They are notable by their absence here. I think this brings us back to that unearthed, unrealistic quality that was inherent in the early planning stage. I think there may be a bit of a gulf between the vision and the reality; there's no sense of how things are going to get done – there is no will to act. I'd guess the very emotional contentment of the dreamy Knight of Cups is fuelling his desire to stay put. This lack of executive will lay latent in the Hermit and Hanged Man: they exuded a kind of stillness, a vacuum of activity which may first have manifested as a kind of passive resistance to action or discussion on this front – now it is surfacing again in the lack of Wands. I think this lack of Wands is central to the problem. Nothing will get done without them.

The card for the most likely future eventuality is *Justice*. She restores the balance and brings us up short if we are going overboard in any way. Here I think she represents the point where discussion and planning have to get down to the nitty-gritty. When, where and how much? Justice is the point where things come down to the ground, usually with a loud thud. The two modifying cards (*9 of Cups, 5 of Coins*) suggest to me that at this point you are going to find you have a lot of love around, a lot of contentment in your present situation, but that your husband may convince you that in material terms the move doesn't look such a good idea. I think you may find there just isn't sufficient financial security to cover the risks involved in moving house and setting up business at the same time. It may be to do with the state of the housing market or business investments. Perhaps it will be possible at some future time when a few Wands have been brought to bear on things. In this context I don't think the long-term marker card (Death) needs much explaining – it's saying the projected move will probably be shelved.

I don't know how you would feel about this, but I think if things do have to be put off it's important not to let disappointment blind you to all you have got or to let it blight your happiness. Your health looks fine as far as this reading goes: *3 of Coins* suggests the solid re-establishment of bodily health, and I think that is partly due to the security and happiness you've found with your husband – represented by the Sun and Lovers. It's also important to keep this 'plus side' in mind, because I think the reason *6 of Cups* is reversed is that your capacity for enjoying life has got rather overshadowed by the difficult events in your past, which have given you a tendency to be apprehensive about the future. It's important to enjoy life to the full, now.

If you'd like to meditate further, the card that should help you toward dealing with all this is the *Knight of Swords*. I don't think I should tell you what significance I would put on it, because it's your insight that's needed here. That Knight always looks to me as if he is rushing into things like a bat out of hell – which may not be the wisest course! Best to just discuss it when you're in a relaxed sort of mood, and, keeping flexible, see if you can find out the basis of your husband's doubts, and between you both get a good objective view of your overall prospects and respective wishes.

Tarot Reader's Notes

I felt from the question that a woman in this position would be feeling pretty insecure, and the Devil seemed to confirm this when I saw him, both by his position and what he was giving off (a lot of projected emotion that seemed a mixture of sexual insecurity and anxiety with vaguely negative traces thrown in). I suppose it would be possible to read the whole spread in terms of sex but I am inclined to think that element is secondary. I felt the Querent's anxiety might be a problem in itself, but that it would be counterproductive to say so or to stress it too much or in the wrong way. So although fears about her continuing sexual attractiveness seemed quite apparent I decided to give them minimal coverage, to avoid embarrassing her. I tried instead to talk about the anxiety generally in the context of what was good in her and her husband's relationship. I hoped thus to put her fears into better perspective and to minimize them while still lifting the lid off her tension.

The Hermit and Hanged Man had a very curious feeling to them, something very hidden, a veiled light that seemed to have several elements to it – hence the many layers of interpretation. I felt her husband may have been hiding his real feelings about the move because he didn't want to rock the boat. I could tell he might be quite sensitive and aware of her anxiety generally, and consequently would tread pretty carefully both because he is fond of her and because he is not very secure in the relationship himself yet. There's a strong sense of reservation around the interplay of these two cards that makes me wonder how keen he was on the move all along – how much his initial (apparent) enthusiasm was born of a desire to please her.

The bottom right-hand corner contained I felt a fairly literal reminder of the break-up of the Querent's first marriage as well as a 'coming up short' against the realization of her husband's opposition. There seemed some sort of rude awakening indicated in Judgement in relation to the modifying cards. In Hermit and Hanged Man I felt there were also traces of the time when she was ill, a time when perhaps she turned in on herself and became isolated; and into this self-absorbed, cocooned state came the shock of her first husband's abandoning her. And I felt this current awakening to her present husband's 'doubts' was bringing echoes of the shock of loss of interest in her.

I think the present husband, as a sensitive Knight of Cups, knows he is not very practical or energetic, but has tried to conceal these deficiencies for fear of losing her. I felt Page of Swords might betoken some bad news monetarily that he hasn't told her about. The lack of Wands made me wonder again about the seriousness of his initial commitment. I think too I have rather taken it for granted in the reading that the Querent herself is not a Queen of Wands type, planning on carrying it all through on her own shoulders.

I think her husband is very fond of her, just from the reflections of him picked up in the Sun, Lovers, Fool, Hanged Man and Hermit, etc. Part of the Devil's anxiety and slightly negative energy may be his – I think he is loathe to spoil things for her.

Looking at the Wheel, 3 of Cups (reversed) and 2 of Swords from the sexual point of view, I think the Tarot might be saying it's time for a change. The first wave of brilliant passion has passed and things are naturally progressing to a more low-key level. The fact that the husband is initiating this change may be worrying the Querent.

I would make sure the Querent wasn't going to take anything I said as holy writ before I started, and be especially careful with regard to statements about her health. Since I feel that the 3 of Coins does imply a good and stable situation I would hope to make her feel a sensible and temperate optimism rather than any flooding conviction that everything is fine, which could later get shattered by a return of her illness.

The 2 of Coins gave me the feeling that just getting his marriage established had made the Knight of Cups feel he had his hands full. It is quite difficult getting used to living with someone, especially when you're middle-aged I think. The juggler in 2 of Cups seemed fairly tottering about in relation to the Knight of Cups, and the Knight seemed to be riding away from the juggler partly because he had had enough of changes for the time being. I didn't think it would help the Querent's sense of security to say all this. It feels to me as if both

parties need to take the plunge and be honest with each other. Maybe
it is the first crisis in their married life, hence all the hesitation. I would
expect their fondness for each other to see them through.

If the Querent is interested in the Tarot I might suggest (in addition
to the Knight of Swords meditation) that she lay out the vertical strip
of five cards that represents herself, substituting either Temperance or
one she finds good and positive for the Devil and turning the 6 of
Cups the right way up. I'd explain what each level symbolized and
suggest that she mull them over to get a more positive sense of where
she is and to balance her inner self.

The Postal Reading

Dear ....,

The question of change does appear to be quite pressing in your life
at present. The three issues you brought up in your question do in fact
weave into one another.

The reading indicates that you presently feel somewhat stuck in life,
almost a puppet of Fate and circumstance. If the business proposition
you were pursuing was originally your husband's idea and the
business itself very much his project, this would account for your
present feeling of being in a difficult situation but being unable to do
anything about it. Since it is his scheme it is hard for you to know
whether his doubts are sensible or exaggerated. The cards relating
directly to you include the *Sun*, which shows you have a great deal of
strength to draw on. On the business front one useful way forward
might be to take a more active role than you have done in the past.

One of the cards that comes up in the immediate future for you is
Justice, signifying an important decision. Relating this to your business
worries it would seem appropriate to seek independent, professional
advice. Try to do so in a way that indicates to your husband that you
are trying to help and further this joint project sensibly rather than
going over his head for a decision. If the situation turns out to be
positive then you will both be freed from that financial anxiety, even
if thriftiness is called for in the immediate future, and be able to make
the move with a firm heart.

Coming back to yourself I wonder if some of your worry is that the
decision to move would be financially unstable? I sense that you are
a woman who values physical security highly. Though it may be
difficult at first to see the connection there is an impression that your
focus upon physical security occludes a deeper desire for emotional
security which you believe you cannot attain. This creates in you a

certain defensiveness, a withholding of yourself so that you don't get hurt. Likely this is related to your feelings of hurt and suffering as a result of your former husband's behavioiur. As things stand there is a definite danger that you may be unconsciously casting your present partner in the same mould. Now that he has voiced some uncertainty you are immediately seeing your past repeat itself. Try to stand back and look at the relationship objectively with the same careful consideration and unbiased appraisal that you would expect the business professional to apply when considering your business scheme for you. It may well be that your husband is uncertain now because he is hoping for some lead from you, some indication that you are committed to the idea and the relationship. If you can find that you are and can overcome the tendency to hold yourself back emotionally you will likely find that your worries about the business and the marriage diminish.

Many cards from the Major Arcana, the Trumps of the Tarot, have come up in the spread and they all circle around you, which is why I am inclined to stress that the real focus of the change going on is within you rather than out in the environment. If you can make that shift in attitude, opening up to the love and creative force you intuitively know is within you, then it does seem likely that the rest will take care of itself!

As far as your health is concerned there is nothing here to indicate ill-health, on the contrary I sense a lot of bursting energy that is desperate to get into action. It may be that this doubt of your husband's has caused you to wonder if the whole scheme is not foolish, especially if this is a criticism that has been levelled at your plans by other people. Despite that I can't help feeling that you want to go ahead, that there is a side of you that would love the excitement and the thrill of trying something new. All that is awaited is the decision to do so.

To sum up, the underlying issue is one of commitment, a decision to overcome your defensive habit of holding back. A far-reaching change is indicated, which would seem to suggest the business move is a good one but only if this is echoed by a change within you that allows you to leave old fears behind so that your commitment can be deeper and so that when you move with your husband you feel you are moving to a new *life*, not just a new place.

Tarot Reader's Notes
The Devil as Significator points to a critical situation: illusions appearing within a sense of possession and a sense of being swept along by Fate or Destiny – which ties in with the 6 of Cups Reversed as an unconscious drive to separate herself from all union. She is

withholding her trust, she can't let herself go. Yet her capacity for joy is there at gut level in the Sun (creative optimism), and the 3 of Coins indicates a stable base.

Her present preoccupation centres around both the possible folly of her departure into this business venture and her underlying worries about her marriage (the Fool flanked by the two Knights). She is influenced deeply both outwardly and consciously by her husband's preferences; perhaps she is waiting for him to act. She sees the present as a financial balancing act – the 2 of Coins – and perhaps she also sees there is no easy link between one lifestyle and another.

Past links tie in to waiting on her husband's will in the Hanged Man (= hanging around). Her habit of looking but not initiating could be useful now in helping her re-evaluate herself. The Last Judgement card stresses that the situation cannot continue as it is but will be brought to a head by her passivity (the Hanged Man) and her husband's loss of wisdom (the Hermit Reversed). This could indicate the end of the 'honeymoon' period of their marriage, and also colludes with the Devil, who represents the end of the old attitudes that are soiling her present relationship. Judgement leading to Death = something must end, either through deep change and rebirth or, as I suspect, the stagnation in her attitude will deal a deathblow to her marriage. (The Death card here does *not* indicate her health.) The root card is the 4 of Coins: this speaks of her need for material security. Maybe she has fears regarding the business move, so sits back, hoping it won't come off. I suspect this ties into the 3 and 6 of Cups Reversed – the masking of her emotional insecurity by a desire for physical security. She may also associate financial worries with her own ill-health.

Unacknowledged circumstances underline the need for change (Wheel of Fortune) but still there is a holding-back, she feels she can't have pleasure (3 of Cups Reversed) and anticipates conflicts (2 of Swords). Unconsciously she is casting her husband as the adversary – his doubt makes her life hard, his show of weakness forces her to face up to issues in herself. Her general defensiveness (Page of Swords) makes her hold back.

The intuitive realm repeats the need for her to make a serious commitment to her relationship (the Lovers and 6 of Cups). Her future prospects are good, with Death bringing the conclusion that the cards push for. This should happen through the decisive action and clear vision of Justice – and relates to a decision about both her business and her husband. The 9 of Cups shows that she will opt for emotional fulfilment despite financial restraint (5 of Coins).

Working Plan

Exercise 1

Lay out all the spreads described in this lesson (Figures 22, 23 and 24) and go carefully through the readings given, taking note of where you agree or disagree.

Exercise 2

Do the same with as many other spreads as you can (referring to those that have been published in books with commentaries). Where would you have disagreed with the reader and made a different interpretation?

Exercise 3

The rest is up to you. Do as many readings as you can, and record them for assessment later.

AFTERWORD

Towards an Advanced Study of the Tarot

There are two paths to more advanced study with the Tarot. One is in the realm of divination; the other is using it to guide you on a symbolic quest in search of psychological and spritual integration. That is, as a western form of *yoga* (which, translated, means 'union') – a unification of all the disparate parts of ourselves on all levels: spiritual, intuitive, intellectual, emotional, instinctive, and physical. The first path can indeed lead to the second, for no one who works persistently with the Tarot is going to be unaffected by it, just as one could hardly fail to benefit from close association with any trustworthy guide, philosopher and friend.

We have imparted the general principles of reading the Tarot in a way that can lead to ever-expanding horizons of realization, developing naturally your own intuitive and imaginative faculties. Further knowledge about divination by Tarot may be gained from other books, but as we have said repeatedly, the best teacher is the Tarot itself. Thus ideas will come to you as you work (or play) with the cards. It may, for instance, come into your head to design other types of spread for your own use. By this means you may eventually develop the facility to use a whole-pack spread, with its consequent subtle and comprehensive readings. Developing your own contacts of wisdom with the Tarot will be more effective than putting too much reliance on other authorities, which can often serve only to dilute and confuse your own inner perceptions.

There is not a great deal to be gained from memorizing a whole host of different 'spreads' (some Tarot texts are rather like cookery books in this respect). And there is little point in collecting spreads the way hobbyists collect postage stamps; one or two tested and tried methods that you understand are quite enough to work with as a general basis. My own preference is for Waite's Celtic spread or my own Spiral one, for simpler or more complex questions respectively. You too may evolve your own methods, but make haste slowly, one proven step at a time.

Similarly, the second road to advanced work with the Tarot is not one that can be condensed into a short curriculum of exercises or reading matter, depending instead upon your own application over a period of time. However, the pattern of the Tarot that we have described does show the general direction in which to work, and we can at least outline this path, or quest – the treading of it is then up to you.

The Tarot can perform this dual role by its very nature, being a system of symbols to which are linked evocative images that portray archetypes of an inner reality located behind the external world. These archetypes have been known from ancient times, and are sometimes referred to as Platonic Ideas (after the Greek philosopher Plato who formulated much of the general theory). It has been given practical application throughout the ages, generally under the name of *Neoplatonism*. Platonic Ideas are not the same as the everyday thought-processes that we nowadays call ideas. Platonic Ideas have an inner, objective existence and might be called 'Ideas in the Universal Mind', or 'Ideas in the Mind of God'. When we approach them, therefore, and take them into ourselves, we are linking our own small, subjective minds to the great principle of creation. Platonic Ideas are objective, bigger than us, beneficent and eminently practical. To give some idea of their power and importance, it has been suggested that we could well describe them in terms, not of 'I have a great idea', but 'a Great Idea has me!'

We ought perhaps to point out that Platonic Ideas are not necessarily the same as 'archetypes of the unconscious' discussed in certain schools of psychology. There is indeed a certain validity to the psychological approach to these matters, and much practical help can be gained from Neoplatonism by those in search of psychotherapeutic techniques, but we must avoid the inherent limitation that characterizes much modern psychology – namely, the assumption that the great psychic and spiritual worlds are confined within our own heads. Our work with the Platonic Ideas leads us to an expansion of consciousness, not its narrowing; to wider and greater worlds of being, not merely to the integration of our own psyche, although that may well be a fringe benefit along the way!

It is by means of the imagination that we perceive the realities of the inner worlds. And when we use this term 'inner worlds', we are speaking of the internal aspect of objective reality, not our own personal subjectivity. It is indeed commonly assumed that the imagination is just a personal picture-house of subjective fantasy. To a large extent this may be true, but there is also present a genuine awareness of worlds beyond the physical. It is our task to fine-tune our awareness so that we can distinguish the objective from the subjective in our imaginative life.

Thus the name of the game is *the attunement of consciousness*. We can do this by concentrating on certain key images. These images represent and act as channels for interior realities. This is another way to arrive at the definition of what we mean by a 'symbol'. It is something that carries great truth. A myth or legend is a system of such symbols, and thus is a system of great truth. It is a great error to use the word 'myth' to signify something erroneous or unreal.

In the Tarot we have a specially constructed system which is, in a sense, the equivalent of a myth or legend. All myths and legends, as well as other Neoplatonic symbol systems – from Qabalah to Astrology and from the I Ching to the Runes – are maps of the same inner terrain, cast in different sets of images. We would probably do best to concentrate upon one set of symbols rather than many, when it comes to concentrated work. All the hares bolt through the same hole eventually, but it can be a considerable exercise in time and energy to try to follow each and every one. Such eclecticism may lead to a formidable amount of theoretical knowledge but may take the focus of action to the wrong level – that of intellectual speculation rather than imaginative experience. We have no desire to add to the ranks of armchair occultists.

The line of our work is an invitation to adventure under the direction of an experienced guide, that guide being the beneficent force behind the Tarot. As a result of this adventure, or quest, we can go through a process of attunement of consciousness whereby we come to an actual experience of the forces, powers and beings of the inner worlds. The aim of all this, it must be said, is not to satisfy an idle curiosity, but to make us, as human beings, better able to serve the forces of light – those invisible forces that strive to bring about the expression of the greater good. It is therefore an invitation to service as well as to adventure.

The Four Elements

In surveying generally the ground that is to be covered we turn once again to the Fool as our guide and initiator. We may again meet him on the clifftop, but this time he will not lead us over the cliff (which served us before to demonstrate faith in action), but will take us with him back up the path to the place whence he has come. This might be termed his Father's House, in which there are many mansions, some of which are the Tarot halls. We may envisage this as a high-towered castle, with many peaks, spires and turrets as in a fairytale

palace. It is only one of the towers which will concern us, however;
the others contain other systems of Platonic Images, alternative to the
Tarot.

In the Main Hall of this Tower we shall meet the Magician, and in
this Main Hall we may study at some length the various powers that
he has at his disposal. These are represented by the 56 cards of the
Lesser Arcanum (the numbered cards of the suits), overseen by the
Court Cards. Each suit is allocated a particular quarter, and each is
represented by one of the Four Elements: Air, Fire, Water and Earth.
These are living Elements, or conditions of being, not just ancient
concepts of outmoded science. Upon these four principles all of life is
founded, and we need to understand their nature before we can work
with their actual powers.

The principles of Elemental expression are based upon a tenfold
pattern. At each quarter of the Magician's chamber, located at
ground-level of the tower, there stands a magic tree. Each of these
trees has magical fruits or flowers upon it, and it is the nature of these
(and whether they are in bud, in full flower, heavy with fruit, or in the
quiescence attendant upon seeding) that will be our first concern. To
aid us we will have the service of an Elemental Guide. In the formal
structure of the Tarot this guide is called the Page of each suit.
However, when we use our inner vision these Pages drop their
anthropological convention and appear as the beings they really are:
sylphs for the Element of Air, salamanders for the Element of Fire,
undines for the Element of Water, and gnomes for the Element of
Earth.

The Powers of Inner Earth

Once we have formed a general understanding of the basic structure
of the four trees and their elemental guardians and guides we can start
upon the process of invoking the force that gives them life and causes
the elemental sap to rise. We do this by taking a journey downwards
into the lower reaches of the Tower. It is not always understood by
those who aspire to higher knowledge that by virtue of our place on
Earth and our human condition we must needs go downwards before
we can ascend. Those who seek the heights without first knowing the
depths are like seeds that fall on shallow or stony ground: They send
up short-lived, weedy growth that is not enriched by the deep earth.
There are unfortunately many students of spiritual enlightenment
who have yet to learn this fundamental lesson. It accounts for the
many highly idealistic individuals and groups who actually achieve
very little within the material world. It is only by making this journey

downwards that we meet the real guardians of the Mysteries. These are the great custodians of all the powers that lie within the Inner Earth, and their underground chamber may be called the Hall of the Guardians.

These Guardians are represented by appropriate images within the Tarot Trumps. The Initiatrix to the Hall of the Guardians is represented by Justice, for none may enter into this portal of the Mysteries without the equilibrium of forces that her scales signify, nor without proper motive and pure intent. This is signified by her sword, for, as the old adage has it, the Way of the Mysteries is as straight as the blade of a sword and as narrow as its edge. The figure of Justice gives us access, once we have passed her scrutiny (which is by no means a mere formality), to the beings within the Hall of the Guardians. There are four of them, and together they make up what is often referred to in esoteric literature as the Dweller on the Threshold. This accounts for their somewhat menacing aspect in their Tarot Trump guise – as Death, the Devil, the Lightning Struck Tower, and the Hanged Man. Each indeed has a lesson to teach the aspiring soul seeking to pass their scrutiny, and a test to prove that this lesson has been learned.

Upon passing their watchful guardianship successfully we may be permitted to make contact with the powers of the Inner Earth, which in the terminology of the Eastern mysteries is called the Kundalini, or Serpent Power. It has its equivalent within the psychic structure of the human body, at the centre, or chakra, located at the base of the spine. However, we are more concerned with the Mysteries of the Western Tradition, and this force's more objective aspect as the power within the land. As such it is often referred to as the Dragon Power, or, particularly in spiritual alchemical texts, as the Green Lion or Red Lion. (A Red Dragon is still the heraldic emblem of Wales, and the Saxon emblem of old was the White Dragon. These are the two polar forces that Merlin revealed under the base of Vortigern's tower, in ancient legend.) Similarly, in more modern times we see the forces rising into popular consciousness through nursery rhymes as the figures of the Lion and the Unicorn. It is appropriate therefore that the Initiating Power that leads us to these forces is represented by the Tarot Trump of Strength, with its associated image of a maiden controlling a lion.

The lowest chamber is sometimes seen as a crypt, to which we are led by the lion and the maiden, and the forces within it can also be referred to as the Ancestors. They are closely associated with the land, and tend to be conservative forces. They are also connected with the family and with the welfare of the tribe and of the country. In Greek mythology they were called the Erinyes or Furies, and also the Friendly Ones, for they guarded the ancient values as part guardians, part ancestral forces. It is these forces that are unleashed in times of national emergency, when they can be strongly protective, morale-building, and beneficent. However, they can also have their adverse mode of expression, with a tendency towards narrow nationalism, racism and even neo-fascism. If the 'old gods' get out of control, as in Nazi Germany and also in repressed nationalist movements, they can, operating through terrorism, be frighteningly atavistic. That is why, in the system which we are using, they are presented in a fourfold balanced structure, and under the guardianship of one of the traditional cardinal virtues (Strength), and after due scrutiny by one of the other virtues (Justice), which together provide equilibrium in two directions – Strength the vertical polarity of higher and lower, and Justice the horizontal polarity of law and compassion, or love under law. The ancestral powers as represented in the Tarot system are either male or female, and of either outer or inner mode of expression. Thus the Emperor and the Hierophant are male, outwardly and inwardly biased respectively. The Empress and the High Priestess are their female equivalents.

Having come to terms with these forces, which, it should be said, are fundamentally natural and friendly, despite their power and antiquity, we can return to the Hall of the Magician where we may approach the tenfold Elemental powers again, but now in an active and not merely philosophical way. We have, in other words, contacted the power that runs in the channels we learned about in our first sojourn within this hall. We have, to use another metaphor, gone down into the basement and started the generator, so that we can now press a switch in the Hall of the Magician, and see all the circuits light up. Our instructor is no longer the elemental being met earlier at each quarter. We are now in a position of trust, and so we make the acquaintance of a higher type of being, traditionally described as an Elemental King. In the outer structure of the Tarot these four are, by virtue of their activity, represented by the four Knights. Their esoteric names, however, are Paralda for Air, Djinn for Fire, Nixsa for Water and Ghob for Earth.

We may now learn how to operate the various forces present in the Hall of the Magician, by means of sounds, colours, and various techniques ranging from mantra to ritual movements. Also, now that we are in balanced self-control and in touch with the deep forces of the Inner Earth we are able to work upon the plane of Earth (this working is in some alchemical texts likened to the preparation of philosophical silver). We are, too, in a position to invoke the extra-terrestrial beings and forces, and ultimately to work consciously upon higher spiritual levels, in cooperation with the high beings upon those planes. (This, in spiritual alchemical terms, might nowadays be termed as 'going for gold'!)

The Powers of Higher Consciousness

The mediating and intermediary forces whom we have to meet on the way may be compared in function to the Guardians whom we met on our journey downward. These however are of an angelic form of consciousness (this is a somewhat inadequate word for a vast range of intelligences, but is sufficiently well-known a term to be generally understood). It is therefore appropriate that to meet these beings we are conducted by a guide or initiator who is given an angelic form, namely, the Tarot Trump known as Temperance. In the Hall of Angelic Principles, to which we are now conducted by climbing to the next stage of the tower, we are opened up, via the imagination, to higher realms of consciousness. These realms verge on the 'formless', although to true spiritual consciousness they are very solid indeed, and it is our physical world of assumed realities that, by comparison, is composed of evanescent clouds.

The imaginative channels which are provided for us at this level are provided by the four Tarot Trumps of the Hermit, the Wheel of Fortune, the Lovers and the Chariot. The beings represented by these images control the conditions under which human life is lived upon the Earth, and can be divided into four main categories.

The Lords of Time are contacted through the image of the Hermit, who on early cards holds an hourglass, and thus represents a Time Lord as well as a wise inner guide. Another category of angelic beings might be termed the Space Lords, and their call-sign or emblem is represented by the Wheel of Fortune. Together these two types of being encompass the primeval angelic powers known in esoteric cosmology as the Lords of Flame and of Form, for all space and time as we know it are under their presidency. They are therefore guardians in the higher sense that is hinted at in the Biblical account of a cherub with a flaming sword who guards the gates of Eden from unregenerate man. That is, they stand between the world as we know it (which they have done much to create) and the realms of Eternity.

The other beings at this level are represented by the Tarot images of the Chariot and the Lovers. They represent forces that are expressed *through* humanity rather than in the exterior, existential conditions of life on Earth. That is, they are concerned with relationships, and in terms of esoteric cosmology they encompass those beings known as Lords of Mind. More specifically they represent, as the Trump images suggest, Love on the one hand – for it is love that quite literally in the cosmic sense makes the world go round – and the opposite pole to this, that of individuality, or free will, which is represented by the Chariot. So it will be seen that on this level we have once more a fourfold system made up of two sets of polarities.

Operating at this level comprises not only working upon our own inner selves and developing a higher consciousness, but cooperating with the folk and 'national angels' that control and influence the destinies of nations. These beings are also responsible for movements of conscience and consciousness within humanity as a whole. At this level are those who have been called the Lords of Story, who work through the ideas that have been impressed upon human conscious-ness by works of fiction and by the arts. This also encompasses movements such as the ecological consciousness that has swept the world over the past couple of decades, and movements towards the maintenance of world peace and good governance. This not only includes such major institutions as the United Nations but all well motivated national or charitable agencies.

We learn to work consciously with this level of being as a result of the power contacts we have made at lower levels, and this in turn leads us into crystal lore, candle-and-mirror work, and similar techniques, often aligned or associated with various sacred sites or other power centres upon the surface of the Earth.

The Powers of the Cosmos

Having learned to work efficiently at this level, that is with the forces of higher human consciousness upon the Earth, we move to an even higher level. This is introduced by a being whose emblem is the Tarot Trump known as the World or the Universe. In fact these terms are two sides of the same coin, for we extend our consciousness out of the world and into the greater Universe.

The being who works behind the figure of the World is known in the East as Sanat Kumara, which means Ever-Living Young One. Under the aegis of this great being, who is associated with the major planetary etheric power centre known as Shamballa, we are enabled to make contact with the Rulers of the Spheres, or their agents, represented in the Tarot system by the Trumps of the Moon, the Sun, the Star and the Angel or Last Judgement. At this highest level of the tower, we are enabled to assist in the mediation of cosmic powers to human consciousness on Earth.

Using the dynamics behind the Moon and the Sun Trump images we can contact the forces behind the natural tides of the Earth. These are inner analogues of various outer forces known to science, for instance, the effect the Moon has on tides and growth patterns, or the electro-magnetic effect of the solar wind and sun spots that emanate from the Sun, resulting in diverse phenomena, from the aurora borealis, where forces come in at the North Pole, to the very greening of the Earth in the course of the seasons. These two images form polar opposites, a powerful pair of forces originating within the solar system.

The other two images, of the Star and the Last Judgement, give us access to more remote contacts, although the term 'remote' is something of a misnomer, based on the assumption that space is a lifeless void. As C.S. Lewis so brilliantly described in his theological science-fiction trilogy *Out of the Silent Planet*, *Voyage to Venus*, and *That Hideous Strength*, space is vibrant with inner life (as we have said, much inner truth is fed into human consciousness through fiction).

The image of the Star is a gateway by which we can attune consciousness to stellar forces which are 'translated' into terms the human consciousness recognizes by means of the traditional star names and constellation patterns. This is not merely a matter of zodiacal signs, which have become almost trivialized by popular superstition (although it must be said that trivialization does not debase the actual powers themselves, any more than the image of a beautiful face reflected in a distorting mirror has any effect upon the face itself), but also the great star patterns such as the Pleiades, the Great Bear, Draco, and many others. This is the domain of sidereal astrology, which is an esoteric extension of the more geocentric, 'tropical' astrology practised by most popular astrologers.

These star contacts have as their complement the forces represented by the image of the Last Judgement – emanations from the 'uncreate realities' of eternity. Perhaps some intuitive realization of this level of being can be gained from the words of St Paul, taken up in Handel's *Messiah*, to the effect that the trumpet shall sound, and we shall be changed, as in the twinkling of an eye. In esoteric cosmology this is a level beyond the projected atoms and divine sparks that make up the perceivable universe as we know it. It marks a fundamental change of state.

Whilst we are in incarnate life in the created universe we cannot know of the paradisal levels whence all causation ultimately springs. However, 'intimations' of this level are, to a greater or lesser extent, picked up and mediated by the greater beings within the cosmos, and this accounts for some of the great esoteric religious traditions, such as the coming together of the forces of the Buddha and the Christ at the annual Wesak Festival. Something similar to this, reflected in the denser levels of popular consciousness, is to be found in 'the spirit of Christmas' and other 'magical' associations and feelings of wonder experienced at festivals celebrated by other great world religions, usually most easily perceived by or in the company of children.

Should we be able to pass in our conscious state to this un-create level, the image that will meet us there will be that of the Fool, though at a higher level – and perhaps seen as 'upside-down', from the standpoint of our reflected universe. In this form, resembling the Hanged Man, he is guardian of the Uncreate Universe of Eternal Paradise.

Other Paths of Progress

The synopsis of study and inner experience that we have just outlined is by no means the only true one, although its general principles hold good for most avenues of progress.

Other ways of exercising the visual imagination in patterns of the conventional Tarot have been outlined in my book *Tarot Magic* (Destiny Books, 1990); wherein I give examples of a brief excursion up and down the structure of the Tree of Life using Tarot symbolism – in the first chapter on 'Tarot Pathworking', and then in a more extended fashion in the section that is called 'Journey to the Centre – Working with the Archetypes'. For a full treatment of Tarot symbolism as applied to the Tree of Life in the classic manner of the Hermetic Order of the Golden Dawn, there is of course my work of some decades ago, *A Practical Guide to Qabalistic Symbolism* (Weiser, 1978). This is theoretical in nature and can be supplemented by the more accessible guide to treading the paths of the Tree of Life *The Shining Paths* by Dolores Ashcroft-Nowicki (Aquarian, 1983).

The Tree of Life element is treated in various other texts, for instance *Discover Tarot* (Aquarian, 1990, first published as *The Tarot Workbook*, 1984) and *Tarot Prediction* (Aquarian, 1991, first published as *Tarot for Tomorrow*, 1988) both by Emily Peach. Here the system is closely integrated with divinatory work. More theoretical esoteric treatments can be found in Robert Wang's *The Qabalistic Tarot* (Weiser, 1987), a textbook of mystical philosophy that discusses the traditional Marseilles cards, the Golden Dawn Tarot Mr Wang produced in association with Israel Regardie, A.E. Waite's designs, and those of Aleister Crowley, (these last three men were all Golden Dawn initiates at one time or another). Aleister Crowley's own *Book of Thoth* (Weiser, 1981) might also be mentioned in this context, although it can only be recommended to those who feel particularly attracted to Aleister Crowley's 'Thelemite' philosophy.

Other treatments of the Western tradition of esoteric training and philosophy are to be found in *The Tarot* by Paul Foster Case, founder of The Builders of the Adytum, an organization that still exists as a teaching agency specializing in the Tarot. There is also *The Magick of the Tarot* by Melita Denning and Osborne Phillips (Llewellyn Publications, 1983), a particularly practical approach that includes group work. Recently there have been books produced that continue practical philosophic teaching with specialized Tarot designs. It is not possible nor would it serve any useful purpose to try to outline and evaluate all that is currently on offer. A visit to a specialized Tarot bookshop and dealer is recommended, to look the stock over personally and see what appeals. There are approaches to suit almost everyone, whether interested in Jungian psychology, femininism, witchcraft, psychedelics, shamanism, Greek mythology, or Mayan or Amerindian legends.

I should say that my own tastes incline to the conventional and traditional Tarot, which has stood the test of time. However I feel there is much to be said for the approach of Bob Stewart's *Merlin Tarot* (Aquarian, 1988) and John and Caitlín Matthews' *Arthurian Tarot* (Aquarian, 1990), both of which are very practical systems based upon the general Arthurian tradition, which readers of my book *The Secret Tradition in Arthurian Legend* (Weiser, 1996) will know is close to my own heart. As regards a practical technique of personal investigation and development using conventional cards, there is much to be said for Edwin Steinbrecher's system, outlined in *Inner Guide Meditation* (Weiser, 1988). Here, starting from a representation of Plato's cave, and led by a personal totem animal, we are taken into a sequence of inter-reactions with those Tarot images that align closely with our personal astrological birth chart in light of traditional Golden Dawn symbolism.

When all is said and done, the number of paths open to the serious student is sufficient to form a labyrinth. This is something of a change from the old days, when the path was more of a faint track through a featureless desert that threatened always to peter out or to lead nowhere. The present embarrassment of riches brings its own problems, however. Discretion and discrimination are the preliminary virtues to be exercised when trying to decide on which is the right first step. The choice is yours. If in doubt, why not ask the

Tarot rather than rely on so-called 'authorities'? Who knows, it may one day lead you to produce your own book and Tarot deck. And that for certain will be the best one for you.

INDEX

BIBLIOGRAPHY

Ashcroft-Nowicki, Dolores. *The Shining Paths*. London: Aquarian, 1983.

Butler, Bill. *The Definitive Tarot*. London: Rider, 1975.

Case, Paul Foster. *The Tarot: A Key to the Wisdom of the Ages*. Los Angeles: Builders of the Adytum, 1947

Conolly, Eileen. *Tarot*. London: Aquarian, 1990.

Crowley, Aleister. *The Book of Thoth*. York Beach, ME: Samuel Weiser, 1974.

Denning, Melita and Phillips, Osborne. *The Magick of the Tarot*. St. Paul, MN: Llewellyn Publications, 1983.

Dummett, Michael and Mann, Sylvia. *The Game of Tarot*. London: Duckworth, 1980.

Fenton, Sasha. *Fortune Telling by Tarot Cards*. London: Aquarian, 1985.

Gray, Eden. *The Complete Guide to the Tarot*. London: Bantam Books, 1971.

Greer, Mary K. *Tarot for Yourself*. London: Aquarian, 1987.

Hall, Manly P. *Secret Teachings of All Ages*. Los Angeles: Philosophical Research Society, 1962

Kaplan, Stuart. *Encyclopaedia of Tarot Vols.1-3*. Stamford, CT: U.S. Games Systems, 1978, 1985, 1990.

Knight, Gareth. *A Practical Guide to Qabalistic Symbolism*. York Beach, ME: Samuel Weiser, 1978.

———. *The Secret Tradition in Arthurian Legend*. York Beach, ME: Samuel Weiser, 1996.

———. *Tarot Magic*. Rochester, VT: Destiny Books, 1990

Masino, Marcia. *Easy Tarot Guide*. San Diego, CA: ACS Publications, 1988

Peach, Emily. *Discover Tarot*. London: Aquarian, 1990.

———. *Tarot Prediction*. London: Aquarian, 1991.

Pollack, Rachel. *The Seventy-eight Degrees of Wisdom Vols. 1 & 2*. London: Aquarian, 1980, 1983.

———. *Tarot Readings and Meditations*. London: Aquarian 1990.

Steinbrecher, Edwin. *Inner Guide Meditation*. York Beach, ME: Samuel Weiser, 1988.

Waite, A.E. *Pictorial Key to the Tarot*. York Beach, ME: Samuel Wieser, 1973.

Wang, Robert. *The Qabalistic Tarot*. York Beach, ME: Samuel Weiser, 1987.

Williams, Charles. *The Greater Trumps*. Grand Rapids, MI: William B. Eerdmans Publishing Co., 1976.

Gareth Knight has been active on the esoteric scene for many years as author, lecturer, publisher, teacher, general activist, and enjoys an international reputation. He lives in England, has two grown children, a granddaughter, and plays jazz. Knight is the author of *A Practical Guide to Qabalistic Symbolism*, *Experience of the Inner Worlds*, and *The Secret Tradition in the Arthurian Legend*, also published by Samuel Weiser.

Look for these tarot decks in the New Age section of your local bookstore:

Standard and Traditional Decks:

B.O.T.A. Tarot—Contains traditionally styled, uncolored cards which students of the tarot are encouraged to color as they learn the significance of each card.

Marseilles Deck—One of the most popular traditional decks, based on medieval motifs. Recommended for beginning students of the tarot by Gareth Knight.

Rider-Waite Deck—This best-selling deck was concieved in 1910 by A. E. Waite in collaboration with Pamela Colman Smith. Features pictorial representations on the Lesser Arcana.

Swiss Tarot—The most popular deck in the USA, it is based on 14th century illustrations.

Tarot Classic Deck—Traditional deck based on original woodcuts made by Claude Berdel in 1751. Companion deck to Stuart Kaplan's book, *Tarot Classic*.

Visconti-Sforza Tarot—Reproduces earliest extant tarocchi deck, circa mid-15th century. The allegorical trumps in this deck are the basis for the Major Arcana found in many of today's tarot decks.

Esoteric Decks:

Crowley Thoth Tarot—Designed by Aleister Crowley in collaboration with Lady Freida Harris, this deck contains Kabbalistic and astrological attributions described in Crowley's *Book of Thoth*.

Gareth Knight Deck—Combining the work of Dutch artist Sander Littel and the occult knowledge of Gareth Knight, this deck illustrates tarot principles and esoteric philosophy.

Tarot of Ceremonial Magick—Each card shows Zodiacal, Ceremonial, Goetic, Tattvic, and Elemental components, along with the card's place in each of these systems and its relationships with the other cards.

Stylized Decks:

Aquarian Tarot—Popular contemporary deck combining medieval and art deco motifs.

Hanson-Roberts Deck—The artist gives new relevance to the tarot with her magnificent illustrations in the Rider-Waite tradition. Titles in English, French, German, Italian, and Spanish.

Morgan-Greer Tarot—A modern interpretation of the classic Waite presentation, this contemporary deck is based on the teachings of Paul Foster Case and A. E. Waite.

Sacred Rose Tarot—Contemporary deck designed by Johana Gargiulo-Sherman, inspired by medieval stained glass and Byzantine icons.

Tarot of the Spirit Deck—This colorful new deck presents each card with a unique artistic expression of its arcane significance. Designed in conjunction with the book *Tarot of the Spirit* by Pamela Eakins.

Universal Tarot—A new deck which presents traditional tarot images with illustrations drawn from the whole spectrum of the world's cultures and religions. This tarot embraces the truth at the heart of the world's diverse spiritual paths. Sold as deck and book package only.

If your local bookstore does not carry these
decks and will not order them, you may
order directly from Samuel Weiser:

Samuel Wieser, Inc.
P.O. Box 612
York Beach, ME 03910-0612

Tel. (800)423-7087
Fax (207)363-5799
e-mail: weiserbooks@worldnet.att.net